The Last Little Citadel

A STUDY OF HIGH SCHOOLS

Horace's Compromise:
The Dilemma of the American High School
by Theodore R. Sizer

The Shopping Mall High School:
Winners and Losers in
the Educational Marketplace
by Arthur G. Powell, Eleanor Farrar,
and David K. Cohen

The Last Little Citadel:
American High Schools Since 1940
by Robert L. Hampel

Robert L. Hampel

THE LAST LITTLE CITADEL

American High Schools
Since 1940

*The Third Report from A Study of High Schools,
Co-sponsored by the National Association of Secondary
School Principals and the Commission on Educational Issues
of the National Association of Independent Schools*

HOUGHTON MIFFLIN COMPANY

Boston

1986

Library of Congress Cataloging in Publication Data

Hampel, Robert L.
The last little citadel.

(A Study of High Schools)
"The third report from A Study of High Schools,
co-sponsored by the National Association of Secondary
School Principals and the Commission on Educational
Issues of the National Association of Independent
Schools."
Bibliography: p.
Includes index.
1. High schools—United States—History—20th
century. 2. Education, Secondary—United States—
History—20th century. I. National Association of
Secondary School Principals (U.S.). II. National
Association of Independent Schools. Commission on
Educational Issues. III. Title IV. Series.
LA222.H25 1986   373.73   85-27028
ISBN 0-395-36451-5

Printed in the United States of America

Q 10 9 8 7 6 5 4 3 2 1

The quotation on pp. 6–7 is from *Making It* by Norman Podhoretz. Copyright © 1967 by Norman Podhoretz.
Reprinted by permission of Harper & Row, Publishers, Inc.

The quotation on pp. 17–18 is reproduced by permission from
the Minnesota Teacher Attitude Inventory, copyright © 1951
by The Psychological Corporation. All rights reserved.

On p. 87, "Sweet Little Sixteen" by Chuck Berry © 1958 by
Arc Music Corp. Reprinted by permission. All rights reserved.

For my high school
English teachers
Virginia Dailey
Edward Wingler
Mary Belle Zillman
Beverly Gallup

Contents

Foreword by Theodore R. Sizer   ix

1 Formalities   1
2 Informalities   23
3 The Persistence of the Old Order   43
4 No One Can Really Tell You What to Do   78
5 We Don't Grab Them   103

Epilogue   142

Acknowledgments   157

Sources   161

Notes   167

Index   204

Foreword

The Last Little Citadel. This 1944 image for the high school belonged to the educator George Stoddard. His vision was of a secondary school of taste and intellect, a bastion against a rising sea of
vulgarity and cant, a place for the last shot many young people
would have at an education to prepare them for a difficult, often
hostile world. The high school was an adolescent's Last Best Chance
to gain the beliefs, critical abilities, and commitments necessary
for citizenship. Stoddard clearly implied that these Jeffersonian ideals for education were embattled. Indeed, he felt that this little
bulwark — the last available — might be overrun.

Stoddard used the diminutive. Did he mean a "little" citadel
for little people? "Little" implying slight, fragile, delicate, sentimental? One sees a little citadel high school on a *Saturday Evening
Post* cover by Norman Rockwell. It is an appealing picture, a place
both gentle and sure of itself, vulnerable and essential, rearing youngsters in an American way in a turbulent time.

Of course, Stoddard's vision was in part an illusion. By World
War II the American high school had taken firm political hold
and shape. Secondary education for all was an accepted American
right (and rite) and was fully achieved by the 1960s. However, its
mass form was not what Stoddard would have liked; the citadel
was altered to accept the masses. How and why it altered even
more since the 1940s is told in this book by Robert Hampel.

Considering the pressures attendant on its inclusive character, though, the citadel high school in some ways has proved remarkably sturdy. Its structural framework was erected in the post–Civil War years and formally legitimated by the prestigious Committee of Ten of the National Education Association in 1893. The course of study, with an intellectual aim for all (those going on to college as well as those not going, asserted the Ten's chairman, Charles W. Eliot), was built along five "main lines" (Eliot's words) — English, mathematics, science, history, and foreign language, with peripheral concerns for several other subjects, such as the arts. These areas were to be packaged into courses, each to be presented, *seriatim,* in classes of a bit less than an hour each day. Committees of scholars and schoolteachers were to design these courses and the texts for them. The colleges would examine the best of the students. (The College Entrance Examination Board was founded in 1903 by several members of the Committee of Ten.)

This pattern of a core of "mainline subjects" has, at least in its overall structure, withstood decades of potential erosion to an astonishing extent. Few American institutions have retained their routines so tenaciously as has the secondary school. The Committee of Ten pattern remains the curricular design for college-bound students, that most visible and praised sector of schoolgoers. Stoddard would not be surprised by the schedule and routine of a 1986 high school. Nor would Stoddard's parents. But he would be surprised — and often dismayed — at what now has been put into those little pedagogical boxes that Eliot and his committee blessed. Though the form remains, the substance has changed considerably, as have the ways and means of school politics.

The change in substance followed from educators' beliefs about what was appropriate for schools to offer youngsters from all backgrounds, not just the genteel students bound for college. Adjusting to life, to a career, to a neighborhood, became as imperative as Eliot's main lines. The citadel grandly expanded to accept these new responsibilities even as it preserved the customary rites. Everyone went to "class" and everyone "graduated," whatever had been his or her substantive course of study. The traditional caps and gowns, which had been passed down from medieval clerics and scholars, now covered the backs of adolescents learned in Distributive Education.

But it is easy to mock. There is generosity in the expansive American high school, a place in which every interest and taste is respectfully accommodated and from which everyone (or almost everyone) graduates as virtual, symbolic equals. It is a conception no less noble than that of a righteous citadel on a hill. Its populism is particularly attractive. However, its riotous eclecticism — of standards as well as program — has had and continues to have troubling consequences. Stoddard's vision of a citadel has evolved into the reality of the shopping mall, the shopping mall high school.

Robert Hampel's examination of this journey from hoped-for educational citadel to real shopping mall high school is the third in a trilogy of books that has emerged from A Study of High Schools, an inquiry into American secondary education organized in 1979 and sponsored by the National Association of Secondary School Principals and the Commission on Educational Issues of the National Association of Independent Schools. Our purpose in the Study has been to illumine the institution of high school, to make available a richer, more sophisticated picture of what going to school was and is all about. Some twenty of us worked in concert but viewed the institution from different angles. Mine was as school principal; my book *Horace's Compromise* reflected on the routines of schooling (Eliot's 1893 framework, in part) and how these might be creatively changed. It had, therefore, a prescriptive flavor. Arthur G. Powell, Eleanor Farrar, and David K. Cohen focused carefully on the complex present. Their book, *The Shopping Mall High School,* explains how schools make the accommodations necessary to keep their doors open and the rite of graduation intact, in the process serving some adolescents exceedingly well and benignly conspiring with others to retain the form of education while cheating on its substance. The subtitle of their volume announces those "Winners and Losers in the Educational Marketplace."

Hampel's book focuses on the recent past — 1940 to 1984. Complementing David Cohen's concluding and retrospective chapter in *The Shopping Mall High School,* it traces the developments that caused the teacher Horace to compromise and the high school to assume its present form. Hampel argues that, after the mid 1960s, when students and teachers began to make life more agreeable for each other, the friction between staff, administrators, and outside critics increased. As regimentation in the classroom relaxed, relations among decision makers developed a bluntness rarely seen in earlier days, when talk of "rights" and "feelings" was unwelcome and notions of propriety discouraged not only camaraderie between teacher and student but also public bickering among the educators themselves.

A common theme of *compromise* throughout our three books — of the treaties, however genial or confrontational, that teachers and students and parents and administrators make to keep school functioning — emerged late in our collective inquiry. All social institutions require tradeoffs, but those in the modern high school seemed to us — each looking at the secondary school from a somewhat different vantage point — to be often ill considered, harmful, and corrupting, however well intentioned. Horace will always have to compromise, but he should do so in better ways than he currently adopts.

The compromises now made did not arise from chance. There are reasons for them, and we must understand those reasons, must trace the contemporary high school from a vision of a little citadel to the sprawling, lively, contentious shopping mall high school.

Robert Hampel chronicles that transformation. All of us hope that our work serves to deepen public understanding of the high school, this profoundly American institution which contains so many of our national contradictions — elitism and populism, traditional symbolics and raucous realism, generosity and cruel stereotyping. Perhaps thereby we can help a new generation to create institutions that serve its adolescents with a more achievable but equally noble vision than that of George Stoddard's little citadel.

Theodore R. Sizer
October 1985

The Last Little Citadel

1

Formalities

IRWIN KEINON, now an English teacher at East High School in Denver, recalls that thirty years ago none of his high school teachers would have thought of sharing private thoughts and emotions with students. Lessening the distance between student and teacher was rare, and Keinon remembers the exception to the rule: "One teacher let me move her car once. I thought that was the greatest thing that ever happened." In contrast, Keinon wants his students to see their teachers as people who feel, suffer, and think. "Many times a hug can let a student know that someone cares." Often Keinon will start a class with several minutes of classical music, followed by a short discussion of quotations written on the board.

The comparison between Keinon's experience in high school and his own teaching methods slightly exaggerates the extent of change. Austere teaching was not universal in the 1940s and 1950s, and not every teacher by the 1980s related effectively and comfortably with adolescents. But the direction of change was unmistakable. The formal classrooms with unnegotiable rules of rectitude gave way to a more relaxed atmosphere. As Keinon said, "They're not afraid to talk about sex and death and drugs. They're just not as embarrassed as they used to be; there's much less compunction than there once was." Teachers and students began to talk to one another about ideas previously reserved for gossip in the staff lounge or a furtive note passed to a classmate.

Pulling Away from Youth

The old notions of decorum cramped teachers' lives outside school as well as students' days inside school. Control went well beyond hall passes and dress codes, and students were not the only ones pushed and pulled by moralistic requirements.

Townspeople expected their high school teachers to exceed their own virtue and restraint, and frequently courts sanctioned the local pressures. In 1939, for example, a Pennsylvania judge ruled against a teacher who had been fired for working in her husband's tavern, where she served beer and occasionally played pinball with the customers. The court, equating reputation in the conservative town with performance in the classroom, held that her loss of respect was sufficient evidence of incompetence, "a relative term without technical meaning." Another Pennsylvania teacher secured a liquor license for her father's use when his was revoked. She was fired, and again a court upheld the dismissal, even though the state tenure law said nothing about liquor.

In other states as well, outside of courtrooms and on matters unrelated to alcohol, teachers' personal lives "were circumscribed by taboos, customs, expectations, and obligations that ranged all the way from where they had to live to where they could buy necessities and to how they might utilize their leisure time without creating a chain of gossip." Although surveillance by 1940 was less thorough than before World War I, when citizens were intolerant of almost any recreation enjoyed by teachers, there were still constraints on the freedom of teachers, especially single women in rural schools.

Monastic demands by small towns was a theme of many novels, written before the 1950s, that examined the lives of high school teachers. For example, Sophia Engstrand's *Miss Munday* (1940) sympathetically presented a young and attractive English teacher in River Port, a Midwestern town of sixteen thousand. In the opening scene, Helen Munday is in her boardinghouse room, grading themes at 11:00 P.M., when she hears a man's laughter. "They are having fun," she thinks wistfully, "playing cards and drinking." Recreation for Helen is limited to walks and movies. She wants to tutor a farmer, but her priggish principal, fearing gossip, refuses permission. The principal's shrewish wife expects Helen to donate to charitable causes (from a monthly check of $157.50) and attend boring lectures, like "Education and Its Application to Democracy." Helen realizes that teaching is "pulling her away from life, pleasure, youth," so she boldly decides to date Adam La Fond, an unmarried fisherman whose younger brother Helen had persuaded to stay in school. Adam's common sense compares favorably with her colleagues' jargon: "Amid all this educational flim-flam, his deep, ungrammatical speech rang in her ears with a sound realness . . . He would take her away from the world of teachers and help her to be a woman." But when he tries to do so, with some force, Helen resists, and eventually rejects Adam's marriage proposal. Her middle-class sensibilities finally recoil from the dinginess of his riverside house and the prospect of a life of domestic drudgery there. But the deeper reason for her decision is that "teaching has unfitted me for any life but that to which I am now accustomed."

That bleak assessment by Miss Munday shows how the stated and unstated restrictions, designed to assure the public of a teacher's respectability, actually projected an image of an emotionally stunted person. In the nineteenth century, pious young adults were considered suited to the constraints of teaching; in the twentieth century, the partial eclipse of religion by psychology made many wonder whether only the emotionally impaired could tolerate such confinement. A teacher was in "a class apart," because of a personality that supposedly was "prim in manner, devoid of humor, and frustrated sexually." That suspicion was not just a reflection of taxpayers' peevishness; some educators admitted the need for staff in better mental health. One professional association reported the findings of a study in which 18 percent of the teachers examined were "unduly nervous," 11 percent had suffered a "breakdown," and twice as many women teachers as men were neurotic. The chief medical examiner of the New York City Board of Education insisted that 12 percent of the staff were "dangerously unsuitable" and 4 percent needed immediate psychiatric care. In an admirable study, *The Soci-*

3

ology of Teaching, Willard Waller also discussed the instability of some teachers. Waller frequently heard of maiden teachers giving male names to inanimate objects: "A car is John, an ashtray Mr. Johnson, a fountain pen Mr. Wright, and so on." Although Waller was more concerned about the suppressions of the spinsters, the male teachers were also suspect (notwithstanding the assurances of a group of English teachers who, at a conference, sang a song with the words "We ain't prissy, we ain't prim"). For both men and women, more assertiveness would have been welcome, Waller argued.

> If every teacher should for a period of ten years insist upon being treated not as a teacher but as a human being, the iron stereotype might be broken. If teachers began tomorrow to argue it out and fight it out with their communities, if they insisted upon their right to play golf on the Sabbath, to smoke on the streets, to curse the garage man and kick life-insurance salesmen through the front door, if they invariably met the statement "That's no way for a teacher to act" with a cacophonous jeer, then the social position of the profession might be changed.

Not every teacher wanted to smoke on the streets or golf on Sunday; many enjoyed their cloistered life. The expectation of exemplary conduct seemed to them natural and right, a sensible continuation of the nineteenth-century notion of educators as guardians of virtue. Urban teachers, of course, were less cramped than their rural colleagues. One New York City teacher urged his students to ride with him on the Nazi wave of the future, and his punishment was merely a transfer. Still, the stereotype was of the prim and upright, an image some teachers accepted, many disliked, but only a few defiantly flouted.

"I Give, You Take"

Students and teachers did not join in an alliance to protest their exclusion from full participation in adult activities. Many communities treated teachers as children, but rarely did the teachers regard the children as comparable to themselves. Although teachers like Helen Munday chafed at the ideal of saintly decorum, in their classrooms they demanded self-control from their students. It would have been just as unthinkable for a student to smoke at school as it would for Helen Munday to drink at a tavern. The teen-ager in school was as confined as the teacher (perhaps more so in urban areas). Orderliness did more than ensure efficient school operation. Self-control improved character, obedience marked growing maturity, and discipline prepared everyone for the rigors of work or college.

Even Waller, who wanted teachers to express their feelings and act on their desires, restricted his suggestions to their lives outside the classroom. Waller saw a legitimate place for "dry, authoritative" pedagogy in the school. Because he interpreted classroom interaction as "a special form of dominance and subordination," Waller accepted the wide distance between student and teacher, which, in his words, "excludes possibilities of spontaneous human interaction."

Not every teacher stifled himself in front of students. In some places, especially the private schools, eccentrics became legends. Students both feared and revered teachers like Andover Academy's Georgie Hinman, who frequently told his Latin class to flush their bad translations down the toilet. When W. H. Auden was a visiting instructor at St. Mark's in 1940, he startled one class by giving a writing assignment in which every sentence had to have a lie.

In a survey taken in 1934 at sixty-six public schools all over the country, cheerful and compassionate instruction ranked highest among the attributes of the seniors' favorite teachers. Four of the five most admired qualities involved human relations, and even the fifth ("is helpful with school work, explains lessons and assignments clearly and thoroughly, and uses examples in teaching") had more to do with personality than with scholarship. Indeed, "we learned the subject" ranked ninth.

But appreciation of teachers' cheerfulness did not imply friendship; the virtues admired by the students signaled admiration and respect. Human relations mattered, but there were limits to the intimacy between student and teacher.

5

In many cases where those limits were ignored, the youngsters were subjected to sterner treatment than in the formal classroom. That was the experience in the 1940s of Norman Podhoretz, now the editor of *Commentary* magazine. His sessions with Mrs. K., an English teacher, were anything but relaxed. Mrs. K. mixed encouragement with criticism, and chided Podhoretz with a bluntness no student would have tolerated after the mid 1960s. He later wrote:

Famous throughout the school for her altogether outspoken snobbery, which stopped short by only a hair, and sometimes did not stop short at all, of an old-fashioned kind of anti-Semitism, Mrs. K. was also famous for being an extremely good teacher; indeed, I am sure that she saw no distinction between the hopeless task of teaching the proper use of English to the young Jewish barbarians whom fate had so unkindly deposited into her charge and the equally hopeless task of teaching them the proper "manners". . .

For three years, from the age of thirteen to the age of sixteen, I was her special pet, though that word is scarcely adequate to suggest the intensity of the relationship which developed between us. It was a relationship right out of *The Corn Is Green* . . . But whereas (an irony much to the point here) the problem the teacher had in *The Corn Is Green* with her coal-miner pupil in the traditional class society of Edwardian England was strictly academic, Mrs. K.'s problem with me in the putatively egalitarian society of New Deal America was strictly social. My grades were very high and would obviously remain so, but what would they avail me if I continued to go about looking and sounding like a "filthy little slum child" (the epithet she would invariably hurl at me whenever we had an argument about "manners").

Childless herself, she worked on me like a dementedly ambitious mother with a somewhat recalcitrant son . . . What would she do with me, what would become of me if I persisted out of stubbornness and perversity in the disgusting ways they had taught me at home and on the streets?

To her the most offensive of these ways was the style in which I dressed: a tee shirt, tightly pegged pants, and a red satin jacket with the legend "Cherokees S.A.C." (social-athletic club) stitched in large white letters across the back. This was bad enough, but when on certain days I would appear in school wearing, as a particular ceremonial occasion required, a suit and tie, the sight of those immense padded shoulders and my white-on-white shirt would drive her to even greater heights of contempt and even lower depths of loving despair than usual. *Slum child, filthy little slum child.* I was beyond saving; I deserved no better than to wind up with all the other horrible little Jewboys in the gutter (by which she meant Brooklyn College). If only I would listen to her, the whole world would be mine.

At first glance, the educator Leonard Covello seems just the opposite of Mrs. K. He emigrated from Italy in 1896 and grew up in poverty in East Harlem, New York. When he was a teacher, he would visit a student's home, talk in the family's regional dialect, and sometimes stay for dinner. When he was a principal, in the 1940s, he celebrated multiculturalism long before that idea became fashionable, opening his high school to the community for evening classes and afternoon recreation. Unlike Mrs. K., he refused to make his students discard their families' traditions and values.

But that did not mean that Covello envisioned an alternative school for working-class immigrants in New York City. There was nothing like the freedoms of the early 1970s at Benjamin Franklin High School when he was principal. Covello believed in the value of organizational structure in his school, and he ran that machinery without hesitation. Students called him Pop, but that connoted paternalism, not fellowship. His autobiography criticized advocates of the "no-failing theory and the concept of uninhibited self-expression." Covello's reminiscences about his own teaching indicated that he prized an "efficient transfer of knowledge" in which authority was clearly demarcated:

I am the teacher. I am older, presumably wiser than you, the pupils. I am in possession of knowledge which you don't have. It is my function to transfer this knowledge from my mind to yours. For the most efficient transfer of knowledge, certain ground rules must be set up and adhered to. I talk. You listen. I give. You take. Yes, we will be friends, we will share, we will discuss, we will have open sessions for healthy disagreement

7

— but only within the context of the relationship I have described, and the respect for my position which must go with it.

Former President Lyndon B. Johnson taught public speaking to white middle-class Southerners. His one year at Sam Houston High School was an interlude between college and politics, not the start of a career. But like Covello and Mrs. K., he laced his keen personal attention to students with severity. He heckled student speakers and criticized their appearance as well as their arguments. The rebukes did not stem from cruelty or from indifference. Indeed, after his team lost its final debate of the season, he ran backstage and threw up. On road trips, Johnson was jovial, but as one of his students later recalled, "Lyndon was always the teacher, and I was the pupil. He was always in a position of command, and he acted like that."

Johnson, Covello, and Mrs. K. rewrote the rules so that they could get closer to particular students, but only to jolt the youngsters into greater awareness of their own potential, not to make their lives easier. Their intervention reinforced the distinctions of age and authority, and clearly did not encourage relaxation.

Covello's ground rules — "I talk. You listen. I give. You take" — indicate that he lectured, but he probably also badgered his students with questions. Stenographic records of classroom performance reveal that teachers relied on rapid-fire quizzing. Pupils were asked to give short answers, bits of factual information from the assignments. Verbatim transcripts from a Wisconsin high school in 1940 tallied eight teacher questions for each student question, and other studies confirmed the same pattern of teacher domination based on drill and recitation. The dozens of surveys from the 1930s and 1940s — exhaustive evaluations of urban systems by nonresident university professors — usually reported extensive reliance on textbooks. Covering the subject was the paramount goal, and justification rested largely on a persistent belief in the theory, already discredited, that learning was strenuous exercise that built up brain muscles. In a 1939 survey of the St. Louis schools, the field staff described the climate of the classrooms, at that time the norm in the city.

When a pupil asked a question not immediately pertinent to the topic, the teacher immediately brought the discussion back to the lesson; pupils are called "dull" in their presence if they cannot read up to standard; socialized recitation consists in having one pupil call on others to recite; pupil participation limited to answers to teachers' questions; no evidence of the use of the experiences of children as a basis for reading; when pupils get restless they are put to work filling blanks on mimeographed sheets.

College course work probably seemed less regimented by comparison. In a filmstrip produced by the National Education Association, a bright high school senior enrolled in a college chemistry course spoke warmly of his new freedom. "It's all up to you," he said; "in high school, the teachers are always looking over your shoulder, threatening you with bad grades."

The typical textbook fostered the sit-listen-remember-regurgitate learning. David S. Muzzey's widely used *History of the American People* is a case in point. In his preface, Muzzey chided educators who voiced skepticism of the value of memorizing facts, a skepticism Muzzey called a "dangerous indulgence." There was a lot to memorize in the *History*. Names, dates, places, events, and people clotted each chapter. Numbers were everywhere. A student would read that "before 1820 more than fifty steamboats were plying up and down the Mississippi, doing a business of $2,500,000 a year, and 66,000 settlers had established themselves in the lower valley of the Mississippi." That sentence represents Muzzey's standard blend of precision and vagueness. Each section of the book had specific items well suited for multiple-choice and true-false exams. But there was little explanation of what the data meant. To what did 66,000 or $2,500,000 contrast? At what rate did those figures change? The text never invited student participation by providing charts with the figures so that the readers could work out answers to their own questions. Furthermore, Muzzey offered little stimulation in the form of pictures; the illustrations were primarily maps. The book was a dry compendium of facts.

Books like Muzzey's *History* were uninviting in another respect: they often were not the possession of either teachers or students.

9

Throughout the South state boards decided which books to buy; elsewhere local and state administrators made the choices more frequently than did the teachers. Whoever decided, the winning entry usually bore the admonition "Do Not Write in This Book." By 1940, most of the students signed for books rather than buy their own copies. Tearing a page set off worse consequences than missing test questions on its contents. A student who penciled dissent in the margin was violating school rules.

High schools also directed students' lives by dividing the curriculum in particular ways. The arrangement of courses was not haphazard. By 1930, roughly half of the high schools offered academic, commercial, general, and vocational "tracks." Each was designed to prepare students for either work or college. (The undecided could hedge by taking the general track, a mishmash of courses less sequentially structured than the others.) The larger the school, the stronger the commitment to tracking. Some large schools had additional specialties, and smaller schools had less variety. The median number of tracks was four. In any school, the selections usually correlated with the parents' social class. Blue-collar families often routed their children into the nonacademic tracks. Switching tracks was possible but unusual, especially after the sophomore year, because the majority of each track's courses were prescribed rather than elective. The selection of track powerfully influenced how a student spent his time.

Ability grouping also sorted and sifted students. School people coped with diversity by putting students of similar intelligence and achievement in the same sections of a course. Smart sophomore mathematicians could take intermediate algebra, the worst readers would meet in remedial English, and so on in other subjects (although few schools grouped by ability in every department). Some schools with tracks used groupings within the tracks; in others, grouping was substituted for tracking.

Whatever the method, the way high schools packaged and labeled students was not designed to bolster self-image and pride. Tracking encouraged snobbery; academic students often scorned their classmates. A girl in Indiana said, "Those who take a general course are neither here nor there. If you take a commercial course, you don't rate." (The same snootiness, a bit less intense, also separated academic and vocational teachers.) But the authority of adults to categorize was not questioned. Whether by tracks or ability groups, the school people maintained an organization that openly classified students as superior or inferior. It is true that students and their parents influenced track selection and, to a lesser degree, students' placement in particular ability groups. Schools often accommodated the clients' preferences. But if the correctness of a placement was disputed, administrators could point to test scores as corroboration. Americans believed that native and acquired intelligence could be gauged accurately. That faith was often intense. One Harvard professor stipulated in his will that the size of his sons' inheritances would be commensurate with the IQ of their wives. Another professor, in 1930, prophesied (wrongly) that tests of intelligence in the high school of 1960 would be as precise as tests of reaction time. The school men's authority to sort and slot ultimately derived from trust in the validity of intelligence measurement, the most sophisticated and quantitative branch of educational research by the 1940s.

In various ways, then, adult control in the school was firmly in place by the 1940s, and challenges to it were unacceptable. An autobiography by Joan Dunn, who taught in New York City schools from 1949 to 1953, warned against the "submission of the school to the student." She ridiculed the idea of encouraging teachers to fraternize with students: "You teach me. Tell me of your wonderful and vital experiences. Do not think of this as a class. This is a wishing well. I am not a teacher. I am a buddy. We are all pals together, so tell me all." She was furious when a student called her Joan. Her book, which openly satirized the street argot of her multicultural students, made it clear that teen-agers who acted like adults exasperated her. That was why she was upset that educators might consider one thirteen-year-old girl who ran away from home twice, stole money, and had syphilis to be a problem in hygiene.

Joan Dunn's belief in the importance of unquestioned adult authority is more typical of midcentury American education than the conditions she described in her classrooms. Few teachers were faced with thirteen-year-old syphilitics, and few were called by their first name. Task-oriented teachers questioned students on their homework, and discussions about personal experiences and feelings were rare. As one veteran Ohio teacher recalled, "There are parts of me . . . that I have ostracized from Room 106." The community put virtuous teachers on a pedestal (to the teachers' discomfort), and, whatever the reservations about teachers' psychological wholeness, adults expected the young to sit quietly and respectfully.

Rationalizations and Rewards

The regimentation in high schools was widely accepted *not* because students received a first-rate education. The diploma was a reward for time dutifully served rather than evidence of the mastery of particular skills. Neither students nor teachers gained a purchase on wisdom. For instance, the *New York Times* in 1942 reported that college freshmen knew little American history. Only 6 percent could name all thirteen Colonies. Fewer than half recalled two congressional powers granted by the Constitution or remembered four of the freedoms bestowed by the Bill of Rights. One-fourth did not know who was president during the Civil War. Two years earlier, in 1940, results of the new National Teacher Examination revealed that one sixth of the teachers thought farmers' planting practices were directly affected by the moon. Education majors in colleges usually scored slightly lower on standardized tests than their classmates did.

In fairness to the schools, it should be said that the society viewed intellectual pursuits with some ambivalence. Intelligence was fine, but practical know-how and a nice personality seemed to many a better guide through life than a keen grasp of abstract ideas. Even the brightest children were constrained by adult expectations of conformity and adjustment. A widely known example of the effect of those pressures was the behavior of the participants in the popular "Quiz Kids" radio show. The program featured four contestants, ranging in age from seven to fifteen, who were questioned on everything from mathematics to presidential wives to Shakespearean clowns. The young prodigies were undeniably sharp, but they were also personable. Wholesome boys good at sports were stronger applicants than brighter bookish classmates. The staff circulated pictures of regular panelists doing all-American chores like washing floors, baking cakes, and selling war bonds. As one panelist later recalled, "We were expected to be not only abnormally brilliant but brilliantly normal." The weekly show emphasized recall and memory, not abstract reasoning, since most questions sought specific bits of trivia. What mattered was that the audience knew that smart kids were not freaks. The brains of these bright children were extraordinary, but everything else was reassuringly normal.

If the tense ambience did not guarantee intense engagement, by teacher and student, with the material at hand, what then explains the texture and feel of the high schools? What accounts for the willingness to prescribe and to take the daily dose of sternness? Two reasons for the acceptance of the dry high school atmosphere involved nineteenth- and early-twentieth-century ideas and practices. A distant legacy obligated schools to attend to the cultivation of virtue in the young. The strong association between evangelical Protestantism and nineteenth-century schooling cast a long shadow on the twentieth century. The earliest justifications of high schools combined religious appeals with economic and nationalistic themes. Secondary education promised to promote the work ethic, spread patriotism, and encourage piety. School administrators, when evaluating one another, awarded more points for moral character than for special training. In the early twentieth century, the vogue of scientific school management retained parts of the nineteenth-century heritage instead of totally abandoning the past. In place of evil, educators wrestled with problems, but with the traditional zeal for setting the world straight. Many superintendents and education school professors were sons of ministers. For "professional development," reading religious periodicals was more common than attending conventions, according to a survey done in 1929. Religious commitment throughout the profession was substantial, which helps explain why, in the 1930s, the pregame cheering assemblies in Middletown's Central High School were called pep chapels.

Another reason that high schools of 1940 did not seem unduly coercive was the relatively greater severity of the previous generation's secondary education. Commands to stand and recite assignments became less common and were replaced by a sea of waving hands. Corporal punishment was less frequent. Fewer chairs were bolted to the floor; after 1934 more than half of the new seats purchased were portable. Filmstrips and movies offered relief from teacher-dominated drills. Parents who had worked during their youth would not have considered high school regimented. Teen-agers' jobs in the early twentieth century had been much more onerous than the shorter, safer days in high school enjoyed by their peers who did not work. The older generation hardly pitied the plight of students. Indeed, in 1934, one poll found that 54 percent of the people queried agreed with the statement that "quite a few boys and girls now in high school would be better off at work."

A broad extracurricular program was another means of lightening the atmosphere in school. In exchange for the students' submissiveness from 8:00 A.M. to 2:30 P.M., high schools provided dozens of athletic and nonathletic activities after the final bell. That time was the students' favorite part of the schoolday. Then they could be closer to friends and to teachers; the relations between coaches and players, sponsors and members, were more informal than the classroom hours. Certainly there was competition within extracurricular activities; teams and clubs perpetuated the adolescent obsession with popularity. But high status usually had little to do with learning, so the classroom formalities lacked the social significance that students accorded the extracurriculum. The most prestigious pursuits — athletics, particularly football and basketball — were non-academic, and the community's interest in varsity teams boosted their status. Replacing a mediocre English teacher was seldom an issue; community pressure to remove the coach of a losing sports team could be intense.

Most important, when teachers and students looked at the wider world, they could feel special. Teachers knew that on the ladder of prestige, many others stood on lower rungs. Students knew that only three of five teen-agers graduated from high school in 1940. High school teaching and graduation were accomplishments not universally available, and that had its advantages.

It is true that the percentage of teen-agers in high school rose steadily throughout the first half of the twentieth century. In 1900, only 11 percent of the fourteen-to-seventeen-year-olds were in school; by 1940, the figure was 73 percent. The number of graduates doubled every ten years; the 1,228,000 diplomas of 1940 meant graduation for approximately 60 percent of the seventeen- and eighteen-year-olds. The more selective European systems, in contrast, kept only a fraction of the elementary school graduates. In 1939 in France, only 12 percent of the high school age population attended a *lycée*. At age eleven, four of every five British children failed the entrance examination for the college-preparatory grammar schools. The American increase was due to many related factors: fewer jobs for unskilled youth, higher educational requirements for white-collar positions, fewer families in need of an extra income, the growth of vocational and technical courses, college expansion, and the belief that more schooling of any sort was a good thing. More teen-agers than ever before went to high school. Since black, rural, and poor areas recorded lower retention and graduation rates, the overall increase meant that white urban and suburban schools were graduating the vast majority of their students by the eve of World War II.

But even if those privileged students were not exceptional within their age group, the high school graduate could feel superior to his elders. Most adult Americans did not have what most of the next generation would receive. In 1940, only 24 percent of the population twenty-five years old and above were high school graduates. Sociologists later estimated that a high school diploma in 1940 had roughly the same status as a college degree awarded in 1970. Particularly impressive was high school graduation by children of unskilled laborers; by 1940, only one third of that group even began high school. Some working-class parents shared the middle-class faith in education as the fastest path up, and their children, convinced of the importance of homework, sacrificed other pastimes to study.

Regardless of class, there was not much glory in dropping out. Unemployment awaited nearly half of the unschooled. In 1937, 46 percent of the seventeen-year-olds not in school were unemployed. Before World War II, there were very few military training programs to provide young people with an alternative way to pick up vocational skills. For older teen-agers in the federal work programs, the routines were even stricter than high school.

On the other hand, there was not much shame in not going to college. Because of the difficulties of college attendance, completing an education at twelfth grade was respectable. More students took the college-prep track in high schools than later matriculated in college, an imbalance largely explained by the scarcity of financial aid. College attendance often reflected wealth as much as ability. Managerial positions in business rarely required a degree. In 1940, more boys joined the Civilian Conservation Corps (a New Deal work project) than began college.

In a major 1947 study of occupations and their relative prestige, public school teacher ranked just below economist and building contractor and just above railroad engineer and agricultural agent. In the 1930s, rising enrollments meant job security, an attractive prospect to bright novices who might otherwise have pursued college teaching or another profession. Even an editor of the high-brow *Partisan Review* considered high school teaching a coveted position during the Depression. The percentage of male teachers rose from 35 percent in 1930 to 44 percent by 1940. Many young people hoped to become teachers. In a survey of Maryland adolescents, Howard Bell found that teaching was on the list of the ten occupations most desired by both boys and girls. It was particularly attractive to lower-middle-class youths, for whom a teaching career marked the greatest proportional gain in status in terms of the ratio between investment and reward. Lloyd Warner, a sociologist, studied the backgrounds of female students in teachers' colleges, and learned that only half as many had parents in the professions as in skilled and unskilled jobs; most of the fathers were farmers.

There were other dimensions to the teachers' social position. On the one hand, men, who were a bit less happy than women were with teaching, knew that they could aspire to become administrators or could teach in junior college. On the other hand, women lacked attractive job alternatives; they considered teaching an excellent insurance policy if, once they got married, their husbands died. Both men and women knew that the salary differentials favoring high school over elementary teachers clearly made high school teaching more desirable. Also, the position required higher educational achievement, which in turn reflected on their status. Ninety percent of high school teachers in 1940 had at least four years of college, as compared with 33 percent of elementary teachers. (Of Americans twenty-five years old and over in 1940, 4.5 percent had college degrees.)

Although the emphasis on virtue and self-control rather than on creative thinking perpetuated the traditional evangelical mission of nineteenth-century teaching, the modification of some of the former bleakness by 1940 seemed to mark progress in the direction of livelier and less formal classrooms. Extracurricular diversions allowed students to shape a significant fraction of their school time and resources. And in comparison with the alternatives, students and teachers both knew that places other than school might be less hospitable. These justifications rested on contrasts, juxtapositions with the past, with afterclass time, with nonschool options. The joy of a stimulating lecture, the give-and-take of sprightly discussion, the intrinsic satisfaction of learning: these were not the foundation on which high schools in 1940 built their authority to run each day with bell-ringing precision. It is wrong to memorialize yesterday's high schools as citadels of order fortified by strong minds. Order, yes, but its acceptance was not contingent on academic excellence; often the strength of young minds was a secondary consideration.

Progressive Education

Teacher-dominated instruction bothered some reformers who envisioned more discussion, small group projects, student choice of instructional material, and a share in decisions about classroom rules and regulations. Student-centered initiatives were often championed by pedagogical "progressives," a label loosely applied to almost everyone in favor of less authoritarian instruction.

Progressive theories excited education school professors. Journals were full of exhortations for democratic schools geared to students' interests, which usually implied more vocational and social preparation and less academic drudgery. Crusaders promised an education at once more pleasant and more practical, a prospect they considered attractive and useful for the increasingly diverse population in the schools. A litmus test of progressive sympathies, the Minnesota Teacher Attitude Inventory, gave points for disagreeing with statements like the following:

- Pupils have it too easy in the modern school.
- The low achiever probably is not working hard enough and applying himself.
- Difficult disciplinary problems are seldom the fault of the teacher.

- A teacher should never leave the class to its own management.
- Grading is of value because of the competition element.

The year before publication of the inventory, the senior author, Walter Cook, criticized the traditional "tense, pin-dropping atmosphere of the classroom" of the past, where "the commands 'attention,' 'position,' 'sit,' 'stand,' 'wait for the order,' 'march' controlled the packed pupils as they squirmed their way through the narrow aisles." Cook taught at the University of Minnesota, a bastion of progressivism. Elsewhere in the educational fraternity the vision of the future also featured kind and patient teachers sensitive to student needs and experiences. Classes would be friendly rather than tense. Schooldays would become enjoyable, never unpleasant.

Yet the purpose of progressive education was not uninhibited self-expression or group therapy. Most progressives sought socially acceptable behavior. They felt that students "need a glowing faith in the rightness of life's essential purposes if they are to experience the normal, healthy attitudes of youth." In the Detroit public schools, for example, English teachers during the 1930s encouraged oral reports, panel discussions, and the reading of contemporary literature, but the instructors banned "tawdry trashy stuff." One new elective (for upper classes only) was named Personal Standards, a title more value-laden than an alternative such as Adolescent Psychology. The course covered dress, diet, etiquette, jobs, and sex — but the frank discussions took place in separate sections for boys and girls. Only a certain degree of frankness was possible.

The impact of progressive ideas on classroom practice was shallow and uneven by 1940. The reformers got attention mostly from private and elementary schools. Elsewhere, they often met resistance to substituting projects and conversations about the needs of real life for the familiar concentration on textbooks. In the Denver high schools, a much publicized progressive program yielded very modest results. Some students — a minority in each school — enrolled in a course that covered English, history, sociology, economics, civics, and personal relationships. (The group also met together for counseling.) This experiment promised "a continuous attack upon the problems which are persistent in the lives of adolescents." Traditional college preparatory work was de-emphasized, and students asked for information on many topics. Are tempers hereditary? How can I overcome jealousy? Are nervous diseases ever caused by the environment? Exactly what is meant by feminine hygiene?

Student-centered instructional techniques were somewhat more common in the experimental than the traditional classrooms, but it was not easy for a school to change the routines, however modestly. Parents fretted about the progressive label, "synonymous in many minds with poor academic achievements and irresponsibility." Some teachers noted "evidence of a respect for personality in the activities of our classrooms," but others noted its absence. Some teachers abandoned "old recitation techniques," but others scorned "socialized discussion that . . . consists primarily of the pooling of misinformation." Faculty members felt too busy to revise their lesson plans and counsel students. They were often unable to relate the new material to other subjects or to life outside the school, and those who taught traditional courses were not always cooperative. The paradoxical legacy of the experiment was that in 1941 all Denver junior and senior high schools mandated a two-year "general education" requirement for graduation. If child-centered class work was valuable for teen-agers, then it was appropriate that adult-directed high schools tell them to do it.

A professor from Columbia University who studied innovations in Pennsylvania concluded that many obstacles faced the reformers. Two thirds of the parents questioned felt that student-centered work would "result in aimless activity and waste of time." School board members, sensitive to the cost of innovations, were even more conservative than the parents. Teachers were also cautious. Often they labeled as experimentation such minor changes as new globes for a geography class. Administrators were too ready to voice progressive slogans without "really accepting any modernizing movement in a wholehearted fashion. They frequently do this by supporting one particular adaptation, leaving the rest of their school traditional, in most respects." In regard to a program that took into consideration feelings and emotions, both teachers and administrators

> cling to stereotypes associated with terms like "will power," "self-control," "listening to reason," "a person's feelings are

his own business." People recognize their "private" problems and somehow can "manage" them. This characterization is often supposed to apply especially to "well-educated" people. Varied as people's backgrounds are, they seem to be uniform to the extent that a large sphere of human behavior is regarded as "one's own business," and as something that each person is supposed to "take care of" himself.

The same wariness of intruding on private terrain marked several sessions of the Harvard University committee that drafted *General Education in a Free Society* (1945), a major statement of the purposes of secondary education. The book eloquently defended the liberal arts. Courses in English, social studies, science, and mathematics would better equip students to shoulder personal and social responsibilities than would classes on manners. The writers took a gentle swipe at progressive reform.

> Our point is that in a proper scheme of general education the mind will acquire the capacity to meet various particular and concrete problems in matters of health, human relationships, and the like. In this view the education of the mind leads to a maturing of the whole person. The schools cannot do everything. Other social institutions are concerned with helping the individual develop personal competence, while the schools have the special and major responsibility of furthering the growth of intellectual abilities.

The committee's private deliberations sounded the same warnings. One resolution to teach "family relationships" initially passed, but eventually the committee tabled the section, noting that the United States Public Health Service, sponsor of a praiseworthy pamphlet on venereal disease, could properly attend to the subject of family life. When the historian Arthur Schlesinger, Sr., asked whether sex education was feasible, his colleagues singled out social taboos, nervous school boards, and unprepared teachers as the major obstacles. "We must go softly" on the issue of emotions, concluded John Finley, a professor of classics.

In addition to intruding on personal and family privacy, progressive education could perpetuate the way students rated and berated each other. Having youngsters involved in school projects risked encouraging more categorization and stigmatization. In one Minnesota high school, the squad leaders from girls' physical education classes constituted the Posture Week Committee. They began their activities on a Monday morning by awarding small black or white tags denoting bad or good posture. During the week teachers and student council members could switch a student's tag. The entire school, on Tuesday, watched a skit on posture. On Wednesday and Thursday, the faculty and student councils elected forty students with the best posture. They made up the Friday Posture Parade during an assembly on clothes. A Friday night Posture Party crowned a king, a queen, and eight attendants.

A project like Posture Week targeted everyone as its beneficiary: carrying it out taught a lesson more easily grasped than translating one of Cicero's orations. But if diversion of attention to personal appearances relaxed academic demands (English classes wrote posture limericks), the way the diversion was run put some students at their classmates' mercy; many were publicly labeled as being deficient. Centering on the child, in other words, did not necessarily bring about noncompetitive cooperation. That was said to be the goal, but the result was not a relaxed, tolerant environment.

Progressive reform never dislodged traditional schooling; the regimentation was too deeply rooted to give way easily. A classroom picture in one book on the curriculum made the point. The authors of the book espoused core courses, experiential learning, group projects, and other familiar progressive ideas. The photograph showed two boys at a blackboard, giving their joint report on trails, their contribution to a unit called Westward Expansion and the Civil War. One boy had on a crumpled hat, eye patch, and beard. He pointed to the map with a long wooden stick. But just above his head, inches over the blackboard, was a sign reading, TIME WILL PASS. WILL YOU?

Paternalistic control was firmly in place in the 1940s. From the castle-style architecture of the school to the hall pass required of a student to walk through the fortress of virtue, the institution powerfully reminded teachers and students alike that submissiveness and propriety were expected. As one textbook warned, "The school must not be merely a pleasant place in which pupils will be encouraged or permitted to establish through practice whatever predisposition they bring to it." Even the young screen stars enrolled in M-G-M's Little Red Schoolhouse were overseen by a no-nonsense spinster. When a magazine arranged shots of a graduation party there, featuring Elizabeth Taylor and Jane Powell, the teacher screamed at the photographer to forbid Elizabeth to throw her books in the air.

2

Informalities

THE HIGH SCHOOLS described in the preceding chapter were theaters of virtues. The daily performances featured teacher-directed drill on textbook assignments. Unscripted interruptions were jarring, because the play's themes were self-control, discipline, and responsibility. Students and teachers knew their parts, and both felt rewarded, in different ways, for their work.

Behind the educational stage, the adult producers were less restricted than the young cast by the script. School governance included negotiations, compromises, and purposeful evasions that the public rarely saw or heard. Administrators dealing with powerful colleagues abandoned the tense rectitude displayed in the daily performances. That is, there was more cozy clubbiness in the front office than in the classroom. But in both places, the adults were freer to wield authority over powerless students in schools than they were to ignore powerful people outside. The constraints on both teachers and administrators were primarily the bonds of local traditions, especially the custom of maintaining the appearance, if not the reality, of orderly consensus. Efficiency was not believed compatible with saying publicly how one truly felt.

The distribution of power, in both classroom and front office, was not nearly as widespread as educational theorists claimed. Both formality and informality characterized secondary schools in the years before the egalitarian initiatives of the 1960s. No metaphor of schooling was more common in the 1930s and 1940s than democracy, but egalitarianism was talked about, not necessarily practiced. Supposedly the way people dealt with each other exemplified textbook notions of participation and representation, embodying every day the abstractions that a civics class might memorize. Adherence to in-class rules, of course, bred a decidedly undemocratic formality. The informalities among decision makers led to genial agreements that made life as comfortable as possible for them and were certainly at odds with the metaphor of school as a democracy. The point is not to indict administrators and lawmakers for enjoying freedoms unavailable to their classroom subordinates. What is significant is that this customary method of doing business later gave way, in many schools, to a confrontational style not conducive to quiet, offstage compromise.

"You Just Have to Wink at Things"

At the turn of the century, indignant critics deplored the complicated and corrupt management of the urban schools. There were too many people on the school boards, and there were too many boards, thanks to ward-by-ward decentralization. Politicians supposedly subverted education for partisan advantage. Self-serving boards often overrode their superintendents' advice in order to give staff jobs to cronies and award building and supply contracts to other friends. Frequent elections exposed education to the vagaries of campaigning in the closely balanced and competitive two-party system of 1900.

Reformers identified corruption and the lack of expertise as the worst problems of educational administration. They wanted to separate politics and education by hiring disinterested managers to run a meritocracy. This vision combined early-twentieth-century business methods with nineteenth-century evangelical exhortations against the perils of industrialization, immigration, and urbanization. The reformers mobilized coalitions of university presidents, lawyers, businessmen, upper-middle-class professionals, and education school professors. By 1920 most urban schools were being run by credentialed professionals shielded from the pressures that had swayed their predecessors.

24

That change is well known and has been described by historians, but what is less appreciated is that a new set of networks, loopholes, and quid-pro-quos formed within the nominally meritocratic structures.

A book by David Tyack and Elisabeth Hansot revealed the veiled power of the "placement barons" from major universities, in the early twentieth century, who sponsored students and colleagues for the choicest urban superintendencies, and who in turn received information, consultantships, and other favors. It was a snug arrangement that rewarded loyalty, forged an informal national network of like-minded white male Protestant school chiefs, and curtailed the indiscretions of earlier administrators. The web included prominent educational theorists who met with administrators at various conferences to philosophize, make friends, and gossip.

Tyack and Hansot could have expanded their discussion of the national "education trust" to include local and state parallels. There is much evidence of quiet bargaining at the regional level during the 1940s and 1950s. Unwritten agreements let the alert slip through the barriers set up to protect the schools from partisan meddling. An astute insider could negotiate the maze of rules and regulations that baffled most outsiders.

Relations between board members and superintendents were more casual than the visions of dispassionate and structured mutual consultation. As one small-town chief recalled, "We'd argue a point and when it was over we'd all go down to the bowling alley and have ice cream together before we went home." Board members could circumvent the administration. In Massachusetts, 19 percent of the members of all boards gave direct orders to the superintendents' subordinates during the 1952–1953 school year. Massachusetts superintendents rated their boards so favorably — 49 percent excellent, 33 percent good — that they must not have been too displeased at being bypassed.

High school principals could keep outsiders happy without disrupting their daily routines. Matthew Gaffney, after serving as principal of New Trier Township High School in Winnetka, Illinois, recalled several parries with legal restraints in his 1959 reminiscence, "School Laws and Pressure Groups." An Illinois law stipulated instruction on safety in the ninth grade, but

25

like most schools we got around it by claiming that every time
a child was in swimming he was learning safety, that in his
shop classes he was taught safety, that we got out bulletins
on fire prevention and so forth. The intention of the bill was
that a special class be organized, but very few schools did it
and there was little or no follow-up.

Gaffney also managed to comply in his own way with a law
requiring both teachers and students to pass an exam on the state
constitution. A local lawyer prepped the seniors, and "in advance
we distributed an outline of his talk and the next day we gave a
test on the outline. The school law made no provision as to who
was to give the examination or grade it, so the [American] Legion
was satisfied to have it on the books." Even so, not everything in
the township could be finessed. Conservatives denounced a multira-
cial mural as communistic, and the board ordered the offensive
wall boarded over.

Institutional accreditation could be as improvisational as New
Trier's constitution class. Before 1959, private schools in New England were consulted on the selection of their "outside" observers.
Short visits by cronies were more social than inspectorial. A campus
tour might end with a leisurely glass of sherry; the strolls yielded
short and positive reports, in contrast to the more thorough and
critical evaluations written in the 1960s and afterward.

Textbook adoptions often invited pressures unrelated to intellectual excellence. Selection by a state board meant very attractive
sales for publishers willing to accommodate regional whims. At
least one major company told its authors to use the phrase "the
War Between the States," because no Southern board would choose
a volume with a unit on "the Civil War." National firms sometimes
lacked the influence of smaller, less renowned, but better connected
firms. A "bad setup" for the American Book Company in Texas
in 1940 was "due, in part, to the little local publishers who have
not yet revealed their hand and who are pretty likely to get what
they go out after." Criteria for selection were sometimes unusual.
When one board split evenly between two books, "those who liked
our book better threw the other one at the wall, taking turns with
the others throwing ours. Eventually the cover came off the other
book and we got the adoption."

There were other ways to retain insider control. The early days of court-ordered desegregation were full of subterfuge; for example, many Southern states introduced teacher competency exams, under the guise of meritocracy, to bar or demote black staff. Colleges sometimes received transcripts with vague and often misleading designations for high school courses that would probably not have met admission requirements. Aspiring administrators in New York City took tests written by New York City principals, after prepping in classes taught by the same principals, and after they had been promoted by the principals to interim administrative jobs, like acting assistant principal. Parents with questions and doubts could be held at arm's length by teacher and principal acting in concert, though wealthier parents were placated, not blocked. The best case study of an early-1940s high school relates an instance of a parent intervening in her child's behalf. In the pseudonymous Elmtown, one girl told the principal that she had missed her detention because she had to get a permanent for the upcoming country club dance. Her mother chatted with the superintendent's wife, and the principal, too scared to defy the women, overlooked the absence. But the superintendent (who had earlier warned the principal that "there are students who simply cannot be sent to detention. Their families will not stand for it") hit on the head the son of a fertilizer plant laborer who skipped his detention. Indeed, one board member in Elmtown wanted to fire a teacher who kept his daughter after school to finish her homework. The superintendent told the researchers, "I used to be a reformer and stood for strict ideals, but as I've grown older I've learned you have to give a lot and take a lot in this business. I don't mean to say I have abandoned all principles, but you have to work with people, and so at times you just have to wink at things."

On balance, the regimentation common in classrooms was less prevalent among the decision makers. Relations were more casual. The formal rules of the game could be quietly revised or carefully ignored. Live-and-let-live agreements were more comfortable than confrontation. Give-and-take between adults was common; similar negotiation between teachers and students was not. The opportunities for adult maneuvering later diminished. By the late 1960s the administrators' world grew more legalistic. Often the ground rules became explicit, and more rules, made by new umpires, complicated the game of governance. More adversarial public disagreements often superseded the old style of informal bartering.

To Conform to the Community

In the 1940s and 1950s, frequent contact between small-town school administrators and the citizenry was an important aspect of school governance. The educational executives kept in close touch with their constituents. Of the superintendent's tasks, community liaison was particularly crucial. He worked with ministers, policemen, social workers, town officials — usually without the help of specialized staff. The tactful and sociable superintendent was much more effective than an administrator who was closeted in an office and had no contact with local notables.

Local influence applied to certain aspects of school life more than to others. As we have seen, sports were very important. Local pride in winning teams was intense, especially in the Midwest, where on occasion defeated referenda for school construction funds later passed in appreciation of a good basketball season. For adults, the school doubled as a convenient social center. One old-timer in Hamilton, Ohio, stated, "There wasn't a damn thing to do in most Midwestern towns once the hunting season ended, so the local gym became the town hall for a few months." Morality was also critical. In one town, a minister asked his parishioners' children to report any comments by their teachers that they thought irreligious. He recorded them in a file he shared with church board members. A minister in a different town asked the principal of a black high school to cancel the dancing classes. But few curricular offerings raised such passion. As late as 1960, a rural teacher could say, "I know evolution is correct because so many babies are born with tails, which the doctors cut off." A study of southern Illinois high schools reported academic complacency on the part of students, parents, and teachers. Only twelve of the thirty-nine high schools indicated a desire for new courses. Their most popular electives were band and chorus. Elsewhere in the Midwest, in the pseudonymous Plainville, the high school satisfied townspeople that their town "either is, or is trying to become, especially in educational matters, just as up-to-date as other communities." In practice, the symbols overshadowed the substance. Renaming history "social studies" transformed nothing. Nor did the introduction of vocational courses reshape students' lives, because there was no local market for typists or bookkeepers.

During the 1940s and 1950s state legislatures frequently offered financial incentives to rural school districts to consolidate. Many observers considered the curriculum of towns like Plainville too narrow; moreover, rising enrollments threatened unacceptably large school construction costs if every hamlet built or even renovated its own facilities. Before the Southern black migration to Northern cities in the 1950s, the worst horror stories about impoverished schools and inept teaching featured villages in the middle of nowhere. Benjamin Fine, a journalist and the author of *Our Children Are Cheated,* published in 1947, reported one befuddled teacher's fear that women might soon get the right to vote. Statistical research spelled out the huge rural-suburban disparities in expenditures per pupil. (Racial and regional differences were also substantial.)

Consolidation of small schools between 1940 and 1960 reduced by two-thirds the number of districts. That reorganization primarily affected districts with elementary school jurisdiction only, but in a period of rising enrollments the total number of high schools stayed roughly the same. Consolidation eliminated some high schools, and the process agitated villagers with an intensity that is mistakenly remembered solely in connection with integration. The passions described in the following story from a 1950 issue of *Life* magazine were not unlike the bitterness of later racial confrontations. The rival Indiana towns of Walton (population 835) and Onward (171) fought to an impasse when Onward residents barricaded their high school.

Last summer, School Trustee Virgil Turner of Walton, an elected official who is responsible for all township schools, announced consolidation. Turner's plan: one grade school (in Onward) and one high school (in Walton) to serve both communities. Onward bellowed in protest at the thought of losing its high school to Walton. Turner insisted that the consolidation would save $20,000 a year. "It is my duty to make these deci-

sions," he said. "There isn't anything bull-headed about it."
When school started on Sept. 5, Walton grade school children
came over to Onward without any fuss, but Onward high school
students, except for nine apostates, stayed away from Walton.
When Onward parents heard that Turner was planning to take
their high school furniture off to Walton in a truck, they recruited a defense brigade and dared him to try. They guarded
the school twenty-four hours a day, manned a portable air-
raid siren and scouted the road to Walton with a small plane.
Argument and vituperation flew between the towns. Said Onward truck driver Edgar Grant, "There's too much delinquency
over there. Walton children run all over the streets and the
poolrooms of Kokomo." Farmer Calvin Albers, a leader of
the Onward group, said he thought the Walton children lacked
moral training. "There are no vulgar poems or markings on
the toilets at Onward," he observed pointedly. Mrs. Russell
Price said, "Walton isn't qualified to run a high school." Re-
torted Trustee Turner, "The people at Onward just don't want
to lose their basketball team."

Even if, in similar situations, the state did step in, localism usually
survived and occasionally flourished. Towns and villages could use
outside agencies for their own purposes, a valuable agility in light
of the increase in the states' educational expenditures (from 16.9
percent of all school expenses in 1930 to 30.7 percent in 1940).
In 1941, in Ohio, for every nonlocal policy, the "local community
is making at least two policies to implement that outside policy."
The disproportionate clout of rural legislators enabled some towns
to busy their representatives with small chores. In Texas in the
mid 1950s, for instance, one legislator introduced a bill setting the
salary of his school's custodian. Existing state law could be turned
to local advantage. A farmer in Illinois opposed to consolidation
bought a schoolhouse for $1600 and hired a retired teacher for
his three daughters — all with state approval.

The cordiality among colleagues thrived in small towns possessive
of their schools, but the unobtrusive resolution of conflict also characterized many of the largest cities in the 1940s and 1950s. Urban
superintendents held firm control of their sprawling systems; open
and abrasive confrontation was the exception rather than the rule.

Officially, administrators were credentialed experts who had the professional skills necessary for hiring, budgeting, testing, and the like. They stressed to the point of overemphasis the intricacy of their work, and persuaded state legislatures to mandate strict certification requirements for administrators. Actually, perpetuating the mystique of expertise was only one of the methods by which urban superintendents quashed dissent. Problems were often avoided or redefined, protestors co-opted by piecemeal changes, and reforms delayed or poorly monitored. In New York City, the bewildering size of the huge system benefited the insiders, who used their positions to play reformers off against one another, kept the board too busy with details to set policy, and hired old friends to evaluate new programs. In Boston, white male administrators promoted so many like-minded subordinates that lower-middle-class Irish Catholics, reared and educated in the city, still ran the schools when the population began to change dramatically in the 1950s.

The noisiest debates about education jangled the suburbs more than the cities or the villages. Setting educational policy and managing the town's finances were the major activities of a suburban government, but they were not seen as just two of many duties. Independently elected school boards and separate school tax levies caused the town fathers to view education as a separate issue (and the suburban preoccupation with teen-agers intensified the concern). Because of their special place, school issues were often regarded as above partisanship, and school debates frequently raised basic questions of principle usually avoided by politicians. One writer aptly said, "School politics [in the suburbs] take on the color of a constitutional convention that is continually in session always discussing fundamentals." As a result, a budget item for, say, a machine shop could easily spark a heated debate about the pernicious lowering of standards.

Even so, the suburban din was muffled by frequent applause. Exemplary systems like those in Palo Alto, Winnetka, Scarsdale, and Shaker Heights were unmistakably suburban. Educators there crowed about fine new physical plants and rushed to offer new courses. In 1950, *Life* magazine publicized the achievements of New Trier Township High School, with pictures of photography classes, outdoor seminars, and an enormous library. Schools like

New Trier paid their teachers well, their principals were prominent in national educational societies, and their students won a disproportionately large number of National Merit Scholarships every year. Contentious school politics, then, did not signal the unraveling of suburban education.

Throughout the country, the superficial peace of the past depended on unsigned agreements between school administrators and their powerful constituents. The precise terms of the uneasy alliance differed from place to place; rural, suburban, and urban politicking were not the same. Localism nurtured the decision makers' negotiations, but the maneuvering was not confined to rural hamlets and small towns.

Courtesies Extended

Not every principal had to forge local alliances or placate influential villagers. No school men enjoyed more untrammeled power than the headmasters of the best-known New England prep schools. They and their heirs ruled their fiefdoms by virtue of extraordinary energy and the moral commitments they imprinted on their schools. Terms of thirty or forty years in office were common, and frequently the headmaster was free to hand-pick his successor. At Deerfield Academy, Frank Boyden had a switchboard in his home, and for years every call that came through at night rang in his bedroom. At another school, the head flatly ordered a teacher with a speech problem to stop stammering. Regardless of their relations with outsiders, the headmasters seemed to rule by divine right inside their schools, and often had no need to bargain or compromise with anyone.

Headmistresses also fashioned their own benevolent autocracies. Beulah Emmet, for one, launched the High Mowing School, in 1941, in the barn of her summer home in New Hampshire. High Mowing espoused ideas of child development psychology and exemplified many aspects of pedagogical progressivism, especially the emphasis on activity periods in place of rigid blocks of time for each subject. Extracurricular activities were unusually lively. The student body celebrated Michaelmas by harvesting vegetables at a nearby farm. The school cooks composed and staged an opera. The faculty arranged the entire senior prom, including music, food, and escorts. Mrs. Emmet donated annual gifts of $50,000 and did not bother with audits or accountants. She kept sparse records on her teachers. As one member of an accreditation team said, "Up to now, of course, a great deal of this information is in Mrs. Emmet's head." When another member of the accreditation team asked to meet Mrs. Emmet, he was ushered into her bedroom, where she lay under a large canopy. Asked for the student records, Mrs. Emmet pulled open a bureau drawer by her bed.

Emmet's casual record keeping was a kind of informality, to be sure, but to call her whimsical managerial style informal is to overlook dictatorial administrative methods rarely employed by public school principals. Her power did not depend on careful alliances with other powerful people. Yet quid-pro-quos and gentlemen's agreements also characterized many elite Eastern boarding schools. Differences between public and private schools notwithstanding, the pattern of powerful administrators reaching comfortable compromises with colleagues cut across American secondary education in the 1940s and 1950s. Decisions later subject to greater constraints and complicated procedures were more negotiable before the 1960s.

A case in point is the heads' work with powerful college admissions officers. The relationship was neither whimsical nor tyrannical. Headmasters and admissions officers knew each other well, but favors were sought and bestowed with great care. Each side had too much at stake to let it be otherwise.

Headmasters usually oversaw the process of college application instead of delegating the job to counselors. Recommendations and lobbying on behalf of applicants carried heavy weight with the admissions directors at major universities. At Yale, the directors treated respectfully the headmasters and directors of studies at the leading Eastern prep schools, from which Yale drew a sizable part of each freshman class in the 1940s.

In the fall, each senior chose one and only one Ivy League school. If he was denied admission, he had to rush in late spring to find another college. The headmaster sent the director a list of all his applicants, sometimes with metaphorical references to this year's "delegation" or "corps." When the admissions director visited the schools in late fall or early winter, he spent ten minutes or so with individual applicants, then chatted for several hours with the administration to review the strengths and weaknesses of the candidates. Written comments sent later were welcome ("He looks not at all Semitic and is a very good mixer. His close friends here are the finest boys in our senior class"). College Entrance Examinations — the Scholastic Aptitude Tests, or SATs — usually concluded the admissions process. Before 1937, the applicants had to wait until June of their senior year to take the SATs and several written essay tests in different subjects. Even when the date was changed to April, the exams were still the applicants' last hurdle. More to the point, the students did not receive their test scores. Only the college officers and, after 1942, headmasters got them, a secrecy which reinforced the brokering that minimized direct involvement by the students. Sometimes the director offered detailed advice on the exams; one man sent a night letter to the Loomis headmaster recommending particular tests for candidates on the eve of their College Entrance Examinations. The director and staff assigned preliminary rankings of A (yes), B (borderline), and C (no), and often the headmasters posted the director on the progress of the marginal B's. There is evidence that some heads pressed for advance word of the preliminary as well as the final admissions decisions.

But the favors were given by both sides. Heads occasionally discouraged weak candidates from applying (which is one reason that the very high acceptance rates must be interpreted cautiously). The heads also ranked the successful applicants who needed financial aid or scholarships, a form of influence by no means trivial. Each party quantified the other: Yale calculated each applicant's probable college grade point average, and the schools knew precisely how many of their alumni Yale had taken in previous years. The relationship, however, was not rigid and legalistic. A head might write a letter of thanks for summer acceptances from the waiting list of boys he had lobbied for; but later that fall the same man might write stern notes to his graduates with poor Yale midterm grades. There were limits to the courtesies extended. There is a large exclamation point in the margin of a letter from Andover's dean of students with his list of "G.G.B.'s MUSTS," thirty-five boys who "seem to me, for one reason or another, unrejectable." When the Exeter principal proposed abolition of grades for juniors and seniors, the Yale director dismissed the implication that his college could safely accept any Exeter graduate.

Reservations Relinquished, Misgivings Retained

An organization as exclusive as the Eastern prep school was the Educational Policies Commission, a prestigious group formed in 1936, sponsored by the National Education Association, the major teacher association in the country. Professors, superintendents, college presidents, and government officials served as commissioners. They initiated, revised, approved, and publicized scores of influential publications on many topics. The twenty members met several times a year to review position papers, pamphlets, and books, usually drafted by outside authors. The eminent historian Charles Beard wrote the first book, and subsequent publications received respectful attention. In an age unblessed by large public and private research grants to policy analysts in universities, think tanks, or government institutes, the joined voices of the twenty commissioners carried far.

In 1944, the commission issued *Education for ALL American Youth,* a four-hundred-page plan for post–World War II schools.

The plan assumed that all boys and girls had a variety of needs that they and their families could not satisfy on their own. The commissioners favored compulsory education to age eighteen so that schools could provide not just academic but also occupational preparation, and could inculcate the ethical sensibility, patriotism, and self-awareness that students might not acquire elsewhere. Those skills and attitudes, the report claimed, served youngsters better than a fare of Latin declensions and botanical esoterica, which did nothing to mold well-adjusted, employable citizens. Clearly the book expressed many of the aspirations of progressive reformers eager to broaden the curriculum beyond textbooks and move teaching away from drill and recitation, but it was not a radical document. It often referred to *efficiency, competence, cooperation,* and *progress,*

35

all popular words in educational writing of the period. The authors wanted to curb confusion, cynicism, and ornery individualism; the "all American youth" part of the title denoted personality as well as numbers.

The commissioners assumed that paternalism was appropriate, but they believed the high schools of the future would be less rigid. They advocated course work keyed to adolescents' interests. Traditional subjects would promote useful skills (such as film study in English class), and new courses would expand the range of vocational specialties. On balance, "less rigid" meant a wider curriculum; it did not necessarily imply informal student-teacher relationships. The narrowness of schooling would be remedied by the greater scope of subject matter rather than by the open expression of feelings between student and teacher.

The broad scope of the schools would require more staff as well as more time. The emphasis on the needs of youth justified stronger guidance departments, which the commission's report praised as the "keystone" of the model high school. Teachers would meet periodically with advisees to shape an "educational plan," and specialists would have new assignments, such as supervision of student employment. In addition, the model high school would stay open forty weeks each year, with daily activities scheduled from 8:00 A.M. through 10:00 P.M. Consolidation of small rural schools would bring together more students in the same building, and in the summer students would find themselves at school-run summer camps. The commissioners envisioned secondary education as spanning grades seven through fourteen, with the final two years to be known as the "community institute." The larger system would supposedly ensure a truly comprehensive program, with something of interest for everyone.

The counterpoint to comprehensive inclusiveness was the faith that a required two-period course would balance the diversity of the offerings. Despite the longer menu of courses, everyone would have to taste the main dish, which was the "common learnings" requirement. The class took up one third of the schoolday, covered English, economics, civics, and aesthetics, and included frequent field trips and neighborhood visits.

All of these ideas were presented with optimistic fervor. Typical of the book's sunny tone is the description of an American history class, where the central theme would be "man's age-old struggle to achieve freedom and security." The growth of America was "marked by the achievements of men and women of high purposes, prophetic vision, and indomitable courage, and by ever-widening diffusion of the blessings of liberty among the people." The rest of the book was just as earnest.

Several historians consider the work a statement of widely shared beliefs of educational theorists. It deserves attention for that reason alone, but what is particularly relevant here is the existence and the kind of disagreement that marked the commission's private deliberations on earlier drafts of its book. The commissioners debated whether to soften high school austerity by adopting some elementary school practices, especially students' spending longer stretches of time with the same teacher. Moreover, proposals to de-emphasize subject matter in favor of social skills provoked criticism by some commissioners. The customary routines pleased them; more informality made them nervous. To the public, the book seemed a unified call for change. In private, some debaters defended traditional practices. The outward unanimity came from people willing to compromise their differences. Reservations and misgivings about reshaping the schoolday led to accommodations, not to public spats.

The commissioners reviewed the document so carefully that nine drafts were written. Of all the sections scrutinized, the pages on common learnings evoked the sharpest disagreements, primarily because the course threatened the teachers' traditional academic orientation. The chief skeptic was George Stoddard, state commissioner of education in New York, who led an interrogation of Paul Rankin, assistant superintendent in Detroit and author of the section in question. Stoddard summarized the plan for tenth-graders, which originally provided for a three-hour common learnings period. Then his attack began:

> STODDARD: What do the English teachers and language teachers do in the 10th year?
>
> RANKIN: We are using them very largely in the 12th grade, and then —

STODDARD: Let's stick to the question. What do they do in the 10th grade?

RANKIN: Some of them, of course, are teaching in the optional courses that are taken in the individual interest period.

STODDARD: What is the difference between an individual interest period and a class?

RANKIN: There isn't any, if you want to put it that way. Students are taking classes there in terms of their individual interests.

STODDARD: I don't think it is realistic to think that in the 10th grade you can shunt English outside of a basic course, make it an elective, or make it something of just a casual nature.

RANKIN: You certainly will find there is attention to English throughout that common period.

STODDARD: You mean the English teacher is there during the period?

RANKIN: No.

STODDARD: She isn't there? Where is she?

RANKIN: I don't think the English teacher has to be there in order to have boys and girls learn to speak and write English effectively.

STODDARD: Is the mathematics teacher there, the algebra teacher?

RANKIN: No.

STODDARD: Who is there?

RANKIN: One teacher who understands, who is trying to teach children, I would say, and not trying to teach subject matter.

STODDARD: That is where I think it is unrealistic.

In that exchange, Stoddard sounded the alarm against extending elementary school practices into the higher grades. He satirized the notion of tenth-graders visiting local stores, offices, and factories. "That is fine, exactly what they do in kindergartens. I've never seen a kindergarten where they didn't do exactly that same thing." He pressed Rankin to explain how common learnings differed from elementary school curricula. Rankin replied, "The purpose is precisely the same, which I assume is that a teacher, if he is to know and understand children, has to be with them long enough to have some contact." Stoddard was not satisfied. He believed that students enjoyed contact with many teachers, each competent in a different subject, and argued that the logical assumption of a close contact theory was that "our best schools should be the one-room elementary school," which everyone knew was not true.

Stoddard was not sure the core teachers would still be teachers.

> STODDARD: I am trying to get a visualization of the 10th grade from nine o'clock in the morning until twelve, when there isn't another teacher in the room and there isn't another teacher coming in during any part of that particular meeting. This teacher is what kind of a person? What is she trained in, or he?
>
> RANKIN: We hoped she was trained to teach high school.
>
> STODDARD: The nearest I can think to that would be an educational psychologist or guidance expert or adult education expert or child development expert.

Stoddard doubted that the average teacher could successfully double as therapist. He felt that nurturance should be offered mainly in the earlier grades. Francis Bacon, the principal of the renowned Evanston, Illinois, high school, reinforced his suspicions:

> BACON: This whole issue seems, to me, to point right up into the type of teacher you have. We found in our work in this particular area, that we have to have very much better trained teachers. I think, without exception, the teachers in our experimental school are teachers who either have their Ph.D.s or they have at least had courses, advanced courses in educational institutions, equivalent to Ph.D.s as far as time was concerned. On top of that, they are unusual personalities.

Stoddard asked Bacon, "Are we going to say in this report that the success of the whole plan depends on such training of teachers?" Bacon replied, "I think it does." There is no such bold declaration in the final text of *Education for ALL American Youth.*

Stoddard elaborated his doubts about the prospect of teacher-therapists. The drafts of the report never endorsed uninhibited self-expression or urged teachers to be therapists, but Stoddard interpreted a three-hour period without subject specialists as human relations in masquerade. He wanted the elementary school teachers to work on getting along with people and reconnoitering the neighborhood; the high schools should focus on subject matter. In some areas, the high school should be directive; in other areas, less so. He said, "You give the indirection to the subject matter, the expertness, the knowledge of science and art and social studies, and the directness to these purposes and contacts and life ambitions. I should turn it around."

Those reservations paled in comparison with Stoddard's final criticisms. He felt that the high school, to be special, had to stand apart from and above the outside world, which lured students with magazines, comics, radio, and movies, each full of

> surface learning, a tremendous amount of contact, a tremendous amount of stimulation and not much sense of form, not much sense of hierarchy, not much sense of theory or philosophy . . .
>
> If we give up in this last little citadel, in the high school, which is the last education for most of our boys and girls today, and merely try to do what the mother and father and everybody else is trying to do, in terms of health and social relations, and getting along with people and visiting, and being nice, and the rest of it, and forget this glory of the human mind . . . I think we are cheapening education. I think we are giving ground. Nobody will teach anybody any algebra whatsoever outside of school, but everybody will teach everybody else a good deal about social relationships, about health, about personal contacts, about work, about travel.

After George Stoddard finished his exhortation, Alexander Stoddard, superintendent of the Philadelphia schools and chairman of the commission, announced that he too had reservations. His junior high schools taught common learnings, but for some students it was too advanced; for others, too rudimentary. "I don't think it is practical as far as 100 percent of the high school pupils are concerned. On the other hand, the old high school program was certainly not meeting the needs of 100 percent of the high school pupils. Everybody here knows that. So maybe there is a way of reconciling this." After four other commissioners expressed their doubts, George D. Strayer, a professor at Columbia's Teachers College, suggested the need for a compromise statement so that "we are not committing ourselves 100 percent, or suggesting that the schools immediately, all of them, try to put all of the pupils in this kind of program." The commissioners then adjourned for lunch.

While everybody else ate, George Stoddard, Francis Bacon, and Paul Rankin met to draft revisions. They agreed to reduce common learnings from three to two periods in tenth grade, with science as a separate course. They agreed to say that this program was interchangeable with other curricula (without saying just what that meant), and that every subject need not be taught every day. The compromise draft said the proposals were flexible and experimental, and the writers urged teachers to adapt to students' interests.

Then the commissioners voted.

> CHAIRMAN STODDARD: Do you subscribe to that?
> FRANCIS BACON: As a compromise, yes.
> CHAIRMAN STODDARD: George Stoddard?
> GEORGE STODDARD: Yes. As I told Dr. Carr [the secretary], I relinquish my reservations and I retain my misgivings.
> CHAIRMAN STODDARD: Paul Rankin?
> PAUL RANKIN: Just "yes."
> GEORGE STRAYER: I second the motion.

Murmurings

Just as the final text of the commission's book gives little sense of the shaping of that document, so would a history of American high schools based solely on the published professional literature conceal the private politicking that was the other side of public confidence. Many public school educators lobbied discreetly while appearing as nonpartisan managers in public. The zippy tone of their pronouncements belies their hard work and painstaking diplomacy.

In part, the maneuvering took place because educators had genuine doubts and reservations. In the 1940s and 1950s, school people like George Stoddard shared with colleagues uncertainties not broadcast to the wider world. There was no golden age among administrators, when everyone believed that everything was just right in American high schools, or when everyone shared the same progressive vision of less regimented schooling. But often the misgivings were not voiced as frankly and loudly as they were later, when quarrelsome skeptics sought public expression of their grievances. One has to listen closely to hear the troubled murmuring, which from a distance can be mistaken for contented purring.

The jockeying also occurred because some powerful and confident people enjoyed strength on their own ground and wanted to extend their sphere of influence. Local village dignitaries worked with their school administrators, often amicably resolving vexatious issues behind closed doors. Elite private schools yielded a prize group of college applicants, and the headmasters forged respectful alliances with admissions officers.

Whatever its origins, the informal give-and-take was quiet enough to let the formal performance hold center stage. In the theater of virtue, the daily rituals depended on self-control, rote recall, and adherence to the rules. The public audience saw, heard, and applauded tightly run productions. They were less aware of the messier, but effective, work by the directors.

3

The Persistence of the Old Order

THE IDEAS of both Paul Rankin and George Stoddard persisted long after the publication of *Education for ALL American Youth* in 1944. Traditional classrooms with teacher-directed drills and textbook pedagogy continued to exasperate people with progressive sympathies. The idea of more pleasant and practical instruction always excited at least some reformers. Soon after World War II a Life Adjustment program mobilized educators eager to teach useful skills along with lessons on "being nice," as Stoddard had put it. The movement quickly became the most prominent educational reform of the late 1940s, a postwar version of the familiar progressive promise to offer something of interest and value to everyone of high school age.

In 1947, the federal Office of Education established the Commission on Life Adjustment for Youth. Its chief spokesman, the vocational educator Charles Prosser, doubted the strength of the connection between academics and "the real demands of living." Mastering the pluperfect tense would not help future wives raise healthy children or future husbands balance a budget. Abstract skills learned in classrooms did not transfer to situations encountered later in life. Immediately applicable lessons, on topics like recreation, choosing a mate, shopping, home repair, friendship, and other practical matters, educated for life; Latin III led only to Latin IV. As Prosser told a Harvard audience in 1939, "Business arithmetic is superior to plane or solid geometry; learning ways of keeping physically fit, to the study of French; learning the technique of selecting an occupation, to the study of algebra; simple science of everyday life, to geology; simple business English, to Elizabethan classics." By 1945, Prosser went a step further. Instead of useful skills being relegated to separate courses in the less prestigious tracks, he said, every teacher should constantly relate his or her subject to practical applications. This would benefit all students, including those who were baffled or bored by parsing sentences and solving equations.

The ideal high school would also prepare students for adulthood by molding their habits, attitudes, and ideals. Life Adjusters usually described the world as a treacherous place, where only careful planning guaranteed safe passage. Stress assaulted the traveler even before he embarked on the perilous voyage; frustration, confusion, and insecurity supposedly plagued all adolescents. Therefore, "lessons in preventive and therapeutic mental health are vital necessities" for those who wished to learn "how to persevere over a long pull in the face of difficulty." The Adjusters hoped young people would confront life's obstacles as problems whose solutions depended on what was socially acceptable. The good student "must learn to control and channel his impulses so that others accord him approval and respect," and he could acquire these abilities through classroom discussions of topics usually reserved for life outside school.

Although some students probably required Life Adjustment more than others did, the program was defended as good for all. Because only two fifths of the seniors either went to college or became skilled laborers — according to Prosser's calculations — 60 percent left high school without much preparation for anything. They would presumably spend their lives in activities for which their formal education provided no background. Comprehensiveness was said to be a sham if, in a democratic institution dedicated to meeting the needs of a diverse population, the majority walked away empty-handed, with neither the know-how nor the social skills they would later need far more than old notes on *Silas Marner.* The Adjusters claimed that because of adolescents' inexperience, all students deserved lessons on effective living, family life, and wholesome personal relations. Those topics would be not only more useful, but more interesting for everyone. School people knew that most teen-agers were fascinated by themselves and each other, not by Latin translations and chemistry experiments. Since students already cared about subjects like dating and acne, teachers would more easily win their rapt attention by setting adolescent priorities at the center of each period. And the teachers too might welcome an opportunity to disengage legitimately from academic routines in which they had, on balance, demonstrated only average accomplishment during their own high school and college years.

The Adjusters' analysis of the student population and its needs was badly flawed. A postwar boom in the colleges and universities quickly invalidated the 20-20-60 calculation. In a decade when the number of youths did not rise, postsecondary enrollments rose by 74 percent, representing 27 percent of the eighteen-to-twenty-one-year-olds by 1950, up from 14.5 percent in 1940. (Educational aspirations continued to rise in the 1950s. In 1949, 70 percent of American parents "hoped" their children would go to college; by 1959, the same percent "expected" to see their sons and daughters in college.) Even before the great expansion of higher education, the general track never drew 60 percent of the students, nor did as few as 20 percent take the academic track. Also dated was the assumption, born of Depression-era anxieties, that self-doubt and despair were the enemy. Life Adjusters wanted to keep alive the boosterism of wartime, unmindful that the strong postwar economy conquered the alienation due to underemployment and unaware that many sociologists deemed Americans much too "other directed," as David Riesman argued in his best-selling book *The Lonely Crowd,* published in 1950.

Furthermore, Life Adjustment flattered the high schools as it denigrated the intellectual and psychological capacities of its charges. The majority of the school population was labeled unspecial, and Adjusters accepted that stratification as a social and economic fact beyond their control. They did not aim to reduce the 60 percent figure by making the unspecial special. The opinion of Earl McGrath, federal commissioner of education, was typical: "A boy who does not have the ability to be an expert auto mechanic can be taught to be an excellent tire changer and acquire good attitudes toward work in the process." Not only were so many students deemed ordinary; they also required extraordinary pedagogy so that they did not botch the job. The ministrations of the school would be better than common sense or family advice. What interested students outside the classroom was naïvely assumed to hold its appeal as a course with requirements, tests, grades, and a teacher. Life Adjustment patronized the individual while applauding the institution. As Jacques Barzun, the historian and critic, wrote, "To try to adjust the undeveloped inner self to an equally indefinite outer world is presumption."

In one sense, high schools had to belittle their students in order to elevate themselves. The 1940s' combination of condescension and self-aggrandizement came at a time unlike previous eras when proud school people had fussed about untalented students. Early in the century it was not hard to celebrate nonacademic work whenever a large influx of foreign-born or working-class children swelled the high school population; very few observers doubted their genetic inferiority. But the 1940s were the only decade in the twentieth century, before the 1970s, when the high school population fell. As a result of the low birthrate during the Depression, fewer students went to high school in 1950 than in 1940. To be sure, the total number of fourteen-to-seventeen-year-olds in America also fell during the 1940s (from 9.7 million to 8.4 million, from 7.6 percent to 5.6 percent of the country's population), and the 9.8 percent decline in high school enrollment lagged behind the 13.5 percent drop in the adolescent population. *Graduation* rates (gauged as a percentage of the total population of seventeen-year-olds) jumped from 45.1 percent in 1945 to 59 percent in 1950. Even measured from 1940, a year undistorted by teen-agers in uniform, the climb was still significant (from 50.8 percent to 59 percent). In the preceding period of soaring graduation rates (from 28.3 percent in 1930 to 41.3 percent in 1935), enrollments had boomed, so the recruitment and retention of teen-agers then could be credited to bleak job prospects. Life Adjustment, in other words, was an accommodation to declining enrollments by an institution accustomed to relentless growth. Postwar educators thought they had to run faster to stay in place.

Previous reformers had also espoused child-centered schooling premised on low estimates of the students' appetite and ability for academic work, but no one before had stated the case so frankly and merrily, and thus so foolishly. *Education for ALL American Youth* never specified a percentage of youngsters unlikely to acquire intellectual or vocational talents. Paul Rankin praised the skill of his common learnings teachers; Life Adjustment publications often assigned nonacademic staff, especially school nurses and home economics teachers, to the new courses. Although the commission's report recommended experience as the basis of good education, it balanced that position with kind words for the intellectual achievements that Life Adjusters often dismissed as ephemeral and irrelevant. Moreover, the choice of name was ill advised. In a society where the symbolic aspects of both schooling and school reform were not trivial considerations, Life Adjustment stirred the imagination far less than a label like *Cardinal Principles,* the name on a 1918 manifesto for a comprehensive high school curriculum. Life Adjustment lost sight of the strategic value of ambiguity.

The great irony is that the Life Adjusters need not have been so boisterous. The benefits of getting along pleasantly with others were widely recognized by midcentury. In 1950, at one Educational Policies Commission session to revise a pamphlet entitled "Education for the Gifted," Dwight Eisenhower volunteered the opinion that "the greatest gift in the world is personality." High school students ranked social skills ahead of basic skills as the most important point to secondary education. College students also put "gets along well with others" ahead of "brains" when asked why some people succeed. The skillful manipulation of interpersonal relations hardly lacked respect. And many schools already offered a few of the Life Adjusters' favorite courses. Enrollments in those classes rose rather than fell during the 1930s and 1940s, according to national surveys from 1934 and 1949. Topics like orientation, group guidance, occupations, hygiene, home management, family relationships, and consumer buying attracted approximately 10 percent of the students during the 1948–1949 school year (which was when the federal panel on Life Adjustment released its first major publication, *Life Adjustment for Every Youth*). Substantially fewer students had taken such courses fifteen years earlier. Rising modestly were enrollments in the high schools' versions of the social sciences: sociology, psychology, economics, and problems of democracy. (Anthropology was not offered.) That set of courses attracted about one of every three upperclassmen by 1949, up from one in five in 1934. Core courses (which usually combined English and history) could promote Life Adjustment goals through the activities Paul Rankin had described to George Stoddard. About 2 percent of the smaller high schools (under five hundred students) and 11 percent of the larger schools adopted that innovation: just under 4 percent of the students were enrolled in core courses during the 1948–1949 school year. All these figures indicate the presence of some of the reformers' prized courses in some postwar high schools. The effective-living courses were indeed at the edge of the curriculum, but at some point in his four years, a student might take one or another of the classes oriented to personal and social relations.

At least one of those courses, psychology, would have been a respectable vehicle for Life Adjustment ideology. High school psychology teachers and students wanted the course to emphasize personality and personal relationships. Friendship, marriage, and the family roused more student interest than learning behavior, physiology, or statistical methods. Teachers, few of whom had majored in psychology, were willing to accommodate those preferences. "Personal problems" ranked first of seven course objectives on one survey of psychology teachers; the same goal was ranked fourth by a control group of psychologists. Several publications of the American Psychological Association admitted the ascendance of "the study of me in an attempt to understand me (and maybe you)" over the presentation of psychology as an experimental discipline. As a social science, high school psychology was decidedly more social than scientific, yet it was the child of a legitimate academic discipline well respected by serious scholars.

If the most popular textbook is representative, high school psychology courses probably pleased Charles Prosser and his kind. T. L. Engle's *Psychology* featured common sense and cautious admonitions. Engaging anecdotes (a chimpanzee and a child grew up together) were mixed with practical advice (ten pages on better study habits) and an occasional sweeping assertion ("To appreciate a work of art, observers must preserve psychological distance. One function of a picture frame is to set a picture off from its surroundings"). In the chapters on popularity, jobs, marriage, and the family, the author beamed with approval on adjustment and efficiency, and endorsed several opinions — homemaking courses are fine; an overdeveloped intellect can mean bad health — compatible with those of the Life Adjusters. There was no encouragement in the text to march to a different drummer. Engle's book echoed Dale Carnegie's advice on how to be agreeable. (Interestingly, more students took salesmanship and advertising in the late 1940s than took psychology.)

Life Adjusters also failed to appreciate how the tone and style of the traditional teaching they criticized often fostered rather than thwarted their own goals. In English classes, which practically everyone took, most exercises stifled creativity. As one book observed, "Poetry is offered to him as a jungle in which to track down metaphor and metonymy so that he may bring home his specimens in triumph for the approving teacher." For an essay, the typical student "regards an agreeable written style as something like the manners expected of him in dancing school." The favorite prose style was self-conscious and florid; in a word, sentimental. The hallmark of sentimentalism is gushing over the ordinary and the mundane, which were central to Life Adjustment.

Yet another reason for the Adjusters to have proceeded quietly was the good health of several hands-on nonvocational courses. Enrollments rose most dramatically in the 1930s and 1940s in the areas of the curriculum with gadgets. Driver education led the way. Almost nonexistent during the Depression, driver education in some form was present in nearly half of American high schools by 1953. Four of every five schools with driver ed gave credit for it. The number of students sitting in front of typewriter keyboards rose from 16.7 percent in 1934 to 22.5 percent in 1949. More hands found their way to domestic utensils as home economics enrollments rose substantially, from 16.7 percent to 24.2 percent. There were no film study credits available, but the proliferation of audiovisuals let technology colonize the academic areas, especially social studies. One study in 1951 reported that history teachers used audiovisuals more often than they assigned library research projects. Cars, typewriters, kitchens, and projectors never promoted attitudes with the forthrightness of Life Adjustment rhetoric, yet each gadget gave the student an opportunity to avoid some serious academic demand. In the same period, many traditional subjects did not expand at all. General science prospered, biology held steady, but physics drew proportionately fewer students. Geometry classes shrank as general mathematics swelled in size. In social studies, older electives, like ancient, medieval, and English history, practically disappeared, giving place to problems of democracy. Latin enrollments plummeted, slipping behind Spanish by midcentury. The academic departments did not collapse, especially in terms of absolute numbers, but their persistence had not discouraged the growth of new, practical courses.

Despite all those reasons to keep a low profile, Life Adjusters agitated noisily for their program. Over a hundred articles appeared between 1947 and 1953 with Life Adjustment somewhere in the title, and several books on the subject were manuals for curricular revision. The major education associations repeatedly scheduled appropriate workshops and lectures for their annual national conventions. Many states undertook local studies, especially on why some students became dropouts.

Ever since the rise of mass secondary education, someone somewhere usually bemoaned watered-down courses, collapsing standards, and runaway mediocrity, but Life Adjustment sparked unusually vigorous attacks in the early 1950s. Books like Arthur Bestor's *Educational Wastelands* and Albert Lynd's *Quackery in the Public Schools* ridiculed Life Adjustment as pretentious, pernicious, and vapid. Lynd wondered why "something like Progress in Democratic Smoke Abatement is closer to a child's real needs than subjects like Latin and French and English poetry." Bestor asked whether "the American people have lost all common sense and native wit so that now they have to be taught in school to blow their noses and button their pants." In several cities, committees of irate parents (of the top 20 percent) insisted that common learnings and the like not be requirements. A widely publicized controversy in Pasadena caused the ouster of the superintendent, Willard Goslin, president of the American Association of School Administrators, an outsider who failed to make local allies when he tried to import the progressive practices he had developed in Minneapolis.

As a formal movement, Life Adjustment disappeared by the mid 1950s. The scorn of critics like Bestor made it hard for most people to take the reform seriously. The adverse reactions reaffirmed the traditional unwillingness to let teachers and students disengage from academics for the express purpose of discussing social and personal concerns. The tradeoff was unacceptable when it was made openly and treated as an achievement. What was tolerated was the quieter avoidance of academic pursuits made possible by gadgets like typewriters and electives like psychology. How well reformers fared in warring against school routines depended on strategic considerations. Frontal assaults on behalf of pleasant and practical education were doomed. The candor of the Life Adjustment crusade was unwise and unnecessary; many of the program's component parts had already found a place in school. As George Stoddard knew, *direct* instruction in social skills was less acceptable than the *indirect* lessons learned from family and friends, and by following all the school rules.

Working on Johnny

Several progressive stepchildren outlived the demise of Life Adjustment. As long as the offspring were known by other names, their future was bright; association with activities and ideas already valued by the society lent them legitimacy. Even so, moves in the direction of less austerity were cautious steps, not great leaps. What John Dewey wrote in 1952 applied to the rest of the 1950s and much of the 1960s: "The fundamental authoritarianism of the old education persists in various modified forms."

Employment of guidance counselors and school psychologists, together, is an example of conservative reform. The counseling ranks increased faster than the student population in the 1950s and early 1960s. In 1951–1952, 17.2 percent of the high schools had at least one person who devoted half time or more to counseling; by 1966, 65 percent of the high schools had hired counselors. School psychology also expanded rapidly in the 1950s. Membership in the American Psychological Association's Division of School Psychology tripled; another survey reported a fivefold increase. As the numbers rose, so did the quest for professional identity. For psychologists, formal certification and training programs, rare in 1940, increased.

For staff, the major change was the replacement of teacher-counselors by full-time guidance counselors. In the 1930s and 1940s, some teachers counseled for one or two periods, and administrators often shared guidance work. Urban research departments in 1930 provided vocational guidance, ran psychological clinics, and supervised handicapped children. By the mid 1960s, those duties were seldom their responsibility. Principals and assistant principals, deans of boys and deans of girls, were once much more involved with counseling. But by 1960, guidance was carried out by full-time specialized staff. The change spawned so many journals, associations, training programs, and certification laws that no one could look on all counselors as superannuated teachers or popular coaches.

The departments of "pupil personnel" gained from the postwar popularity and high esteem awarded the therapeutic professions. The number of psychiatrists soared by almost 500 percent from 1945 to 1964; membership in other health professions rose only 30 percent. The National Institute of Mental Health, established in 1946, financed several thousand research projects by 1960. Not that this field had languished before 1940; mental disease had already been retitled mental illness, a condition benign enough to be prevented yet serious enough to warrant early care. After the war, however, some prominent psychiatrists exhorted their colleagues to expand their jurisdiction. Malaise as well as pathology was in the realm of the therapists, according to theorists like Franz Alexander, a proponent of "guarded and antiseptic kindliness and reassurance" in place of the more severe orthodox Freudianism. Psychology also expanded its influence on people outside the discipline. Morality and morale edged closer together as more ministers gave soothing sermons, assuaging anxiety and disappointment as well as guilt and defeat. Norman Vincent Peale's *The Power of Positive Thinking* was the nonfiction best seller of 1953. Businessmen found psychology useful. General Motors, for example, hired seven psychologists to analyze the 1957 Chevrolet's smell and sound. More common was the personality test for potential executives, administered by one third of American corporations by 1952. Novels, television shows, and movies often featured the vagaries of the heart and situations of psychological entrapment. As a consequence, school counseling and psychology were connected with an increasingly popular and powerful branch of social and medical science, an association far more beneficial than affiliation with Life Adjustment. Psychologists did not disdain adjustment and middle-class respectability, and they seemed to be reputable professionals, not windy education school teachers.

The guidance departments, however large, were not clinics dispensing survival skills. Counselors rarely analyzed teen-agers' emotions to the extent envisioned by many reformers. Counselors never shouted about curing emotional illness or revamping the curriculum. They were greeted as administrators who would help keep the peace, expanding school services rather than reshaping what was already there. This was the sort of progressive reform that meshed with the traditional priorities and values of the high schools. Yet the rise of pupil personnel services (as they were called) honored the progressive imperative to attend to a broader range of student needs.

In the early twentieth century, guidance concentrated on discipline and vocational placement. By the time of Sputnik, in 1957, helping with course selections and advising on college planning were the priorities. Counselors thus became mediators between students and the bureaucracy, but with a physical and symbolic location closer to the administration. As a result of rising enrollments and larger schools, the facilitator role was necessary, but it left little place for discussion about personal affairs, especially for dutiful students obeying the rules and passing their courses. Students seemed to accept that arrangement. One study reported students' preferences for those helping with personal and emotional problems. Three-quarters opted for someone outside high school, 21 percent checked "other school personnel," and only 4 percent picked the counselors. (When the counselors answered the same questionnaire, only 56 percent picked themselves as being preferable!)

It is true that school psychologists paid attention to emotional woes, but their role in the high school was not a major one. School psychologists before the 1970s spent almost all their time with elementary grade children. High school cases involved the truant and the retarded; these clients came by compulsion more than by choice. Until the mid 1960s, two thirds of one large reservoir of casework — emotionally disturbed and socially maladjusted students — attended public and private residential facilities separate from the regular high schools. Psychologists usually operated from the central office, not the school; often they referred difficult cases to private therapists or public clinics. And rarely did diagnosis go beyond classification based on test scores, which generally confirmed statistically that Susie read slowly, David's IQ was 88 — what teachers already knew intuitively. Labeling offered teachers very little help in individualizing instruction to suit different learning styles.

Psychologists usually respected the importance of institutional order. At the Lawrenceville School in 1947, the headmaster wanted to delay an expulsion, pending a psychiatric report. Deferral was unprecedented; the faculty had never used clinical criteria in considering dismissals. The staff anticipated an "overindulgent and sentimental" report, but when the doctor concluded his talk by recommending dismissal, "the atmosphere thawed perceptibly." The following fall, the psychiatrist addressed the faculty in a series of lectures. He stressed the importance of high disciplinary standards strictly enforced, and reassured the masters that psychiatry was simply "mental hygiene" designed for modest preventive ends. In the early 1960s, the sociologist Edgar Z. Friedenberg discovered the same sort of cautious attitude among students in a public high school. He asked for evaluations of this hypothetical situation:

> Mr. Arthur Clarke, a social studies teacher at your school, is taking his midmorning coffee break. On entering a men's washroom he discovers Johnny Barto, a junior and a somewhat notorious character around the school, smoking. Mr. Clarke knows that Johnny should be in class this hour and furthermore, that he is a troublemaker, is having difficulty with his courses, is on probation, and that he is old enough to quit school. While Mr. Clarke and Johnny are approximately the same size, Johnny is not very strong. His whole attitude, though, is one of arrogance, as if to say, "Show me, buddy."

Of nine possible courses of action — including calling the parents, sending Johnny to the principal, and referring Johnny to a student court — the students chose this paragraph:

> At the faculty meeting that afternoon, Mr. Clarke discusses the "Johnny Barto problem" with the school psychologist, and

the school psychologist agrees to set up a counseling program designed to get at Johnny's "antisocial" behavior and straighten him out. The psychologist then calls Johnny in for counseling.

According to Friedenberg, students thought referral to the psychologist "would show [Johnny] that he had not gotten away with anything, but it would also show that people were trying to help him . . . but the school psychologist is not supposed to work *with* Johnny; he is expected to work *on* him. He is supposed to tinker with him and straighten him out." Johnny Barto needed life adjustment. The place to get it was in a specialist's office, not in a classroom, talking to a teacher. What was unacceptable as the center of the curriculum was fine when it was at the edges of school life.

The class Johnny cut was probably less forbidding than the classes his parents had encountered in their schooldays. Change in the design and furnishing of high schools is another example of conservative reform straddling traditional values and progressive ideals. The structures erected in the postwar years were less austere than the fortresses they replaced, but the new schools were often as stark as the shopping malls they began to resemble. The topic of school architecture is a neglected subject in need of more study, but a few generalizations are possible.

The amount of school construction in the 1920s was not matched until 1950, the year when capital expenses topped $1 billion for the first time. By 1957 that figure tripled. The rapid expansion reflected the pressure of rising birthrates and twenty years of tight budgeting. The nation needed sixty thousand new classrooms for the 1954–1955 school year; in contrast, President Franklin D. Roosevelt's Works Progress Administration built twenty-four thousand elementary and secondary classrooms from 1933 to 1939, which represented 70 percent of all school construction in those years. Aided by postwar affluence and successful local bond referenda, there was a school building boom throughout the 1950s. Architects often relied on the advice of educational consultants affiliated with universities sympathetic to progressive reform. The final product reflected the influence of many factors, especially cost, so no one could declare school architects the agents of an insidious plot hatched by teachers' colleges. Yet the new buildings made manifest educators' visions of the proper environment for learning and teaching. The new citadels offered friendlier settings than the old museums of virtue.

What is most striking about the new high schools of the 1950s is their resemblance to elementary schools. Three- and four-story ponderosity gave way to one- and two-story casualness. Low-rise structures previously found only in the warmest states appeared throughout the country, especially in suburbs with ample land for horizontal expansion. Usually the new schools reduced the older demarcation between outside and inside. Courtyards were popular for single-building schools. Some campus-style sites had breezeways connecting several buildings; elsewhere, corridors radiating like the fingers of an open hand ensured spaciousness. Often the plans mirrored college construction, but the airiness of the one-story elementary school was the closer parallel. The buildings conveyed the impression of greater accessibility than the schools of early years. (The same shift affected the appearance of many elementary schools, but the change was more pronounced for high schools.) On the surface, the architecture announced ranchhouse ease more than cathedral-like solemnity, third-grade playfulness more than college seriousness.

On the inside, new classrooms were indeed less austere than the spaces in older high schools. Chalkboards were often yellow or light green instead of black or dark green. The desks were also lighter — honey and straw were popular colors. The furniture was movable, not bolted to the floor. The ceilings were lower than in the older buildings, and better lighting and acoustics made reading and listening easier. It was also simpler for the student to see outside, because partly glassed interior classroom doors and exterior windows extended closer to the ground.

Yet the sprawl of a one-story institution could be just as formidable as a four-story pile of masonry. In both settings, there were more right angles than curves, more squares of cinder block or brick than square feet of carpeting, little privacy in the Spartan washrooms, and no differentiation of paint colors. There were no places the students "owned." There might be a student store (for selling textbooks, tickets, and the like), but not a student lounge. Long straight corridors banked with rows of lockers emphasized the lack of space belonging to students. An area for quiet reflection was not a priority. Outside evaluators allotted more points for toilet facilities than the combined total for the library and teachers' offices. The persistence of clearly defined classroom clusters for business and vocational education perpetuated the segregation of different types of students. The practice office machines were not next to the chemistry classes; the beauty parlor equipment was far from the language lab.

The new mode of building did not affect all students, particularly those in rural areas. In 1951, only 39 percent of the high schools held more than twenty classrooms. In many small towns students had never spent their days in a fortress. One Southern black high school doubled as a gristmill and canning kitchen; rural schools included buildings converted from barns, grocery stores, poolrooms, and cheese factories. But school consolidations (coupled with rising enrollments) meant that a girl in Iowa might no longer walk to the village school. Instead, she would travel by bus to a larger facility farther from home, full of strangers from other villages, where she might feel isolated and anonymous. Her new school would outwardly resemble an elementary school, but it was a large and remote edifice compared with the local schoolhouse her mother had attended. In many hamlets, the sleek new consolidated high school would not be a relaxed modification of older architectural forms.

School architecture and guidance activities marked a slow and cautious advance of efforts to moderate the schools' chilly climate. Educators acknowledged the importance of students' feeling good about themselves by building sprawling ranch-style schools and expanding the guidance departments, but the changes they oversaw were conservative. New buildings were cheap and efficient. Hiring more counselors solved administrative problems. Working on, not with, Johnny Barto was still the primary commitment of educators.

Reaffirming and Reflecting

In March 1958, a *Life* magazine article, "Crisis in Education," contrasted the schooldays of Stephen and Alexis, high school students in America and Russia. Stephen wisecracked in math class and joked about his clumsiness in typing. Alexis wrote marvelous lab reports and read *Sister Carrie* in English. Stephen needed tutoring in geometry; Alexis visited science museums for enrichment. After school Stephen amused himself with dates, dancing, and swimming. Alexis played chess and piano. No wonder the Russians put a satellite in orbit before the Americans, the article implied. Our schools were softer than theirs. The 1957 Russian space shot intensified the fears that American schools coddled the young. The collapse of Life Adjustment as an organized cause left many people unconvinced that high schools were rigorous enough, and the space launch seemed to heighten the importance of brain power.

In March 1958, James B. Conant was visiting American high schools as preparation for his own analysis of the putative crisis. He gathered a great deal of statistical information, wrote a short book describing what he found, and immediately became the most renowned high school reformer of the 1950s and early 1960s. After twenty years as president of Harvard University and four years as high commissioner for Germany and ambassador to West Germany, Conant was sure to have a large and attentive audience for whatever he wrote on American schools. No educational reformer of that time had his extraordinary combination of careers. In addition to his service in Cambridge and Bonn, Conant was a distinguished chemist who helped develop chemical warfare during World War I, and in World War II served as an adviser to the Manhattan Project, which made the first atomic bombs. His talents looked especially impressive in the 1950s. Cold War tensions enhanced the prestige of weapons inventors and ambassadors, and the combination of national service with the Harvard presidency was multiplicative rather than additive.

During the years of his Harvard presidency, 1933 to 1953, Conant found time to write extensively on public secondary education. He saw great possibilities for the high schools to improve America's social structure; they could identify and encourage academically talented young people and help many to improve their economic and social position. He recognized, however, that a democratic country must not foster class distinctions. Laborers and lawyers had to share common ideals, many of which were presented in courses like English and social-studies, which were required of everyone. Especially urgent was his belief in the "equality of status of all forms of honest labor" (one of Conant's favorite phrases). Conant wanted education to advance competition and cooperation, individualism and social justice.

To encourage both mobility and stability, Conant placed his bet on high schools large enough to offer an array of academic, vocational, and general education courses. He preferred comprehensive schools to private, small, or specialized schools. The ideal school would nurture democratic fellowship, challenge the talented (whom he defined as the top 15 percent to 20 percent on aptitude tests), and train the vocational students. The comprehensive high schools would mix and sift simultaneously, a desirable objective Conant thought impossible in selective or small schools.

Conant returned from Germany early in 1957 to devote his time to a study of the comprehensive high school. The Carnegie Corporation funded the project generously enough to enable him to hire four associates for research, field work, and writing. Conant and his staff focused their search on examples that demonstrated the existence of the type of secondary education Conant already endorsed. The validity of the model itself was not in doubt.

After making one-day visits to fifty-five schools in eighteen states, Conant asked twenty-two of the schools to tabulate the course selections of the seniors whose standardized test scores before ninth grade ranked in the top quartile of their class. (Conant later reported the course work of only the top 15 percent.) Their programs were of greatest interest to Conant. If the best students slid through high school without enough rigorous academic work, then the ideal of comprehensiveness was not being realized. It was crucial that this minority be well served.

In *The American High School Today,* published in 1959, Conant announced that in eight schools with satisfactory general and vocational education, a majority of the academically talented boys took at least seven years of math and science (a load Conant deemed suitably challenging). In only two schools, however, did foreign languages attract a majority of the bright boys for three years. (Girls' language enrollments were higher.) In "all but a few" schools, the sharpest "were not working hard enough." And in only five of the eight satisfactory schools was there "significant interaction" between students of different abilities and career goals. The majority of the twenty-two schools left much undone (and because Conant visited schools with good reputations, the state of affairs elsewhere was surely worse, especially in the smaller high schools unable or unwilling to offer physics, French IV, calculus, and the like). Yet Conant did not despair. "Most of the schools which I found unsatisfactory in one or more respects could become satisfactory by relatively minor changes," he wrote. The existence of a handful of praiseworthy comprehensive high schools was cause enough for him to urge the laggards to reform.

What lessons could others learn from the better schools? *American High School* offered a total of twenty-one recommendations, most of which were designed to provide challenges for the talented students and marketable skills for others. High schools had to match the right students with the proper courses. The 15 percent who were academically talented required a program of four years of English, mathematics, and foreign language, and three years of science and social studies, a program Conant hoped would entail at least fifteen hours of homework weekly. Vocational students needed training in trades with real employment opportunities in the local community. Very slow readers who were not retarded were to be assigned to special teachers and given special textbooks instead of being steered to vocational courses. (For the other end of the scale, Conant proposed segregating the top 3 percent from the merely talented so that they could receive either advanced tutoring or have special classes.) It was true that several recommendations in the book — the use of homerooms, the requirement of a heterogeneously grouped senior-year course in American problems — might have blurred differences, but most of the proposals called for extending distinctions.

The making of *American High School* merits inspection because the book reaffirmed the existing distribution and exercise of power. Conant's writing proclaimed his commitment to high schools strong enough to direct students this way and that. In his opinion, schools were to test extensively, group students by ability, and channel the brightest to the most demanding academic courses. Conant did not advocate a laissez-faire environment with curricular units on dating and mating. Both doubt and dickering shaped Conant's investigations. He worried that some of his own well-publicized recommendations were not tough enough; the public cheerleading masked private hesitations. Moreover, Conant worked closely with prominent educators and politicians, preferring to advance his ideas behind closed doors. His support for school consolidation evoked more opposition than any of his recommendations. That protest underscored the persistence of the devotion to local control. In that particular, Conant did not reflect so much as encounter educational realities.

Whether as a mirror or as a lamp, Conant's published and unpublished writings show that the old order was very much alive. The endorsement of high schools as adult-directed was much more common than the notion that the students' socioemotional condition should shape the curriculum. And the informal style of decision making still marked the educational world of the late 1950s.

Ability Grouping

Grouping by aptitude: that was *American High School*'s major premise, the foundation without which a Conant high school could never stand. As early as the second month of field work, in November 1957, an adviser from the Educational Testing Service (the administrators of several widely used tests) felt that "the main Conant case" rested on grouping. Perhaps his organization had an interest in believing so, but in the same month Conant himself began a long "First Thoughts" memo with a strenuous defense of ability grouping. Without grouping, Conant saw little chance for academic excellence in the classroom. Typical of his opinion was a field note in which he evaluated a school where "social studies is used as an integrating mechanism, and there is no opportunity for ability grouping in this field. Therefore, it suffers to that degree from the intellectual side. You can't have it both ways." Curricular reform was a question of who rather than what or how; Conant said very little about course content or teachers' methods. Because grouping was so important, it deserves close attention.

The most striking evidence of Conant's commitment to ability grouping is in his unpublished correspondence with Henry Chauncey, then president of the Educational Testing Service. At the start of his high school study, Conant hoped to secure separate measures of aptitude and achievement. A letter to Chauncey in the fall of 1957 explained his position. Conant said that he had always assumed that an aptitude test in junior high school gauged "potentialities" for later academic success. But in his initial school visits, he heard many educators question the validity of IQ tests; often they preferred to use teacher evaluations and achievement scores for placement. Conant told Chauncey that reliable aptitude tests would facilitate grouping by identifying the bright but lazy students who should not rest in peace in undemanding classrooms.

Chauncey's reply is missing, but four of his associates wrote memos in which they took Conant to task for "asking for the moon," as one assistant said. They countered that achievement and ability could not be disentangled, nor need they be. At any age students differed in the capacity to benefit from future instruction; the difference might have had "a thousand and one" causes other than genes. The more factors the school took into account, the better; there was no reason to try to isolate something as elusive as raw genetic endowment. Guidance was not to be so "scientific" that it ignored teachers' opinions. Steering particular students to particular courses always involved questions of value, one colleague argued. Prodding the unmotivated might offend schools that prized students who on their own initiative could "keep in step, and maintain the pace, and follow the leader" without constant pushing from the staff. Pressing the bright laggards also assumed that motivation and manners could change quickly, an assumption not universally held.

In 1958, Conant again quizzed Chauncey on the reliability of aptitude tests. Conant asked whether a test of fifteen academically talented boys would identify at least twelve "who really are the most able." Before compiling the inventories from the twenty-two schools, "I've got to be surer about the tests." His staff proceeded with the analysis of the course work of the top 15 percent, but Conant's fretfulness marked a long letter of July 1958, the time he began to draft *American High School.* He reminded Chauncey that "you ought to be able to devise tests" that discriminate between achievement and aptitude, conceding immediately afterward that he and Chauncey had discussed that issue "for years" and that he knew the testing experts would dismiss him as "unrealistic or ignorant."

Conant also sought a ratio between achievement and aptitude that he could offer school boards as a gauge of teaching quality. Chauncey politely suggested the alternative of a "laborious" evaluation with multiple and extensive tests used in tandem with other evidence. Chauncey's advisers were less circumspect. One asked whether a sensible farmer would judge his own skill by dividing yield per acre by soil fertility, ignoring rain, wind, heat, and insects. Another said, "Some influential nontesting person is always trying to push us off the deep end." The Educational Testing Service staff had a keen sense of the complexities of test interpretation, and cautioned against putting technical instruments in the untrained hands of school board members.

The Chauncey correspondence is only part of the unpublished material that illuminates the depth of Conant's commitment to grouping. Conant's fear of diluting various groups with less able students was greater than the book let on. He differed from critics who favored academic courses for the middling group. He said to a Berkeley professor that diligent average-ability students could grasp subjects "reasonably well," but he preferred that they take more vocational courses, which would motivate them and provide them with skills. "I should hate to think of these same students sitting through advanced academic subjects." Conant feared that their parents would force them to take too much math, science, and foreign language. In one field note he mused about the school with an average student IQ of 105. If 35 percent of the students entered college, what courses should be recommended for the middle 30 percent, who were in precollege courses only because of parental pressure? At Ann Arbor High School, all the members of that group took geometry, but "for my money, they'd be just as well off if nearly half of them didn't." About another school, where 40 percent of the boys took physics, Conant wrote, "We almost ought to have it as a separate criterion that if more than 15–20% of the students are taking physics and there is no ability grouping, the physics course is unlikely to be a very good one." He did not want to see college enrollments soar. A first degree, Conant felt, told nothing about a graduate unless one knew something about the college. Conant believed that four-year colleges should not increase too much in size and number but that community colleges should expand rapidly and lure average students.

For the student of decidedly lower ability, Conant considered departure from high school a good choice. According to a field note, Conant felt that students whose IQ was below 90 should be "encouraged" to leave school at sixteen. His "First Thoughts" memo rejected holding power as a measure of school quality. Conant doubted that a slow learner could achieve the sort of mastery of easy material that a brighter pupil exercised over harder matter in the same field of study. He went so far as to say that "for boys in this group, employment may be found in simple tasks in garages, and if this can be done by the school authorities, they have certainly made a social contribution to the community." Later, someone — the handwriting looks like Conant's — scratched out "garages" and penciled in "the community."

Conant briefly flirted with a more drastic form of protection against dilution. A memo of June 17, 1958, titled "An Academic High School Within a Comprehensive High School," described the selective admissions and prescribed courses at Allentown High School in Pennsylvania, which had a very selective admissions policy for its academic program and required difficult courses of those enrolled in it. Conant wondered whether a similar arrangement might work in other high schools. School administrators could at least consider special diplomas for high grade point averages and require high grades of those who wanted to enroll in junior- and senior-year mathematics. Conant said that even if they decided to reject the idea, he "might hint at it in some of my speeches to the superintendents as a sort of trial balloon."

Several other trial balloons are signs of Conant's inclinations. In *American High School,* he mentioned how "proper labeling" of courses encouraged de facto grouping. "First Thoughts," the unpublished precursor of the book, referred to grouping by "partially disguised" namings. Recommendation number twenty-one in *American High School* advocated heterogeneous grouping in the twelfth-grade course on American problems, but in the "First Thoughts" memo Conant said that homogeneous grouping should be used if economics and political theory were part of the course.

Taken together, the memos, letters, and field notes indicate how keenly Conant sought to justify his final recommendations on groupings. He yearned for strict and dependable measures of native aptitude as the surest basis of grouping, worried about blurring the distinctions between the academically advanced and the less talented, and considered the possibility of a school-within-a-school for the talented. On the crucial matter of course selection, Conant was closer to 1940 than 1970, because the administrative machinery and institutional authority necessary for grouping reinforced the power of the school over the students' lives. Conant assumed that any problem with grouping would concern efficiency; justice was not a consideration. He never questioned the right of adults to maneuver students. Indeed, he felt that stratification in American society was merciful and generous. Conant believed that this country "gives losers the widest latitude in rewriting the rules of the contest." Like most school people, he did not apologize for the sorting and slotting done in schools.

Cramped Legs and Tired Eyes

Nor did Conant worry about the taste of the medicines he prescribed. Some people thought his program would frazzle the students. A college president figured that the artistic teen-ager would be busy for eleven hours each day "if everything keeps exactly on schedule and there is no lost time. Can it be done? Surely. But when do our musicians and artists practice, or must they come from the lower 85%?" One of Conant's associates reported that in his Missouri high school, a year of the Conant reforms encouraged neglect of "the heart and emotions," because the curriculum encompassed too much material. A sharper warning came from Paul Diederich of the Educational Testing Service.

> As we advocate a "get tough" policy with these superior students, we should realize that we are advocating a daily schedule for growing boys and girls, at the most social and fun-loving period of their lives, that is a lot tougher than any adult puts in — except a few harassed executives with ulcers. Whenever we teachers go to educational conventions, do we regularly

go to seven or eight meetings per day, sitting on hard chairs in cramped quarters the whole time, and then return to our hotel room to put in three or four more hours boning up on what the speakers wanted us to know, so that we could prove that we understood it and remembered it when they quizzed us about it next day? . . . You may say, "This is sheer exaggeration. Surely going to high school is much nicer than this." No, it is not, and I know whereof I speak. I have just been sitting in classes day after day all over the sixteen excellent school systems participating in the "lay reader study" . . . I solemnly declare that at the end of each day visiting classes — even though I am treated as a VIP, not as a guilty student — my fundament is sore, my legs are cramped, my eyes are tired, my brain is reeling, and I would rather do anything else on earth than study for three or four more hours what these students are supposed to study. It is not that the teaching is bad; there is simply too much sitting down, listening to talk, talk, talk. We say that these students ought to learn to "work hard," and they would not mind that in the least; it is the sitting down and listening all day in a space half the size of a grave that gets them down . . . The teachers come out of it as scarred and tired as the students. The art of teaching is so delicate and difficult that I would be willing to bet that we shall wind up . . . with the fully documented conclusion that no one can do it effectively for more than two hours a day . . .

All this dreary, ineffectual round is based on the assumption that learning proceeds best when administered in doses of five periods a week plus homework for all academic subjects. This assumption is unsupported by a shred of evidence in all experimental literature, contrary to common sense, and contrary to the practice of almost all colleges . . . Dr. Conant does not say one word to justify it.

Conant probably did not lose sleep over the Diederich memo. In 1960 he wrote "good" next to these lines from a colleague: "Altogether too many of us try to make everything easy and painless for our youngsters. We prefer leisure to learning." Aside from the issue of civility between future workers and professionals, Conant did not fret about students' comfort. What mattered most was the delivery of the right educational diet, not whether it tasted good or whether the students were invited to select the menu and help with the cooking.

He hoped that mutual respect would accompany the distinctions made between students, but how they felt about one another was an issue Conant de-emphasized in 1957 and 1958. Even before he began his school study, Conant had emphasized that comprehensive high schools had three tasks of equal importance: challenging the academically talented, providing vocational training for noncollege-bound students, and teaching general education to foster democratic values. *American High School* presented the same triad.

But during the early months of planning his study, he gave less emphasis to the general education portion. Comparison of an October 1957 memo with a letter from Conant to John Gardner, written in December 1956, suggests that the change began before the bulk of the project's field work was undertaken. The note to Gardner indicated Conant's interest in learning whether all the "integrating forces" discussed in *Education for ALL American Youth* "were in fact operating." To ascertain that would have required an extensive examination of student attitudes and friendships. The ambition expressed ten months later, in the memo, was much more modest. General education was mentioned only in connection with heterogeneous grouping of students in homerooms, which Conant hoped would promote social integration.

Conant came to place his bet on good vocational course work as a means to achieve social cohesion. His field notes, full of evaluations of vocational programs, often weighed the advantages and disadvantages of separate vocational schools. In Chicago, where the superintendent opposed comprehensive schools, Conant agreed that elaborate aircraft engineering and bricklaying programs, already in place in some of the vocational schools, need not be incorporated into the curriculum of every school in the system. But outside the large cities, Conant resisted specialized schools. He wanted vocational work to be a part of the comprehensive high school for reasons "largely social rather than educational," as he wrote in a staff memo. Social in what sense? Not relations between blacks and whites; Conant avoided that subject in *American High School.* Not student councils; domination by the brightest "is a phenomenon which repeats itself very often in the schools, and I'm getting used to it." Conant thought that a strong vocational program would so engage otherwise indifferent students that they would take seriously the heterogeneously grouped homerooms and the course on problems of democracy. As he told one friend, "For certain kinds of people [vocational work] provides the only motivation which, I believe, will keep them interested in and benefitting from the education for citizenship on which you rightly lay so much emphasis."

How does school feel? was asked only as a narrower question: Do future blue- and white-collar workers respect each other? Even with that pinched phrasing, Conant gave the question less attention in his high school study than in his previous writings on education. To Conant and others, school climate — a popular topic by the 1970s — was not an important variable in measuring educational institutions. For evaluating a high school, a statistician consulting the front office's files would have been chosen over an anthropologist roaming the lunchroom.

Doubt and Dickering

Conant's method of arriving at agreements exemplified the decision-making process of the 1940s and 1950s. As some of his thoughts on grouping suggest, he occasionally had reservations and doubts that he did not air publicly; his outward optimism covered his misgivings.

In the fall of 1958, when Conant finished the draft of *American High School,* he told his associates that he was becoming more critical of the schools he had visited. "As I now review the situation, I see that I just barely found a couple of schools that were satisfactory in all *three* respects [vocational training, academic challenge, social integration]. If it hadn't been for Sputnik and the general rush, I should have probably looked further and held my report for another six months."

A remarkable admission, and remarkable too that Conant made a similar confession two months later, just before publication of the book. The "torrent of uninformed and unintelligent criticism" unleashed by Sputnik had hastened the release of the report, Conant repeated. But he also admitted a conscious decision that predated Sputnik, that of playing up the positive aspects of American high schools. From 1957 on, Conant "stressed always what should be added to the program and said nothing about what should be eliminated." His sympathy for educators actually declined in 1958; he thought too many of them stressed health, citizenship, public speaking, art, and music. They "have been little interested in pushing the academically talented to develop those talents which this group alone possesses." Schools did indeed neglect the brightest students. "I am afraid the profession must bear the responsibility in large measure for this fact."

An equally striking hesitation concerned girls. Conant privately cared more about the high school course work elected by boys. When he evaluated enrollment figures, what mattered most were the percentages of talented boys who chose the rigorous subjects. As Conant jotted down on a copy of a report stating that 11 percent of Indiana high school graduates completed four years of math, "right kids? boys — girls — what goes on?" After just one month of field work, Conant asked his staff to present separate enrollment data for males and females. Conant believed that most of the bright students not bound for college were girls, "which doesn't seem to me, therefore, to represent a bad situation at all. A good deal of the talk about the bright people who don't go to college may be just the question of the girls." Conant later claimed, in a letter to the president of Bennington, then a women's college, that "national need" justified his discrimination; after all, "professional people will be 97 percent men." He told John Kenneth Galbraith that it was easy to defend his recommendations by invoking the need for more professionals. Galbraith, in contrast, rued the relegation of so many Radcliffe women to "a life in New Rochelle," a fate that Galbraith lamented as "a kind of brood mare doctrine." In a 1959 letter, he told Conant that many girls were "decidedly uneasy" about the prospect, and hyperbolically declared that now was the time for "a stern attack on home and motherhood."

Conant's reply typified his tendency — on this matter and others — to sidestep potentially volatile issues. "I am frank to admit I treat this subject gingerly, for I know strong emotion can be aroused on one side or the other. I certainly don't wish to complicate my educational recommendations" by attacking domesticity, he wrote to Galbraith. Five months earlier, before publication of *American High School,* Conant told his senior associate that he was "not so sure about the girls; I admit [they] are a somewhat different story," and may not need to take all of his recommended program. He tried to duck the question: "I have said an alternative for girls is recommended by some experienced administrators. Perhaps this is a compromise that will please no one." In the published report, Conant did not endorse the alternative; he simply reported it. Elsewhere in the book, Conant actually sounded supportive of girls. "If all the high schools were functioning as well as some I have visited, the education of all American youth would be satisfactory, except for the study of foreign languages and the guidance of the more able girls." His private reservations about the preparation of academically talented girls were not evident in the published text, nor were his gloomier assessments of overall school quality.

Conant was not the only person with misgivings. His book evoked the greatest opposition from the small high schools he wanted to consolidate. In a memo to John Gardner, and again in a note to his advisers, Conant emphasized that his recommendation for larger schools was "the one most vigorously attacked." High school size "is the major issue in many places." The merger of small schools was a key part of Conant's projected reforms, and he knew the idea would meet the stiff opposition of rural representatives in the state legislatures, who fought state aid for larger schools. On the other hand, major educational groups favored consolidation, and the movement was well advanced in many states. In Illinois, for example, there were 646 high schools in 1944–1945, but only 280 by 1960–1961; in Iowa, where there were 819 high schools in 1954–1955, there were 562 by 1960–1961. But staunch rural opposition persisted, which helps explain why the filmstrip Conant made for the National Education Association began with a day in the life of a rural comprehensive high school.

Conant was sure that geography rarely necessitated tiny high schools. One superintendent told him that to meet the specifications of *American High School* he "would have to fly our students to and from school." In such cases, Conant was ready to have students boarded for four days of each week. He hesitated to tell another correspondent how to improve small schools for fear of minimizing the need for reorganization. When a Harvard professor reminded him that local pride in village schools often bred a "cherished" connection between the community and its schools, Conant wrote in the margin of the letter, "Is a high school's purpose to give kids an education or to make citizens proud?" Because Conant accepted the fact of decentralization of American education, he was more sensitive to local differences than were other prominent critics of the 1950s, and he refused to recommend federal intervention beyond school construction money.

The recommendations of his book did not sweep the field, yet Conant worked hard to make the report acceptable. He stayed in touch with educational and political leaders in the large states. The study was a personal report, but he wanted to speak to policy makers and to create a climate of opinion favorable to the sort of education he championed.

After writing an article for *Life* in 1964, Conant told his colleague Merle Borrowman that the issue of most concern was "the old one"; namely, "How hard do I hit the establishment *again* in public." He asked Borrowman, "Is there some way of maintaining my 'third force position' and yet not seeming to give in to the establishment?" That question was particularly serious after the sharp criticisms in his 1963 study of teacher training, but it was not a new question. Conant had always wanted to work closely with professional educators and their associations, but not identify himself totally as an insider. It is typical that when his associate Bernard Miller urged him, in 1958, to "wrap the N.E.A. mantle around yourself," Conant wrote in the margin of Miller's memo, "but lightly."

Groups like the N.E.A. were not the audience Conant sought to reach with his high school study. He focused instead on an assortment of influential men and traveled extensively to speak with local leaders. Those trips began in the spring of 1958, eight months before publication of *American High School*. At that time, Conant visited Indiana, Illinois, and Minnesota. In each state, he gave speeches and interviews, but "the real work is done with the educational, business, labor, and communication leaders in the state who come to the off-the-record luncheons." In Indiana, for instance, the president of Indiana University brought together thirty guests, who heard Conant urge the consolidation of their small schools.

Conant did not rely solely on the state power brokers. He corresponded with various education school professors, especially those whose research paralleled his own. Conant also wrote regularly to school superintendents in large cities. In fact, he told the chiefs of the St. Louis, Chicago, and Detroit systems that he would not release his later book *Slums and Suburbs* if "its publication would do you more harm than good." Earlier he agreed to districtwide rather than school-by-school inventories in Chicago; the latter would have embarrassed the superintendent because of "the problems raised by the racial situation."

But the quirkiness of public opinion bothered Conant. He felt that people clung to blanket condemnations instead of distinguishing the successful aspects of schooling from the mediocre. Conant also feared that no one could simultaneously calm the nervous and goad the sluggish. To his Educational Policies Commission colleagues he depicted, just after the Sputnik launch, the beleaguered educators' dilemma.

> What we are trying to do in part is to say to the American public, "Don't be silly. You're talking a lot of nonsense about the whole thing. You don't know anything about it, your premises are wrong," etc. And we don't have to say that to the profession.
>
> But at the same time, we cannot say — and I am sure nobody would want to say — that everything is satisfactory in the schools. [Yet] the minute you begin to say they are not satisfactory, these other people say, "Aha! The Educational Policies Commission now at last recognizes there is something wrong with the schools." Whatever we say is going to be used against us in this very emotional and irrational debate — if it be a debate — or discussion now going on.

Conant worried about the fate of *American High School* once it was in the hands of book reviewers. What they had to say might not reach his audience, "those in a position to make decisions affecting public education — namely, school boards and superintendents." Conant was aware of the shortcomings of many school boards, but he retained his faith in reform from the top down. Gentlemanly pressure from above was more agreeable (and efficient) than noisy grassroots agitation, he believed. Conant preferred representative government over town meetings.

As a decision maker, then, Conant was a man of his day. Although he did not voice the opinions of all school people, how he went about his study, and the opposition he aroused, reflected the patterns of power. His reliance on information from, and influence at, the top of the educational pyramid encouraged cordiality from those in positions of authority. Conant's struggles with his private reservations were similar to the Educational Policies Commission's deliberations on *Education for ALL American Youth;* in both cases, public optimism held sway over private hesitations. The way things got done was not drastically transformed in the 1950s.

Social Dynamite

In the late 1950s and early 1960s, school people championed programs that presented the academic challenge Conant and others favored. Introducing tough courses and tests took precedence over students' feelings about themselves, one another, and school. Rewriting a lab manual was fashionable; work on affective education was not. Some of the changes began before Sputnik and Conant: early admission to colleges, Advanced Placement college credits for seniors, and National Merit Scholarships. National initiatives immediately followed Sputnik. The federal government provided money through the 1958 National Defense Education Act, and the National Science Foundation educational budget grew from $1.5 million in 1952 to $84.5 million in 1962. There was concurrent activity at the local and state level. Between 1958 and 1960, the number of language labs jumped from sixty-four to over a thousand. State education department specialists in science, math, and foreign languages increased fivefold.

Enrollments reflected the heightened respect for math, science, and foreign languages. In each field, relatively more students took a course in 1960–1961 than in 1948–1949, the year of the previous census of enrollments. Other straws in the wind were the spread of Russian language instruction from one state to thirty-six; the declining percentage of students in business courses (never before had those enrollments slumped); and the teaching of foreign languages and algebra in junior high schools. Not everything bent to the academic breeze. Driver education boomed in the 1950s. Enrollments of mentally retarded students rose substantially between 1958 and 1963. Art enrollments rose slightly, music held steady, and requirements for gym and health increased a bit. As always, the opportunity to take a Conant-style load of serious subjects like physics and French IV depended on where a student lived. More than a third of all high schools in 1960 enrolled fewer than two hundred students, and less than 10 percent of those schools offered a third year of any foreign language.

Among curriculum experts, optimism was stirred by the acclaimed theories of the psychologist Jerome Bruner, who argued that every student could glimpse the underlying structures of each discipline. As he recalled, "The strategy was to find means that would help the learner to get through the surface clutter to the simpler, more beautiful underlying forms. Issues of race and poverty in education had not come into our consciousness. At least not into mine." New projects in math and physics generated much excitement because they called for problem solving in place of rote recall. Social studies reform soon followed; it also required students to study underlying structures and promoted inquiry rather than memorization.

Yet curricular expansion and revision did not transform secondary education. Though committees, talk, and fussing abounded, much subject matter remained unchanged, like the basic U.S. history requirement, physical education, and tenth-grade English. New federal funding for reform projects did not constitute a major commitment by the government. Considering the scale and complexity of school curricula, the investment was small. A concurrent crusade, NASA, received far more money. Moreover, the reformers rarely trusted teachers. University professors put together teacher-proof packages with elaborate instruction guides without seeking the teachers' help. As one sociologist remarked, "This is an attempt to rationalize the instruction rather than improve the skill of the handicraft workers." Also, the new initiatives targeted the best students at a time when cities began to stagger under the burden of educating an influx of new students, many with low elementary school achievement, hostile attitudes toward schooling, and unsupportive or broken homes. The new social studies, for instance, relied on abstract terms and sophisticated language, but not everyone in school was a bright twelfth-grader. Principals and counselors usually discouraged even the brightest beneficiaries of the new curricula from the unorthodox but available option of acceleration by early admission to college. Age grading remained the rule.

Academic enrichment also left the school culture largely unaffected. Customs remaining undisturbed included compulsory attendance, isolation of departments from one another, and graduation in return for a set number of course credits. If public recognition of academic excellence spawned a new student elite, its numbers were tiny. In 1956, only the top 5 percent in each school took the first National Merit Examination. By 1964, anyone could take the test; 800,000 did, but a handful won. Similarly, the rise of financial aid intensified the scramble for admission to selective colleges, which appeared more attainable in light of their national recruitment initiatives, but only a few took the coveted prizes. The rest could not blame their fate on poor parents or stingy scholarships; the responsibility for success or failure, as defined by one's college, seemed to rest on the student. As college attendance soared, the price paid by high school dropouts rose. The broadening of the distribution of the college admissions rewards made failure to compete that much worse. The youngster who left early sacrificed proportionately more than a dropout from his parents' class. In short, the drive for academic rigor in the late 1950s and early 1960s, a trend that Conant encouraged, did not result in more relaxed high schools. A few more cars had been added to the train, but usually the ride still felt the same.

The one place where the trip did indeed feel different offered neither relaxation nor striving for excellence. The Southern migrations of the 1940s and 1950s crowded many Northern city schools with a new population unlike the earlier immigrants. Coping with black children new to city life and trying, themselves, to cope with ghettoes, frustrated educators, who had found the previous generation of immigrants more respectful of teachers. Children living in

75

slums grew up more rapidly than their rural and suburban counterparts; exposure to and participation in domestic strife, street violence, drugs, sex, and other experiences initiated ghetto youth to adulthood at an early age. The rawness of the streets affected the schools. In the mid 1950s, teachers in the largest systems reported four times as many assaults as rural schoolteachers. In most cities, school boards forbade teachers to hit students, and it was the urban teachers who were most insistent on having "rights and authorities . . . to maintain effective control." Even in perfectly safe classrooms, the transience of the student population made continuity and closeness hard to achieve.

A book (later made into a movie) that dramatized the threat of aggressive youth was *The Blackboard Jungle,* by Evan Hunter. In that novel, a first-year teacher unsure of his ability to control a class of tough urban vocational students brought a record player to school one day. Joshua Edwards hoped to meet his students on common ground by playing and discussing popular music. But when he put on his favorite, "Celery Stalks at Midnight," the class hooted and jeered. "Ain't you got nobody singin'?" "Take it off now." Efforts by adults to be friendly seemed fruitless. The book exaggerated the terrors of city schools, to be sure; most students were not as rude as Mr. Edwards's group. But *The Blackboard Jungle* accurately expressed common puzzlement at how to deal with unprecedented urban rowdiness.

Many inner city teachers tried to obviate disorder by using films, worksheets, and in-class "homework" that preserved quiet. But this kind of class period discouraged student-teacher conversation on side issues. Many white urban teachers had no desire to fraternize; they often demonstrated "a withdrawal of energies" bred of "weary pessimism" and "fear and hatred of the students."

In 1961, Conant addressed the problem of black education in the North. One of the sequels to *The American High School Today* was Conant's *Slums and Suburbs,* a comparison of two very different settings. The book announced that "we are allowing social dynamite to accumulate in our large cities." Conant referred to one report that the girls' greatest problem was getting from the street to the front door without being sexually assaulted. The fact that approximately half of black dropouts aged sixteen to twenty were without jobs also alarmed him. Conant's proposals were cautious. For example, he rejected busing as impractical, preferring instead staff integration and higher salaries to attract better faculty. He refused to say that standardized tests might be culturally biased. Conant despaired of achieving in big cities his earlier recommendation that there be enough counselors to advise students individually on course selection.

Slums and Suburbs signaled the start of a decade when older notions of equality were re-examined and reshaped. The high schools traditionally offered students the time and facilities necessary for them to demonstrate innate ability. Educators assumed that "talent presumably will realize itself, even in the face of a culturally alien or impoverished home, indifferent teaching, boring textbooks, obsolete curriculum, and all the rest of it." A stronger notion of equality gave the schools more responsibility for seeding and nurturing the motivation that often wilted in blighted neighborhoods. Instead of waiting patiently for the mind to overcome environmental obstacles, the school was to undertake compensatory tasks. As well as revealing talent, schools had to help create it. The new mission meant paying more attention to sociological and psychological considerations. As one principal said, "The kid we used to call belligerent and mischievous we now call deprived and disadvantaged." That tolerance, indicative of a more charitable attitude toward diversity, helped bring about more relaxed classrooms.

4

No One Can Really Tell You
What to Do

IN THE YEARS after World War II, adolescents and teachers became less confined in their out-of-school lives. Adolescent music and other amusements pulled kids closer together; their customs sanctioned more openness among peers than prevailed in the classroom between student and teacher. The wider world began to loosen up earlier and more markedly than the smaller worlds of Latin II and American history. Being granted full membership in the adult world and enjoying richer personal lives probably mellowed some teachers, but that did not transform the classroom culture. Teachers and kids bound themselves more tightly to people their own age. The student's relationship with the teacher retained elements of deference and dependence.

The first wave of change, cresting in the 1950s and early 1960s, saw the school population relax, but not in the schools. There, the balance of power was still with the adults, and the authority of teachers and administrators was rarely challenged. But that authority had little effect on the extent to which youngsters were drawn to cigarettes, beer, fast and loud cars, louder music, faster dancing, and necking parties — rowdiness that took place off campus.

A second wave of change was only several years away, and it would make the first wave seem small. The perspiration of the

1950s came from the heat of exercise; the sweat of the late 1960s from the heat of fever. In the late 1960s and early 1970s, a combination of related changes modified important aspects of traditional age roles. Because of drug use, sexual experimentation, a welcoming job market, and shifting parental values, adolescents came to enjoy some prerogatives and experiences previously reserved for adults. At roughly the same time, many adults adopted curiously adolescent forms of behavior, undergoing identity crises, job changes, explorations of feelings, and marital realignments. The gulf between young and old narrowed, and educators were not as impervious in the 1970s as in the 1950s to their clients' personal lives.

Power also shifted in the realm of decision making. The old authorities did not collapse, but new players entered the game, and rules for the crowded field were less often written in private. Judicial interventions were especially crucial in uncovering the practical accommodations forged by clever insiders. Teacher associations also challenged the power of administrators, and other groups began to participate modestly in policy and planning. Quiet compromises among colleagues gave way to noisy public confrontations. Court-ordered busing and teacher strikes expressed openly the conflicts previously finessed or suppressed behind the scenes.

The consequence of these developments was that people in school sought new ways to get along with one another. Power inside the citadels was reallocated as both adolescents and adults strove for a caring and equitable school environment. This chapter traces the background of the late 1960s and early 1970s turbulence; the following chapter adds material drawn from four different high schools.

Sweet Sixteen

In the twenty years after the war, most schools adopted a hands-off policy toward the personal lives of staff and students. What the unmarried Helen Mundays did on Saturday night was their business. If Helen's students read *Mad* magazine, listened to the Beach Boys, and watched television, the high school would neither condone nor condemn.

The policy (or, rather, the lack of one) toward Helen was new.

Fewer novelists presented the cramped lives of suffering spinster teachers, and articles like "The Teacher and Zestful Living" no longer appeared in the *Harvard Educational Review*. The image of the female schoolteacher as a suppressed hysteric lingered in films like *Picnic* (1956) and *Rachel, Rachel* (1968), but the old stereotype was clearly in the process of vanishing. In a 1957 N.E.A. survey, 61.2 percent of the high school teachers reported no constraints on their personal lives. "Some restrictions, not serious" was the response of 36.4 percent, and only 2.4 percent felt that local taboos were serious. Rural respondents indicated somewhat more restrictiveness, but the differentials were small.

The waning of personal restrictions owed much to school consolidations, teacher shortages, and tenure. Enrollments rose after 1950, but the number of high schools remained roughly the same because of the merger of small school districts. This meant more teachers in a high school, and often the school was located at a distance from the village, removing both the teachers and the school from the scrutiny of the citizenry. At the same time, persistent shortages of certified teachers made administrators hire married women. From 1941 to 1951, the percentage of boards refusing unconditionally to hire married women fell from 58 percent to 8 percent, and the number of single men and women in one-teacher schools plunged from 73.4 percent in 1937 to 25.3 percent in 1951. The afterschool life of married women was not an appropriate object of Victorian prying. In addition, the extension of tenure (from 28 percent of the teaching force in 1931 to 56 percent by 1951) protected those whose behavior at one time might have resulted in dismissal.

But restrictions on teachers inside the school persisted. School authorities rarely wrote explicit rules against discussion of controversial topics, yet teachers feared parental criticism and pressure-group anger. Sex education was always a touchy subject. Expressing political opinions could incite protests. In California, for example, one couple hid a tape recorder in their son's textbook to document a social studies teacher's liberalism. (The parents belonged to the John Birch Society.)

Laissez-faire policy toward student recreation was *not* new, in contrast to the lessening surveillance of teachers' private lives. Life after the final bell usually relaxed the 8:00 A.M.-to-2:30 P.M. regimen. By 1940, schools had abandoned the sort of rules occasionally observed early in the century, when one Georgia school barred weekday movies and another school told girls not to sit on boys' laps in cars. But in the 1950s, the leisure pursuits themselves began to change.

In 1941, the seniors at the Cambridge (Massachusetts) High and Latin School voted Guy Lombardo and Glenn Miller their favorite bandleaders; other entertainment winners included Bob Hope, Bette Davis, dancing, and *Life* magazine — reassuringly familiar choices to parents who shared these leisure preferences. In 1948, a high school girl told the sociologist David Riesman her thoughts on radio programs.

> Well, I like stories — and "Lux" tells the story of some movie, and the "Cavalcade" tells of some important person's life, "The Greatest Story" tells New Testament stories. At Christmas they told the life of Mary until Christ was born, and the actors were so much like the persons would be.

Her selections were as familiar to adults as the choices made by the Cambridge seniors. There is little evidence of a generation gap in the 1940s with respect to entertainment.

The next decade saw the rise of distinctively adolescent music: rock-and-roll and rhythm-and-blues. The records were louder, unlike the croonings of Frank Sinatra and Perry Como. The lyrics paid more attention to adolescent preoccupations, such as driving and dating. (In fact, Ricky Nelson, then a teen-ager, wrote "I'm Walkin' " to impress a date who "said I couldn't sing and laughed at me.") Many artists stood apart from mainstream America: black singers were popular, and several young stars like Elvis Presley looked and sounded delinquent. Energetic dances like the twist bewildered elders for whom a rhumba was satisfactory excitement. Radio stations catered to the profitable youth market; popular disc jockeys whose patter offended adults adopted nicknames like Cat Man or Hound Dog, confirming their allegiance to the young. The subculture also promoted (and was promoted by) television shows, magazines, and clothing, but the major expression of teen-age leisure was music. It was the clearest sign of the strength of an adolescent subculture that stood apart from at least some adult rituals and values.

A combination of forces shaped the growth of youth culture. The postwar baby boom expanded the ranks of the young. Not only were there more children around, but more of them stayed in school through and beyond high school, strengthening their sense of having something in common. Postwar affluence gave teen-agers the money necessary to buy Madras shorts, *Seventeen* magazine, and 70 percent of the records sold in 1958. The economy in 1947 began such sustained growth that in only one year of the next two decades did the gross national product drop by more than 1 percent. Not everyone prospered, but international comparisons were always reassuring: the median income of black Mississippians exceeded the Puerto Rican average, and both figures ranked in the top quartile in the world. Postwar surveys found increased satisfaction with the standard of living, a trend that reached a plateau only in 1959. An average American teen-ager in 1958 had four times the weekly spending money of a 1944 teen — but parents made the major purchases that let youngsters pursue their own recreation. The number of cars per hundred Americans jumped from twenty-four in 1940 to forty in 1960. In the same twenty years, telephones per capita increased by 150 percent. Communicating and traveling with friends became easier, and entertaining one another probably became simpler, thanks to the recreation rooms in the larger houses suburban parents bought in the building boom of the 1950s. New television sets also required adult money. That particular purchase reduced the number of adult radio listeners, leaving more stations to the ears of the young.

Prosperity may have encouraged another peculiarly adolescent ritual — rating each other without primary reference to parental wealth, occupation, and status. In the 1930s, student popularity correlated significantly with parental social standing. As one Midwestern girl described her well-off classmates, "They can do things that we can't afford, and they hog all the offices and are in all the activities." In Muncie, Indiana, the public high school nearly required uniforms because the attire of poor girls was so different from that of middle-class girls that shame or snobbishness affected almost everyone. By the 1950s, the stratifications rested more on good looks and athletic skill than on parental income. Fewer students feared schoolday embarrassment because of shabby wardrobes; fewer students had to work after school to supplement the family income. Ranking each other was relentless; as David Riesman said, "Much is at stake — and still more *seems* to be at stake." But the evaluation standards no longer featured money as prominently as before. Money was not irrelevant in the ratings, but there was a wider class spread in high school cliques than in adult friendship groups. Parental social standing was not a result of a forty-five-year-old's basketball prowess or nice hair. Adolescents sized up each other according to different standards from those their parents used. These shifts in adolescent values were not as sudden or extensive as the musical revolution, but they served, like music, to widen the distance between young and old.

Parents wondered about their ability to monitor adolescent pastimes. Particularly troublesome was the prospect of lower-class rowdiness subverting respectable middle-class enthusiasm. A singer like Elvis Presley walked a fine line between surly defiance (his "duck-ass" haircut was a big hit with greasers) and wholesome adjustment (he did preach loyalty to country and family). His position was underscored by Ed Sullivan's refusal to televise Presley's hips, although Sullivan was willing to pay $50,000 for three Presley appearances. (Natalie Wood's parents almost refused to let her accept the part in *Rebel Without a Cause* because the movie cast adults as ineffectual bumblers.) Talk of rampant juvenile delinquency was an expression of adult fears of docile youth led astray by peer pressure. After an arduous climb into the middle class, the last thing ambitious parents wanted was betrayal by backward slippage from the next generation. The doubling of juvenile arrests between 1947 and 1957 intensified those fears.

Social life in Levittown, New Jersey, is an example of adult anxieties over unbridled youth. Teen-agers in that suburb had few recreational facilities — a candy store, a bowling alley, and a luncheonette. Parents knew the inadequacies of the afterschool amusements, but they feared any diversion unsupervised by adults. After one party at which the chaperons insisted on slow music, the dancers signed a petition to dismiss the adult DJ, but the parents refused to receive the petition, "fearful that petitions to fire the superintendent would follow." On the other hand, the Miss Levittown contest was permissible (but not a Mrs. Levittown pageant. "The idea of married women parading in bathing suits was thought to be in bad taste, especially by the women"). Adult fantasies about teen-age hormones accounted for rumors of orgies in the shopping center, on rural roads, and in the school playground. One gossip circulated a wild story of forty-four pregnant senior girls. The image of over-sexed teens stirred both outrage and envy, an ambivalence that helps explain the fussiness of the parents' benevolence.

To be sure, earlier generations had worried their parents because of their energetic pursuit of good times. In the 1920s, there was overwrought attention to "flaming youth" who drank, danced, smoked, and necked. But at that time, the supposedly frenzied social-izing imitated adult practices. Youth sought rather than rejected the symbols of adulthood — monogamous relationships, spending money, drinking liquor. The presence of fraternities (often illegal) in high schools was one sign of how teens revered older role models. The idea of a different style of leisure was not a hallmark of the 1920s.

Whatever their nervous reactions, adults in the 1940s had fostered more outspoken offspring by virtue of gentler methods of child-rearing. The ideals and practice of child-rearing prescribed more tolerance of children's impulses, fuller expression of affection, and less physical punishment. Whipping a son for lying gave way to more subtle chastisements, like the withholding of the weekly allow-ance and the reduction of weeknight privileges. A less repressive attitude toward masturbation was part of a larger aversion to sham-ing. Dr. Benjamin Spock's best-selling advice put parents at ease because he insisted that anxious, fretful child-rearing was unneces-sary. More fathers demonstrated more affection, trying to be friendly ("Dad") rather than patriarchal ("Father"). These characteristics of modern parenting were initially middle- and upper-class traits, but working-class mothers and fathers by the 1950s had adopted the more relaxed style of child-rearing. Together with more acute responsiveness was a more democratic tone in family life. Sweet reasonableness replaced the mailed fist. Ward and June Cleaver, on the popular television series "Leave It to Beaver," represented the ideal of even-tempered respect for the children's reasonable requests. Unlike the guardian of the writer Mary McCarthy in the 1920s, June Cleaver would never tape Beaver's lips at night to prevent mouth breathing.

The sudden rise of television gave young viewers easy access to information previously restricted to print. In the 1950s, a typical high school student watched eighteen hours of TV each week. Teens usually liked the programs seen by adults; "children's shows" lost everyone over ten. Many series featured the violence, sexuality, domestic strife, or conniving which most adults traditionally tried to keep from their sons and daughters. Discussion shows on topics like reforming children's television alerted the young to adult scheming to shield their innocence. Because of TV, it became harder for parents to deny that adults manipulated (and stole, murdered, and divorced), a fact not as readily gleaned from comics, radio, or library books.

Admittedly, most American teen-agers still shared with adults common values and activities. More often than not, girls objected to first-date kisses. Adolescents' political opinions matched the electorate's moderate-to-conservative views; for example, most students opposed the idea of a school newspaper free of staff approval. Like their children, most parents celebrated athletic victories more fervently than the classroom triumphs of the academically talented. Half of Dick Clark's home audience for "American Bandstand" was adult, and lots of youngsters liked the McGuire sisters.

But adolescents' weekends and evenings featured more rambunctiousness than their parents had experienced. Whining electric guitars, *Hot Rod* magazine, and the twist enlivened teen-age recreation. Joining the Boy Scouts seemed dull in comparison (the average scout age dropped throughout the 1940s and 1950s). Outside school, youngsters seemed less inhibited than ever before. The rise of 1950s' youth culture actually distanced adolescents from adults, even though parents in various ways made the changes possible. Orderly recreations shared with adults were no longer so obligatory. Instead of promoting closer adolescent-adult relations, youth culture provided alternative forms of socialization to those offered by the school, forms more easygoing and outspoken than the in-class dutifulness. In short, a teen's time after 2:30 P.M. took on more exuberance by virtue of new rituals unwelcomed by high schools.

The Last Little Citadel

The citadel remained largely unaffected by the major shift in how its clients spent a large part of their waking hours. What seemed a bland contrast to recreational excitement was the persistent commitment of educators to traditional notions of self-control and conformity. As one teacher in a Washington, D.C., high school said, "There is little room for the individual who cannot successfully adjust." Although teen-agers were less inhibited, that frankness did not appear in many classrooms. One student recalled the unwritten early 1960s' rule against too much outspokenness:

> All the English teachers proclaimed the virtues of James Joyce. You know — "*Ulysses* is a masterpiece, a great book." I read the book. It's trash. It's garbage. It's crap. And I know it! But I couldn't say that because I didn't have the assurance to go back to class and just face the teacher and say, "This book is crap. Period. End of report."

In 1960, an N.E.A. survey reported 97 percent of teachers in favor of having schools prohibit blue jeans and tight sweaters. During a Democratic administration, politically conservative teachers outnumbered liberals. High schools were not about to welcome the distinctive music and other rituals that pulled adolescents closer together without simultaneously transforming student-teacher relationships. In any typical week, the hoopla of fun — sports and clubs and pep rallies — disguised the students' fundamental powerlessness. The world of adolescents changed faster than the regularities of their high school.

Scholarly research on schools continued to lack an anthropological and sociological sensitivity to culture and ethos. Ethnographic reports from insiders or outsiders were much rarer than statistical compilations of questionnaire answers. Organizational theory almost never informed studies of organizational subsystems like tracking or extracurricular activities; most research had no conceptual foundation. There was more good research on teachers' past lives than on their present working conditions. The social origins of teachers received more attention than their attitude toward their current environment.

More teen-agers graduated from high schools in the same years that a vigorous subculture won their deeper devotion. School was becoming less central to students' lives. The weekly top forty records often mattered more than trigonometry or chemistry. In the same years that Conant and others called for more rigorous academics, the youth culture rivaled formal classroom education for the job of socializing the young. The hands-off policy toward personal affairs of students and teachers permitted less constrained lives outside school, yet everyone was still expected to exercise self-control inside school. The last stanza of a Chuck Berry hit record captured the contrast.

> Sweet Little Sixteen,
> She's got the grown-up blues,
> Tight dresses and lipstick,
> She's sportin' high-heel shoes.
> Oh, but tomorrow morning,
> She'll have to change her trend,
> And be sweet sixteen
> And back in class again.

Adultifying the Adolescent (and Vice Versa)

Although some adolescent social behavior copied adult activities, teen-agers still seemed inexperienced. Cigarette smoking, drinking beer, reckless driving, raucous music, and unchaperoned parties explored but did not exceed the boundaries of "stopping short after overstimulating yourself." Radio and television afforded intriguing glimpses at, not active participation in, adult life. "Knowing when to stop" remained a norm through the mid 1960s. The rock star Janis Joplin, a high school senior in 1960, withheld her favors from her boyfriend. Girls who went all the way were usually not nice girls. Petting, not intercourse, increased during the 1950s. Sanctimonious teen romances like *Fifteen* and *The Luckiest Girl* were much tamer than the candid *Up in Seth's Room, Dinky Hocker Shoots Smack,* and other 1970s' realistic books aimed at young readers. The sentimental and euphemistic 1950s' music did not mobilize rebellious youth for a cultural revolution. Song hits fostered generational differences, not conflict. "American Bandstand" had a dress code.

Dress codes began to disappear around 1970, as did some other traditions. Contraception and abortion made girls who unzipped acceptable rather than sleazy. Drug use accelerated the fall from innocence. Rising afterschool teen employment also started adulthood earlier. Changes in adult lives — divorce, more working women, attempts to look youthful longer — allowed many children to observe parents who were openly working through, at forty instead of sixteen, their own developmental crises.

As a result of those changes, few teen-agers today will be able to write anything like Sue Allen Toth's reminiscences of mid 1950s' Ames, Iowa, a Midwestern city unscarred by poverty, crime, or drugs. Adolescence was quiet and gradual. There was only one black family in Ames, and one prostitute. Toth overheard a discussion of one suicide attempt, and she knew of one divorce ("no one would say why"). Public morality mattered. In private, necking was unobjectionable, but at the Ames high school dances, if a couple danced too closely, "plump Mr. Post would waddle self-consciously onto the floor and tap them on the elbow. 'Tut, tut,' he would try to joke, 'light! Let there be light!' " Mr. Post had little reason to fear further intimacies. There was no glory in going too far. When the sophomore Snow Queen runner-up became pregnant, "we all felt as though she had died." It is true that Toth's first courtship was in sixth grade, but she and Doug did not smoke reefers and fornicate. When she walked by his desk, he would try to stab her with a pencil.

In 1956, Arnold Gesell, Frances Ilg, and Louise Bates Ames published the latest in their series of books on child development. In *Youth: The Years Ten to Sixteen,* the physician and psychologists offered confident generalizations about the habits specific to each of the seven years. Sixteen-year-old girls were chaste and pure. If a boy "gives signs of being excited, she knows it's time to 'brush him off.' " In that year, approximately 3 percent of white American sixteen-year-old girls had had premarital intercourse. In 1976, one-sixth had. The change affected girls more than boys. The shift was not simply numerical; it involved new notions of the relationship within which sex was allowable. Although most girls continued to prize love and commitment, the casual attitude toward sex in the 1970s had not been acceptable earlier. Birth control was also treated casually; the number of teen-age pregnancies rose dramatically during the 1970s. Another crucial change was in the socioeconomic background of the sexually active teen-ager. Before the 1970s, a lower-class sixteen-year-old dropout was more promiscuous than an age peer headed for college. Teen-age sex was not unknown in the 1940s and 1950s, as Dr. Kinsey discovered, but it flourished outside high schools and was closely identified with unrespectable girls. Premature adulthood was the blessing and curse of the lower classes. By the 1970s, middle-class girls no longer lost their respectability and virginity simultaneously. One important threshold of maturity could be crossed at an earlier age without fear of disgrace and punishment.

When the singer Grace Slick joined the Jefferson Airplane, she declared, "You've got to be able to move and do more than just sing the notes . . . You just can't stand there and pat your thigh and expect people to get off on it." Thigh patting had ceased to shock by 1970. Indicative of the swift pace of change was a pair of meetings at Abbot Academy, a private girls' boarding school in New England. In the early 1960s, when only seniors could wear loafers or earrings, the faculty discussed how to tell, at a distance, whether the girls were wearing stockings, as required. In the late 1960s, a lecture series on sex prompted a student to ask whether masturbation was harmful (at which point a French teacher put on her gloves and left the room).

The availability of drugs coincided with the sexual revolution. The percentage of teen-agers smoking marijuana soared in the late 1960s and early 1970s, then reached a plateau, and fell modestly later in the decade. Getting drunk was no longer the only chemical rite of passage. Unlike drinking, drug use, with a little effort, could be concealed during the schoolday. Approximately one in ten students was stoned during a typical schoolday, meaning that a significant number of students were unlikely to give their best attention to cognitive tasks. Alcohol remained popular. (Between 1960 and 1973, arrests for alcohol-related offenses by teens rose 135 percent, but not during the schoolday.) Getting high not only gave kids the previously adult prerogative of changing their state of consciousness; it also gave them an opportunity to be "adult" whenever and wherever they wished (as long as they were somewhat discreet).

Working for money was another marker on the passage to adulthood increasingly familiar to more and more adolescents of the 1960s and 1970s. In those years, the percentage of sixteen- and seventeen-year-olds in the labor force rose substantially. The increase of girls with jobs (from 22.6 percent to 39.1 percent) exceeded the boys' gains (34.0 percent to 45.6 percent). Fast-food and clerical jobs accounted for most of the new opportunities (although for teens out of school seeking full-time positions, the job market actually became less favorable). One figure that fell was time given to homework. The typical senior in 1960 devoted nine hours per week at home to his assignments; in 1980, the time was four hours. For the senior class as a whole, the ratio of homework time to job time plunged to .2 in 1980, from slightly over 2.0 in 1960. In contrast, the hours given to television remained basically unchanged — around eighteen to twenty for younger teens, fourteen or so for seniors. Television held its audience, the job market recruited better than ever, but the unpaid, unamusing, and specifically adolescent task of doing high school homework took less and less time. The greater time spent by teens in workplaces populated by adults and their continued exposure to programs keyed to adults contributed to the blurring of age roles.

Another important development was the waning of emotional innocence. Adolescents' exposure to divorce was never greater. The rise of single-parent families (from 7.4 percent in 1950 to 19.5 percent in 1980) saddled children with more responsibilities. The same effect resulted from mothers with school-aged children taking full- or part-time jobs. By 1982, two thirds of the women with children still in school held jobs outside the home. Adults, caught up in their own passages, concerned themselves with matters formerly considered of importance to teen-agers. Adolescence was no longer the only transitional stage in a healthy life. As a literary critic noted, adolescence had "gradually enlarged its metaphoric reference," because exploration, becoming, growth, and pain were no longer predominantly teen-age characteristics. Physical fitness appealed to many adults, as was evident in the popularity of jogging. Change in emotional ties was also appealing, as was seen in the rising divorce rate. Career shifts at midlife became a legitimate option instead of an embarrassment. Even fashion varied less according to age and generation than before the 1970s, according to Kennedy Fraser of *The New Yorker*. Adults may not have yearned to be sixteen again, but more of them than before (usually by choice, but not always) had the plasticity of that age.

The 1972 revision of Coronet Films' *Personal Health for Girls* (originally issued in 1952) reflected changing notions of teen-age empowerment. The remake was more candid about the body. There were remarks about menstruation. In a shower scene, the covered armpit of 1952 was uncovered in 1972. The definition of good health was broadened to include time for relaxing; the original urged constant observance to detail ("Even my shoes need lots of attention"). The remake followed two girls through a department store; teen-age consumerism had been unacknowledged in 1952. The original included the girl's mother and her words of advice. She was not in the revision, but the narrator's words — "No one can really tell you what to do" — explained why Mother was gone.

No one can really tell you what to do. As youths became more adult, and adults more youthful, older forms of control were harder to maintain. Some parents openly decried overprotectiveness; they were less willing to sacrifice for the children and more eager "to get their children to understand, to agree, to forgive, instead of simply telling the kids what to do." Some observers deplored the abdication of traditional vigilance, but if parents did try to exercise their lost powers, children might treat the interventions as unwelcome. In some states they could and did sue parents for emotional as well as physical abuse.

It is easy to overemphasize the starkness of the transformation of the relationship between adults and teen-agers. In many families, the change was gradual and pleasant. It is wrong to dismiss all the results as cause for regret. The earlier roles, often predicated on adult hypocrisy and adolescent repression, should not be glorified. Indeed, it is the subtlety of the shifts and the mixture of results that make them interesting and important. Adults did not become wholly powerless; children were sometimes passive. But the sharpness of the distinctions had blurred, and that affected how adults and adolescents came to terms with one another. It was harder for an adult to sermonize about self-control when some of the congregation smoked hash in the pews. Teachers no longer faced docile naïfs uninvolved in adult ups-and-downs. By 1970, a best seller would proclaim that high school had too long been "a brutal machine for destruction of the self, controlling it, heckling it, hassling it." The old constraints began to chafe as teen-agers took on more adult characteristics than their older brothers and sisters had manifested fifteen years earlier.

Unlike the impact of 1950s' youth culture, the later definitions of age-appropriate behavior directly affected life inside high schools. Instead of expelling pregnant girls, many schools set up parenting programs. Alcohol-abuse workshops and drug counseling were widely available. Work-study and afternoon release allowed more students to hold jobs. School nurses dispensed birth control information. The relationship between teacher and student after 1970 was not the same as it had been in the 1940s and 1950s; changes had altered the balance of power. The partial disappearance of childhood, coupled with the adolescent flavoring of adulthood, undermined the old paternalism. Authority had to be rebuilt on new foundations.

Feelings and Rights

Because of a growing awareness of adolescents' feelings and rights, school people no longer expected students to be quiet in school about their out-of-school lives. In any case, so many court rulings clarified the constitutional rights of adolescents that rule by fiat became difficult.

The first issue of *Psychology Today* appeared in 1967, coinciding with a popular quest for personal fulfillment that did not rely on stereotypes, societal roles, and organizational affiliations. The relational aspects of marriage, parenthood, and work mattered more than the badges of respectability. The scope of the therapeutic professions increased in the 1970s. Many practitioners exalted growth above healing, and welcomed patients who wanted to feel better, not get well. That change in goal had begun to take shape earlier, but though it was somewhat familiar, the 1970s witnessed a proliferation of methods for reaching it. In addition to analysis and counseling, the innovations included family and sex therapy as well as such exotic techniques as bioenergetics, primal scream, encounter groups, and transactional analysis. One critic groused, "The sheer revelation of someone's inner impulses became exciting." Fewer people felt compelled to cover up dark secrets. As the psychologist Thomas Cottle wrote in 1974, "What was for me as a child unknowable material — stuff that I might have suspected but could always avoid because it never was openly announced — is now blatant and irrefutable." One large quantitative study reported less denial of personal problems, based on data about the decline of private prayer and the greater frequency of personal discussions with friends and professionals.

The changing sensibility was evident in several movies made by Coronet Films. *Control Your Emotions,* a 1950 film for high school students, began with a roaring forest fire, followed by a stern warning: "Your emotions can be your greatest enemy." The narrator was a psychologist, wearing a white jacket that suggested laboratory work, as did his behavior. Thwarting leads to rage, loud noises cause fear, affection breeds love: it is all stimulus and response, the doctor declared. If an irate boy decides to "reason it out" by means of "straight thinking," then he won't get angry (and anger was the main emotion — "a violent emotion" — in the film). The movie ended with a family roasting marshmallows over a small fire, and the narrator reassured the audience that nature can and should be controlled.

The 1971 version of *Control Your Emotions* was retitled *Managing Your Emotions,* a change indicating that the film was less judgmental. When a boy afraid to use a high-dive board wondered why he was afraid, a psychologist in a handsome sport coat cautiously began, "All I can do is make a considered guess." This was a far cry from the previous narrator's certainty. The anger in the movie was tamer; inner turmoil replaced rage. In the 1950 film, a boy chased his younger brother with a wooden coat hanger to retrieve a letter; in 1971, a girl quietly left a room, irked by her friends' choosing as the day for a party a time when she'd be out of town. *Managing Your Emotions* also presented a couple discussing whether or not they should sleep together, a sharp contrast to Coronet's 1949 *Dating Do's and Don't's* (in 1972 retitled *The Dating*

Scene), in which the narrator interpreted as crude and lustful a boy's clumsy lunge on the front steps for a first-date kiss.

The changes discussed earlier — experiences of and attitudes toward sexuality, drugs, work, and family roles — occurred in roughly the same years that American courts recognized that some adult prerogatives belonged as well to teen-agers. In 1930, a Tennessee court declared that a student was "entitled to as much protection as a bootlegger." In 1945, a Midwestern superintendent told an ornery student, "Strikes may be legal in industry but school [student] strikes are not legal. The procedure is to dismiss from school anyone fomenting a strike and then to have him arrested for contributing to the delinquency of minors." By 1973, teen-agers could learn otherwise by picking up *The Rights of Students,* an American Civil Liberties Union publication. Such a booklet could not have been published earlier, because the judicial decisions summarized in it were recent ones. By affirming that young people had procedural and substantive rights once thought to belong only to adults, the courts had taken away some of the authority of the school people.

From 1909 to 1968, there were fewer suits by or on behalf of public school students challenging teacher, principal, and school board practices than in the years from 1969 to 1978. The percentage of cases decided in favor of students rose dramatically, from 19 percent (before 1969) to 48 percent (1969 to 1978). The type of case also changed. Before 1940, the few suits concerned parental rights. In particular, there were the cases against mandatory vaccinations, on the grounds that the parents' religion forbade them, and flag salutes, which some people considered authoritarian. In the 1940s and 1950s, the most frequent type of case involved student fraternities, and the courts sanctioned rules against those organizations. In the 1960s, the rights of married students replaced the existence of fraternities as the most frequent issue litigated (marking a transition from the earlier concern with unacceptable *group* behavior). The courts waffled on these cases. Judges usually refused to condone the expulsion from school of married students, but rulings often sustained their exclusion from extracurricular activities. Administrators feared the influence of prematurely experienced teen-agers on their supposedly innocent classmates. As Professor Lawrence Friedman wrote, "The locker room talk of married students could hardly be worse than that of the unmarried, but what the school boards really feared was legitimating teenage sex. The ideal was chastity and strict morality, obedience and respect for authority." One Michigan school board hoped the exclusion from extracurricular activities would "humiliate and ridicule" the married students.

The case in 1969 upholding the students' right to wear black armbands to protest the Vietnam War was a milestone. *Tinker* v. *Des Moines* ruled that neither "students nor teachers shed their constitutional rights to freedom of speech and expression at the schoolhouse gate." Here, the Warren Court was applying a defense of civil liberties drawn from cases that were very different from *Tinker,* because earlier student cases provided little precedent. The magnitude of the shift is best illuminated by comparison with the *Barnette* case in 1942, which gave students a passive right, the refusal to salute the flag. *Tinker* opened the door for active dissent. The armbands themselves were not particularly active, but the Court's decision legitimated vocal and vigorous expression of student opinion.

There were four crucial aspects to *Tinker* that challenged the customary regimentation of high school. First, the Court recognized a student as a person with constitutional rights, a more powerful identity than the dependent creature subject to the vagaries of school authority. Second, the justices felt that the process of schooling mattered as much as the content of course work. It was well and good to teach democracy in civics class, but those lessons had to be honored in practice as well as theory. Third, the Court suggested that some degree of disorder in schools was acceptable and positively educational, because the world itself was "disputatious." The revered goal of clockwork efficiency could no longer excuse suppression of feisty students' words and nonviolent deeds. Fourth, school could not be an instrument of cultural imperialism or homogenization. As another decision phrased the idea, "Is it not more vital to encourage experience with diversity and adaptation to it, in a diverse nation and world, than to encourage homogeneity?"

Tinker and subsequent decisions on dress codes, underground newspapers, and hair length compelled the high schools to make fewer personal demands of their students. Clothes, grooming, and reading material could not be regulated as thoroughly as before. One important case, *Goss* v. *Lopez,* granted modest due process rights for students in risk of suspension. Other cases restrained the school to punishing instead of preventing illicit behavior (such as a scurrilous article in a handout). Students did not win every case, but they felt encouraged by the courts to express themselves more openly than ever before. What the youth culture of the late 1960s promoted — longer hair, less clothing, political protest — no longer had to be set aside for late afternoons, evenings, and weekends.

The judicial recognition of student rights did not sour student-administrator relations in school. By and large, school people did not resist the court decisions. They knew that rules against long hair or blue jeans or armbands could be more disruptive than the fashion. Their acquiescence was paralleled by student satisfaction. In the late 1960s, student agitation unrelated to race focused on symbolic and expressive rights more than on substantive changes in school routines. For example, the right to print and circulate in an underground newspaper a few pages sprinkled with mild ob-scenities and references to dope was more important than evaluating courses, criticizing teaching styles, or discussing student cliques. One anthology of underground high school newspapers had more pages on rock music than on the curriculum. Once the symbolic privileges were secured, the underground newspapers faded away.

What should be remembered about the changes of the 1970s is that they would have been more modest had there not been strong support in the wider world for the therapeutic value of, and students' legal entitlement to, speaking out.

Opening Closed Doors

The old foundations of policy making also began to crack in the 1960s. Gentlemanly agreements among colleagues became less common and effective. Public bickering began to rival private dickering as the style of doing business.

In 1944, only 2 percent of American teachers thought they should not be allowed to see their evaluations. Yet 47 percent of the urban teachers and 69 percent of the rural teachers had never even seen the blank forms, let alone their individual ratings. But in 1969, C. R. Keister, a high school principal, wrote in his diary that he was not permitted to tell his female teachers not to wear knee socks to school. In 1944, teachers could do little to get access to their records, but twenty-five years later the strength of teacher unions convinced Keister that he should "pause a bit before issuing any kind of 'thou shalt not' statements."

Job actions by teachers used to be unusual. The National Education Association rarely condoned any sort of work stoppage. Principals felt comfortable with the N.E.A. because it did not incite teachers to confront administrators; if the N.E.A. was critical, the target was usually a school board. In contrast, the American Federation of Teachers, a smaller, more militant association based in several large cities, challenged administrators more directly. Successful A.F.T. strikes in the early and middle 1960s swelled the federation's membership, which pushed the N.E.A. toward more aggressive negotiations in local bargaining. The rivalry helps explain the sudden surge of teacher strikes in the late 1960s. From 1955 to 1965, there were only thirty-five strikes. In the 1968–1969 school year alone, the number was 131.

The rise of aggressive unionism diminished the principal's powers. Small but important areas that formerly lay in his domain were now specified in contracts. Issues like teacher transfers, evaluations, and afterschool duties began to be spelled out, alongside grievance procedures. Relations between staff and administrators often became adversarial. In one school, a special education teacher filed a grievance charge against a principal who took some of her sink sponges. In another district, a principal could not request a meeting with a teacher without giving the reason for the meeting beforehand. Furthermore, central office administrators assumed more power, and principals rarely participated in the bargaining with teachers. When a grievance was filed, the teachers and the central office usually knew about the complaint before the principal did. When cutbacks of staff became necessary, the officials downtown decided who would and would not be on the principal's staff the next fall. Yet the lessening of the principal's power did not expand the time and energy he had available for instructional leadership. His organizational chores remained burdensome, even though the crucial decisions were being made elsewhere.

Not every point of teacher-administrator contact became a conflict, to be sure. Many principals valued cordiality with teachers above the enforcement of regulations handed down by central office negotiators. In the settlement of strikes, good personal relationships shaped the proceedings. Informal interpretation and renegotiation of contract provisions remained possible in many places. There was still much aversion to publicity. One study found that "open negotiations allegedly provoke grandstanding, while privacy facilitates thorough discussion of technical points." Despite this flexibility, teacher associations increased the probability of conflict by their readiness to strike if negotiations broke down.

Before the mid 1960s, another option — keeping schools racially segregated — was not too hard to exercise. Many Southern districts openly established separate black facilities. There were no political or legal barriers to their doing so. In other regions, administrators, school boards, and local politicians could perpetuate racial discrimination by policies that seemed both professional and color-blind; drawing attendance lines and deciding the location of new schools supposedly required special expertise. Decisions that in practice discriminated could be defended by mystification of the intricacies of capital spending and demographic change.

For ten years after the 1954 *Brown* v. *Board of Education of Topeka* decision against separate but equal schools, the old discriminatory practices persisted because of ingenious new evasions. The Supreme Court had ordered desegregation with "all deliberate speed," an ambiguity designed to coax rather than force the Southern states to act. There were no deadlines set, no quotas calculated. That policy of gradualism failed. By 1964 only Texas and Tennessee had more than 2 percent of their black students in integrated schools. Tactics of resistance varied from place to place. Virginia withheld state funds from integrated school districts, redistributing the money as tuition grants for private school students. More subtle (and successful) were complicated "pupil placement laws," stipulating an elaborate appeals process for transferring students between schools. Integration plans were based on intricate rules made to confuse parents. Another powerful weapon was the threat to require higher

National Teacher Examination scores for new teachers, thereby depriving blacks of jobs and promotions while letting whites crow about educational excellence. In the North, some districts flimflammed with district boundaries, hiring policies, and school construction in order to maintain segregated schools. As the president of Columbia's Teachers College told Conant in 1962, "I am finding the whole business a badly confused mixture of tough problems, honest error, misunderstanding, and a fair amount of subterfuge."

The 1964 Civil Rights Act helped unmask the customary evasions. Enforcement of the law strained the traditional coziness between state and federal officials. The small staff of the federal Office of Education previously relied on state departments of education to administer the few federal programs. They treated each other cordially, as fellow professionals. If the local administrators began to distrust the distant authorities as zealous social reformers, no federal program would be in safe hands. At first the Office of Education simply monitored local progress and trusted Southern avowals of good intentions. Freedom-of-choice plans satisfied many Southerners, who found ways to continue to thwart integration by various tactics (lack of publicity, complicated paperwork, pressure on black teachers to urge students not to transfer).

In 1966, however, the federal government insisted on measuring satisfactory progress by demonstrable results, not by sweet talk. Accompanying the stiffer standards of integration were millions of dollars of new federal aid; stubborn segregation thus jeopardized the release of money for school improvements most needed by rural Southern schools, the bastion of segregation. Federal authorities hesitated to cut off funds in cases of noncompliance with the Civil Rights Act, but the occasional freeze badly strained valued personal relationships between people in the federal government and those in the communities. Fears of arbitrary federal meddling grew stronger. The government's sending investigators from Washington, D.C., to the hinterlands marked its refusal to trust local white leadership. The old bartering among colleagues was also changed by the fact that the federal contact might now be a lawyer rather than a fellow educator. Shrill rhetoric marked the deteriorating relations. Representative Mendel Rivers of South Carolina called the commissioner of education a "misfit"; a Virginia politician accused President Lyndon Johnson of planning to send children to compounds to learn socialism; and Georgia governor Lester Maddox told parents to let the air out of school bus tires. Prominent Southerners did not hide their hatred of federal reformers.

Controversy persisted as desegregation suits affected Northern schools in some cities, which by 1970 were more segregated than those of the South. Court rulings set more stringent and complicated criteria of integration. Typical of the interventions were those affecting Detroit, which had to revise its disciplinary code, devise new tests, hire human relations specialists and bilingual instructors, and open more vocational schools. Several aspects of most desegregation cases challenged covert decision making. First, racial policy was a complex legal and political issue transcending the administrators' skills at school construction, curricular revision, budgeting, and the like. Outsiders felt perfectly qualified to shape crucial decisions governing the daily lives of the insiders. Judges and legislators asserted unprecedented control over educational policy, vitiating the traditional hegemony of administrators and boards. Second, many lawyers tried to strengthen their suits by documenting a pattern of willful segregation by local authorities. Those investigations often turned up solid evidence of intentional discrimination throughout the previous twenty years or more. What that suggests is not just good historical research; rather, the decision makers had been careless about covering their tracks. They wrongly assumed immunity from outside scrutiny. The mutual administrative backscratchings might have persisted longer if they had been less overt. Third, media coverage of integration and busing featured episodes of hostile confrontation. Nightly TV news programs showed pickets, snarling dogs, and broken bus windows. The public consequently overestimated the divisiveness of racial policy, unaware that most communities accepted desegregation peaceably. Nor was the conflict among decision makers as extensive as the public believed it to be.

Outside voices were heard in discussions about yet another development related to racial issues: the emergence of quantitative research on equal educational opportunity. Scholars began to study carefully the relationship between the school's contributions — such as environment, facilities, staff, extracurricular activities, counseling

— and the student's achievement, and the research yielded some startling results. Especially provocative was the finding that family background mattered more than the school itself. Poor kids in a new and well-equipped building often did worse than rich kids in a dilapidated one. For years professional educators had said that facilities were a reliable index of educational quality. It was all a matter of resources, they argued. This major assumption was challenged by the research. A library of twenty thousand books made less difference than the social status of the borrowers. Social science ruled out measuring opportunity just in terms of the school's contributions. The educational process was shown to be intricate and subtle; the researchers expanded the number of variables and acknowledged the difficulties of evaluating some of the available evidence. Should the percentage of teachers with master's degrees be classified as a factor in school policy (discriminatory hiring), a resource (a differentiated pay scale), or neither (the effect of the local job market)? How should an econometric model be adjusted to take into account the fact that a student is both a consumer and a producer? If teacher morale correlates with student achievement, wouldn't the causal relationship run both ways and thus be harder to measure? By raising such questions, research from the mid 1960s on complicated the sociology of education, but the relationship between social scientists' findings and governmental policy was less harmonious than the earlier one between education schools and state departments of education. Educational research was less often an in-house brief on behalf of expansion; maybe more was not necessarily better. The old public solidarity among optimistic school people was easier to maintain when researchers quietly compiled charts on salaries, retirement laws, tenure provisions, and other data unrelated to cause and effect.

Other outsiders — parents, legislators, foundations — pressed the schools to share power, but it was desegregation and teacher militancy that had the greatest impact in opening the doors of the decision makers' offices. The change primarily reflected the growing entitlement in the 1960s of a broad assortment of minorities and special interest groups. The disenfranchised no longer relied on the benevolence of authorities who covertly managed education by welding coalitions of the enfranchised. The old assumption of a basic unity of interests was superseded by a more wary attitude toward authority. As the historian David Rothman wrote, "To claim to act for the purposes of benevolence was once sufficient to legitimate a program; at this moment it is certain to create suspicion."

When students took on adult characteristics, they too could resist unwelcome intervention carried out in the name of benevolence. Teachers, administrators, and parents wielded less discretionary power, and adolescents had legal recourse in cases of the abuse of power. The traditional and ritualistic displays of self-control receded in an age when judgmental interference became suspect.

The fortresses had tried to protect many things: opportunity, virtue, learning, community pride. But the regimentation inside their walls did not allow for those on guard duty to ask people how they felt or to question whether such and such a command was legal. Propriety, or at least the semblance of it, seemed to require austere classrooms and covert decision making. Talk of rights and feelings had not been welcome in the citadels of middle-class respectability. When those concerns began to influence school practice, the high school became an accessible citadel.

5

We Don't Grab Them

"IT'S THE LEG THING that makes her difficult," the home economics teacher noted as one of her plumper students paraded across the auditorium stage in a new dress. In another part of the school, an administrator stopped a student in the hall. "Lunch means lunch; it doesn't mean telephone calls," he warned the boy without a pass. In the front office, the principal told a senior that her prom dress was too short. A counselor agreed, reminding the girl that proper attire was important ("My husband is honoring the youngsters by wearing a tuxedo"). In a sex education class, the lecturer emphasized the importance of self-control, stressing that "you can't have what you want," because, she said, intercourse before marriage supposedly increased the likelihood of divorce.

Those scenes from Frederic Wiseman's 1970 documentary, *High School,* captured the watchfulness of schools in the monochromatic days of hall passes, gown lengths, and unkind references to fat calves. The tense rectitude of a middle-class urban high school was the major theme of the film. Wiseman's portrait of education was a harsh commentary on an era drawing to a close, but anyone who was in high school before the late 1960s would probably concede the accuracy of much of the movie.

If Wiseman had remade the film in the first half of the 1980s, he would have found less quibbling between staff and students, and more arguing among adults. Rather than lecturing on the perils of sex, a counselor would tell pregnant students of a new program for unwed mothers. The assistant principal would be too involved with a court case to linger in the halls, checking for passes. Instead of measuring hemlines, the principal would be on the phone with an angry parent upset by the human development course unit on divorce. For a student, high school became less stressful. For an administrator, daily life was more harried. For teachers, relations with students were usually more relaxed, but interactions with other adults often were not.

To see in detail what changed during and after the late 1960s, we examine the history of four schools. The focus is on the watershed years, 1968 to 1972 (but background information on earlier years draws on the major points in previous chapters). Because different schools are subject to different forces, one cannot write educational history in general terms, unrelated to real people and specific places. It is risky to equate what outside observers said went on with the actual experiences of the participants. And what were those experiences?

The turmoil in high schools in the late 1960s began suddenly, without much warning. Previously, cautious experimentation was the limit of reform. Modest changes usually enlarged the course catalogue without modifying the traditional school atmosphere. The tinkerings made no room for political protest, black pride, or student rights, all issues of great importance to college activists several years before high school unrest flared. Despite the college protests, few public school administrators foresaw the school ferment of the late 1960s. In 1968, approximately three quarters of the principals lacked contingency plans for responding to student demonstrations.

Following the years of tumult, schools restored order and safety. The task was hard because other problems — budget cuts, declining enrollments, teacher strikes, public skepticism, court orders — jolted educators throughout the 1970s. Moreover, teachers pleased with the late 1960s' ferment chafed at reassertions of administrative control. Still, the search for order was successful. The popular image of schools lurching from crisis to crisis badly misrepresents the smooth and efficient administration of most high schools.

The peace treaties did not reimpose the traditional severities.

Many of the traditions persisted — age grading, departmentalization, bureaucratic fussiness, compulsory attendance, the frenetic pace of each day — but the texture of schooling, in and around those durable fixtures, softened and mellowed. Teacher-student relationships, on balance, became more relaxed; so did student-student interaction. In school, students voiced openly thoughts and feelings that had been felt but unspoken thirty or forty years earlier. Teachers' willingness to stray from lesson plans to freewheeling discussions would have flabbergasted Leonard Covello, Mrs. K., and Lyndon Johnson. So would the curriculum. In the 1970s, American high schools became truly comprehensive. Course electives, special programs, and social services started to overshadow the old methods of dealing with diversity — tracking and ability grouping. Instead of sorting students only on the basis of cognitive skills, schools made use of new programs that lessened somewhat the insidious effect of vocational, commercial, and general track labels. To be designated as special no longer meant that one was intellectually superior or inferior. Economic, racial, linguistic, psychological, and physical considerations took their place alongside, often in front of, academics as criteria in the placing of students. The sociological and affective emphases saluted by the progressives in the 1930s and 1940s commanded serious attention long after the formal progressive associations had died. As the report of one conference on controlling student activism avowed, "What matters most is that the school cares." At another conference, a session on the Federalist Papers attracted three people while next door a values-clarification panel drew over a hundred.

Yet the relations between adults were often contentious. Faculties frequently became polarized when principals responded harshly or leniently to the protests, and subsequent policies kept the gap wide. The rise of strong teacher unions brought detailed contracts specifying rules, regulations, and grievance procedures in place of the informal and often unwritten agreements of the past. Teachers and administrators alike increasingly confronted hostile parents, voters, and school board members, wary of the old alliance between home and school.

Academics was not the focal point of high schools' unprecedented attentiveness to rights and feelings. Reformers expended much energy, but the gains made on legal and affective issues did not necessarily bring greater knowledge. Recent changes in American high schools have not been one and the same as intellectual challenge.

"Human Just Like Us"

Between the 1920s and the early 1960s, the two public high schools of Cambridge, Massachusetts (Cambridge Rindge Technical and Cambridge High and Latin), located less than one mile from Harvard University, kept their distance from the university's Graduate School of Education. Irish and Italian politicians controlled both the city and the public schools; occasional fiscal mismanagement and patronage appointments spurred local reformers to campaign for proportional representation in the election of city councillors and school board members. The voters approved the change, unwilling to believe some citizens' mutterings about a local communist plot and unmoved by the pleas of others to make Harvard a separate city. Proportional representation did not oust the traditionalists (ironically known as Independents), who usually held a narrow advantage over the Cambridge Civic Association (the C.C.A.). Independents supported faithfully the cautious policies and insider appointments of Superintendent John Tobin, the politically astute brother of President Roosevelt's Secretary of Labor, Daniel Tobin. To his subordinates, Tobin was stern; with the school board, he sought discreet compromise and friendly conciliation, which resolved most differences. Tobin and the board consolidated their power by hiring local candidates for teaching positions and promoting loyalists from the ranks. In 1946, two thirds of the staff of both schools were graduates of either Rindge Tech or High and Latin, and 60 percent were born in Cambridge. Of the seventy-seven administrators, sixty-three had twenty years or more of service in Cambridge. Married women were ineligible for appointments, and men enjoyed a salary advantage over women of between 15 and 20 percent.

The high schools staffed by those teachers were more traditional and rigid than the nearby education school professors would have favored. In the 1930s, teachers expected silence in the corridors as students passed from class to class. But quiet was not a guarantee of academic competence. Arthur Schlesinger, Sr., took young Arthur out of High and Latin and sent him to Exeter when a tenth-grade history teacher declared that the residents of the European country Albania "were called Albinos because of their white hair and pink eyes." By the 1950s, the hallways were noisier, but inside the classrooms the instruction was regimented. The English department at High and Latin, for instance, offered no electives, and the required courses emphasized dictation and memorization. In foreign languages, course work almost always began with a year of Latin. Not until the 1950s could freshmen elect either Spanish or French. A school board Independent delayed the introduction of Advanced Placement courses because he learned that his children would probably not qualify.

Course selections were not monitored by counselors; indeed, there was no guidance department until the mid 1960s. Assistant headmasters usually coordinated course choices, but during their hours as counselors they concentrated on discipline cases and academic failures. There was no vocational guidance (but there was a five-man attendance department to find truants). What shaped student course selection was extensive tracking and ability grouping. Rindge had nine different technical specialties as well as a college preparatory track. High and Latin offered college prep, commercial (largest enrollment), general, and home economics with practical arts (for the slow. And for the very slow, there were two small separate vocational schools). At High and Latin, students in a particular track took classes with other students in their track, but ability grouping within the tracks further separated the students. There were a few special classes to which teachers could transfer the rowdy and the retarded. But emotional problems and learning disabilities did not receive individualized and sympathetic treatment. Special education was academic remedial work rather than care for affective problems. Most of the sections were for elementary school children, and assignment to them was rare if parents objected. Although there was a psychiatric clinic for Cambridge students, the staff treated the younger children. (In 1964, for example, only fifteen of the 101 visits were from high school students.)

The public image of Rindge as a purely vocational school further compounded the distinctions fostered by tracking and grouping. Earlier, it was harder to overlook Rindge's credentials as a good technical school. Rindge usually sent several graduates each year to M.I.T., and the overall percentage of students who went to college or found full-time employment was similar to the High and Latin figure. In the early 1960s, there were four sections of advanced physics at Rindge, and only two at High and Latin. But Rindge's last eight to ten years (the schools were combined in 1978) were not its best years. Politicized blacks and C.C.A. candidates noted the tarnished image of Rindge as a dumping ground. Guidance counselors reportedly used the threat of a transfer to Rindge to intimidate unruly High and Latin students. By the early 1970s, the perception and resentment of a two-tier system was strong.

Any such reaction would have been unlikely under Superintendent Tobin, to whom piecemeal change marked the limit of reform. Driver education (1949), Career Days (1950), an emphasis on "group living" in social studies (1951), an in-service workshop on "democratic human relations" for administrators (1952), an expansion of citizenship courses (1954): those were the tame progressive-style gestures that left teaching methods, course content, and school politics untouched. In the late 1950s and early 1960s, the high schools again faintly foreshadowed some national fashions. In those years began course work for the brightest (1959), separate guidance departments (1965), and school libraries (1963). Before then, the books were stored in an empty classroom, and there was no trained librarian). But teachers still relied on recitation and lecture instead of discussion and questioning; independent study was rare; and the Basic English classroom was separate from the rest of the department. The pace of change was slow.

John Tobin retired in 1968, and his successor, Edward Connelly, tried to retire the anti-Harvard feelings. Although Connelly had served Tobin loyally as an assistant superintendent, he was receptive to educational innovation. He convinced a skeptical school board to house a small Harvard-originated experimental Pilot School, funded by the federal government. The project featured several reforms recently popularized by the success of "open education" in British elementary classrooms, where teachers permitted noise, softened the distinctions between work and play, let students learn at their own pace, and encouraged group activities. The upward extension of elementary school flexibility and personalization promised to dislodge the old regimen of rote learning. This refurbished progressivism offered the child-centeredness of *Education for ALL American Youth* without its paternalism and bland conformity. Many small private "free schools" abandoned grades, disciplinary codes, homework, and other impositions, but such freedom was so closely associated with the radical counterculture that many parents found it unacceptable, and their children were, instead, exposed to the slightly tamer innovation known as the "alternative school," which invited student participation in governance, extended greater personal freedoms (especially of dress, speech, and smoking), encouraged new courses on contemporary issues, and fostered closer student-teacher relationships. Alternative schools usually deplored alienation and impersonality, and sought an intimate community with greater emotional investment by teacher and student. Usually the alternative school drew only a fraction of the student body and occupied a small part of the building. But the very fact that this option existed marked a substantial change from educators' past reluctance to accept less structured educational settings.

In Cambridge, a broad spectrum of students and staff joined the Pilot School. A lottery admitted the first class of sixty freshmen, with names drawn from hats marked according to sex, race, residence, and academic ability. The staff members (many of them part time) included a Harvard professor, a research associate, fifteen graduate students, six volunteers, four teachers from the Cambridge system, and a secretary. Diversity of outlook accompanied diversity of background, because neither students nor staff had to pass admissions tests of ideological purity. In fact, many students volunteered because they knew they would receive $75 for participating in summer workshops; few eighth-graders could earn that much money that quickly. For several Cambridge veterans hired to fill gaps in the curriculum, their departments' willingness to let them go mattered as much as their educational philosophy.

By assembling a range of adolescents and adults, the pioneers hoped to avoid a problem that had fragmented the public high schools: the stereotyping of whites and blacks, boys and girls, academically talented and vocationally inclined, and teachers and students. They believed that people would get along better with one another, and feel better about themselves, in a climate that consciously celebrated diversity. The founders expected to foster the mutual respect, sharing, and openness absent from the public high schools, in Cambridge and elsewhere, but very crucial to liberal reformers of the time. The staff hoped for a sense of community more substantial than the rah-rah pep rally form of school spirit. Pilot occupied several rooms in the Rindge building, but its ideology stood far outside the school's.

Each "home group" of twelve students and two staff met daily, but not to endure the administrative details of traditional homerooms. Although many periods were spent in reviewing Pilot School issues, the groups also planned trips to museums, movies, campsites, and the teachers' homes. In addition, students and staff shared an office-lounge in a converted chemistry lab, where they could buy tonic water, play Ping-Pong, or study. (There were no Pilot rooms designated as study halls.) Shared interest in the alternative school movement drew faculty and students to a Toronto conference on open education, and several students visited the renowned Parkway School in Philadelphia. Course work included a broad selection of humanities electives — women's literature, race relations, adolescent development — that encouraged the study of interpersonal issues. Students discussed their work in conferences with teachers at the end of each quarter, and teachers also wrote lengthy comments as part of the formal report card.

But the Pilot School was not one big happy family. Some white girls almost left Pilot because of harassment, which prompted a three-day moratorium on classes so that everyone could discuss race relations. Two black girls were expelled after they attacked each other with knives. Some lower-class kids kept to themselves, as did the bright blacks and as did the students with learning problems. Approximately 20 percent of the students lacked friends within the Pilot School. In a new environment with more freedom, according to sociologists of the workplace, many people, especially working-class and lower-class people, prefer autonomy to power. Given the traditional Cambridge distinctions — rich versus poor, university members versus North and East Cambridge ethnics, Catholic versus Protestant — the persistent divisions were not surprising. But given the Pilot School ideology, the schisms were a disappointment. Student factions traditionally ignored each other, but the Pilot premium on candor in all-school meetings made it harder for anyone to avoid recognition of those differences. The transcript of one school meeting contained the following: "faggot," "get 'em, militant," "shut the fuck up," and "drag queen." From one point of view, the students' willingness to speak out was laudable, and the tone of jest and bravura in the jibes was understood to be lost in transcription. From a different point of view, the language was evidence of the precariousness of the Pilot School experiment in town meeting democracy.

There were also divisions among the staff. Black teachers met together informally to share mutual concerns; so did the female teachers. The Cambridge veterans sometimes resented zealous young graduate students. What divided the staff most deeply, however, was the question of authority. Some teachers were task-oriented; others emphasized process and philosophy. When some teachers asked, "What can be done to keep the school clean?" others would reply, "Why is it that students don't take responsibility for cleaning up after themselves?" No one chaired the early planning sessions, which were sometimes interminable. After one particularly long meeting — the staff was unable to decide whether teachers should smoke in the building, in light of the ban on student smoking — it was clear that someone was needed to draw up an agenda, moderate the discussion, and follow through on decisions. Moreover, the ninth-graders were not as eager to participate in group discussions as the teachers had hoped. Early in the first year, their indifference to routine meetings was evident by their absence.

The appointment of coordinators did not eliminate the ambivalence toward authority and decision making. As the very word suggests, "coordinators" were not powerful administrators. One teacher recalled that "the whole area of some people having authority over others was an emotionally loaded one for the staff members." When a coordinator suspended four students in the spring of 1970 for vandalism, the staff criticized his failure to consult them. They also disliked his appointing a powerful committee on hiring and planning for the school's second year.

Extraordinary decisions were complicated by the students' desire to share full voting rights. The staff alone adjudicated the girls' knife fight, but another case was more controversial. Shortly after the theft of $500 worth of videotape equipment, one Pilot student announced that he knew who had stolen it — an outsider — and he carried a message from the thief. The Pilot School could have its equipment back in exchange for $200. Staff and students met to discuss how they should respond, but the question of payment was linked to a second question: Should the staff alone decide? Policy and policy making were under scrutiny at the same time. The discussion went on so long that many students had to go home, an ironic reminder of the limits of innovation. Late in the evening, those who had remained voted not to pay. In most public and private schools, that sort of frank deliberation would have been unimaginable. The go-between would have been pressured to name the thief. But in a regular high school, he never would have let on that he knew the culprit.

The wariness about exercising authority and the reluctance to enforce decisions also marked Pilot's policies on grading and attendance. In the required double-period humanities course, the final grade was the average of the teacher's mark and the student's self-evaluation. Those things which were graded — papers, projects, journals — were selected after negotiations between individual students and teachers. The school briefly adopted policies for cuts and disruptiveness (students could penalize tardy teachers under this system), but enforcement was sporadic.

The lack of a tough attendance policy stemmed from the fear that insistence on daily attendance would threaten the friendly student-staff relations. At the end of the first year, an evaluation of Pilot reported that both students and staff mentioned good human relations most frequently as the best feature of the school. The informal relationships were an important goal of the Pilot School. Kids called adults by their first names, and they shared the couch, radio, and refrigerator in the office-lounge. An undeniable success of the first year was the sympathetic connections established between individual students and specific teachers. In large groups, whether committees or all-school meetings, there were often conflicts or disagreements. One-on-one interchanges were less stressful.

The difficulties of decision making, then, ultimately resulted from the staff's reluctance to jeopardize the cherished informality by imposing rules that told people to do this or not do that. One teacher remembered that "if you say yes or no instead of maybe, you're a villain." Another later said, "In the Pilot School, moral evaluations, if they are made at all, are only informational to the individual, and all morality is relative among those individuals." Most teachers saw themselves as friends and counselors. (The majority were under thirty.) They feared that bureaucratic structures would preclude the candor they cherished and that was so rare in public high schools. Regardless of the factionalism, almost everyone chose the interpersonal life of Pilot as preferable to the style of traditional high schools. Hierarchy, regulations, and unilateral decisions would have threatened the welcome informality. Furthermore, the checkered record of the all-school meetings indicated that inflexible policies might have brought about disorder, not reduced it. Pushing too hard on drugs, attendance, and expulsions would have invited confrontations in an already fragile school.

What modified much of the hesitancy was the employment, in the school's third year, of a full-time administrator to tighten the routines so that the Cambridge school committee would vote to fund the Pilot School when the three-year federal grant expired. For the reform to survive in a conservative and keenly political system, it had to be orderly. That was the price of admission. The liberal C.C.A. board members could defend experimentation but not chaos. The city became more liberal in the 1960s and early 1970s, because of an unusual coalition of university professors, rent control activists, welfare recipients, and black militants, but elections were so close that Pilot's future was never certain.

The new director heeded the concerns of the central administrators and board more than the coordinators had done. As part of his quest for efficiency, he separated the front office from the student lounge. An indication of his assertiveness was his decision to admit fourteen more white students (which prompted such strenuous protests that later six new black students and two black staff were recruited). He knew that the Pilot School had barely survived school board scrutiny in the previous year, when the senior Independent member, James Fitzgerald, assailed Pilot as unpatriotic (an occasional Black Panther circular appeared on a bulletin board), unsanitary (the carpeting was dirty, because Rindge janitors refused to vacuum Pilot rooms), and unsavory (some student had written essays about vampires). At one public meeting, Fitzgerald unfurled photographic enlargements of Pilot classrooms and was incensed by one picture in which painted American flags decorated a room partition. "See," he crowed, "there is no real American flag in the Pilot School! A painted flag is not a real flag!" To his embarrassment, the next picture, of an art room, had a small but unmistakably real flag in the back corner.

The board eventually voted to fund the Pilot School, but the staff interpreted the director's successful external accommodations as a retreat from basic Pilot principles. Teachers believed the director had failed to argue on their behalf for modifications of such central procedures as the systemwide rule that they sign in every morning. Teachers and students knew that he had removed couches from the student lounge after one school board member publicly charged that they were used for sex. Once the Pilot School became a permanent part of the Cambridge schools, the system regulations required an open search to fill the director's position. A committee of students, staff, and parents, after anguished deliberations, chose an outsider in preference to the incumbent. The outsider declined the job; the directorship stayed in the same hands. During the Tobin administration, consideration of outsiders would have been as unthinkable as screening by a committee that included students. The democratic hiring procedure publicized tensions usually masked by the promotion of loyal insiders.

At roughly the same time, school board appointments of other administrators evoked much greater controversy than the Pilot search. Frank Frisoli, an assistant superintendent, was a dutiful insider with strong enough support from the Independents to override the C.C.A.'s wish to look nationwide for a new chief when Connelly resigned in 1970. Frisoli frowned on some of Connelly's innovations and was disliked by many blacks, who considered him racist. In 1971, C.C.A. candidates ran on an explicitly anti-Frisoli platform, and, with their five-to-four majority, fired him immediately after taking office. On the night of the termination hearing (the TV broadcast of it remained on the air for hours as rapt viewers phoned in pledges to pay for more air time), a former city councilor declared the proceedings a conspiracy by Cambridge Protestants, a reminder of the fierce tribalism of a city deeply divided over educational issues and increasingly willing to make those disagreements public. From the perspective of Cambridge politics, the Pilot job search was relatively tame. But in both cases, of hiring and firing, there was more involvement by the public than ever before.

Despite the administrative changes, Pilot School classrooms retained many of their distinctive features. Groups of students met once a week with advisory teams, each comprising a teacher, a student adviser, a community resource person, and Harvard graduate students. Teachers set their own attendance policies; although no one could allow more than six unexcused cuts, staff and students could negotiate alternatives to attendance, such as independent study. Staff meetings still prompted nonjudgmental discussions of private opinions and experiences. At one meeting on drugs, for example, the rule was "that no one's feelings were to be challenged or argued with, rather, heard and understood."

The ceremony in the spring of 1973 for the first graduating class was a particularly gratifying event. Celebration was in order for the substantial achievement of college admission for 80 percent of the students, well above the figures for the regular high schools. True to form, there were no special awards. Speeches were given by parents and students as well as teachers, a democratic and refreshing change from the administrative benedictions and the platitudes of valedictorians, salutatorians, and class presidents endured in most graduation exercises. The speakers had kind words for their involvement with the experimental school. In contrast, the valedictorian at High and Latin, quoting the singer James Taylor, said, "I'd have to be a natural-born fool to want to pass this way again."

The fact that the valedictorian could offer that quote suggests that candor was not confined to the Pilot School. Indeed, one reason for examining Pilot in detail is that it magnified developments found throughout the regular high schools. But Pilot certainly spurred change. It introduced the notion that alternatives deserved a secure place in the school, not in spite of their representing minority opinions on proper education, but because they did so. In the wake of this pluralistic liberalism came the entitlement of many new constituencies, from the learning disabled to pregnant mothers to girl athletes. Groups previously shortchanged, ignored, or punished began to receive more sympathetic attention from educators. Alternative schools were not the only places in the 1970s where customary attitudes were discarded. But all the new initiatives ran into the problem of forging a sense of community while simultaneously encouraging diversity. Although relaxation characterized individual relations, minimal tolerance and civility marked the overall school culture.

The Pilot School was so popular that student oversubscription led to the formation of the Cluster School in 1974. The superintendent initially planned a school oriented to career education, but students and staff preferred a project of Harvard professor Lawrence Kohlberg on adolescent moral development in a "just community," where conflicts and decisions would be scrutinized in terms of ethical principles. Like Pilot, Cluster devoted much attention to issues of governance, discipline, grading, curriculum, and the quality of student-teacher interaction. Like Pilot, Cluster encouraged frankness. As one girl said, "You get to say anything you want, and no one will be offended by it." Like Pilot, a low student-teacher ratio, usually 10:1, blessed the project. Like Pilot, Cluster hoped students would not think of teachers as distant and infallible. In one all-school meeting to discuss a teacher who had stamped on a student's tape recorder because the owner blared music in the teacher's ear, a student expressed amazement that an adult could act in such a way, at which point another student interjected, "He is human just like us, and he is subject to emotions too."

Both schools emphasized communal norms, but Cluster did so more consistently. Attendance at the weekly community meetings was mandatory, and the staff met before each meeting to decide how important issues could be addressed as moral dilemmas. Kohlberg wanted the weekly sessions to present issues as conflicts between competing values, which he believed encouraged greater moral development in adolescents; in contrast, Pilot often shied away from confronting inflammatory issues. Advisory groups, a Discipline Committee, and the core course also dealt with governance.

Notwithstanding the theme of moral development in a self-conscious community, Cluster School students divided into factions. Black-white divisions were particularly stark. In the third year, when students could pick class sections differentiated according to learning styles, the choices seemed dictated by race. At community meetings, blacks and whites usually sat on opposite sides of the room. Most people called for deeper relationships but eventually settled for courtesy. One typical student thought that people should respect each other, "but he did not think they should have to be friends." Making diversity the basis of community was a hard assignment.

The issue of attendance was also difficult, which was not surprising, considering that 40 percent of the students had had poor disciplinary records in their previous schools. At the first weekly meeting, a motion carried to let anyone leave school if he or she disliked the courses. Soon Cluster allowed a maximum of ten cuts per semester, but not everyone endorsed that policy. As one student grumbled, "I like to cut, and if it doesn't hurt me, why should it bother anyone else . . . Who cares. You know it's my business." That same reasoning recurred in school discussions about smoking dope. Despite much rhetoric about insulting the community by coming to meetings with one's "personhood impaired," most students believed in a "be cool" rule, which in practice meant that you could do as you pleased, as long as you did it discreetly. Students defended that position by arguing pragmatically that it kept both the police and the principals of the regular schools "off our back." In exchange for orderly and legal behavior, the students' private lives were left as their own business. As one teacher admitted, "The norm prohibiting drugs is a norm of order to protect the existence and functioning of the school."

Discipline for violations of the attendance and drug rules (and for thefts and fights) was a communal decision. Here is one rule, for classroom rowdiness:

   I. If a disturbance is identified as a disturbance by an individual or by a group, then a vote will be taken to determine whether or not it is a disturbance.

      Teachers should also receive the same penalties as students.

  II. If a person causes a disturbance a second time, the group involved can:

1. assign a composition,
2. have a discussion in class, or
3. another person in the class can take the disturber out in the hall to have a conversation.

More than repeat disturbances or other infractions, poor attendance raised the issue of expulsion, which became as thorny for Cluster as for Pilot. In every expulsion case, the advocates of communal norms debated with those concerned with helping the individual. The belief in the transcendent importance of shared rules clashed with the sense that only this special environment could benefit students unable to cope elsewhere. But as everyone knew, there was no agreement on the definition of helping. Often the word connoted a personal evaluation of the miscreant's honesty. After one student explained his truancy by referring to difficulties with his father, a teacher responded, "I have to judge your sincerity." The therapeutic commitments were as vague as they were strong. At the end of the second year, only five of the sixteen students whose infringements called for expulsion cases were banished, and banishment simply meant re-enrollment in the regular high school. One teacher later said, "The slightest amount of caring about the school guaranteed every student another chance to stay."

Pilot and Cluster both illustrate some of the complications of moving school authority and good personal relations closer together. The candor encouraged in the alternative schools went hand in hand with closer student-teacher relations, but it also legitimated open quarreling previously unacceptable inside schools. The feuding made possible by forthrightness was particularly threatening to experiments like Pilot and Cluster, which fervently promoted the sense of community as a goal. It was in part the extraordinary diversity of the two groups that encumbered the quest for community; the different backgrounds and values fitted together jaggedly. On balance, these two schools achieved more on the counts of openness and good personal relations than on community. Pledging to honor diversity and cherish differences was more conducive to awareness of others' feelings than to a sense of community. Tolerance and pluralism often bred mutual avoidance pacts instead of friendly treaties among allies.

Pilot and Cluster were not alone in seeking satisfactory accommodations to diversity. The regular schools could not ignore the claims of minority groups. Racial issues agitated High and Latin in 1969 and 1970. Fights between black girls and white (often sparked by black boys dating white girls) angered their parents, who accused one another of racism at public school board meetings. The tensions erupted in the spring of 1970, when some black students raised clenched fists for their yearbook pictures. The headmaster and his assistant refused to approve publication of the photographs, and the blacks responded with a sit-down strike outside his office. "That was the first time anyone disobeyed my orders," the headmaster recalled. He assured the superintendent that the blacks would leave; they did, for one day. In the following weeks, the agitation continued.

Racial issues throughout the 1970s flared with regularity. When one superintendent ruled that a Black Student Union excluding whites was illegal, irate blacks demonstrated so vigorously that a school committee member asked the police to send the tactical assault unit. When a black principal lost his job, the black community accused the superintendent of racism (and the principal brought suit, unsuccessfully, for $300,000). Early in 1980, when a black student stabbed and killed a white classmate, the school closed for one week, and on the day of re-opening, a security force of seventy-five included local clergy, plainclothesmen, parents, and counselors. None of those episodes typified day-to-day life, but each received so much publicity that the image of Cambridge high schools remained much worse than the reality.

Race was not the only form of diversity. Student cliques multiplied with the rise of "disco babies," "punks," and "preppies," in addition to the older groupings by neighborhood, class, ethnic background, and athletic ability. The number of bilingual students rose dramatically in the 1970s; legal mandates required that special classes be given in the students' native languages. The law also stipulated individualized programs for students with learning disabilities, physical handicaps, and emotional problems. (Nationwide, special education teachers between 1971 and 1980 climbed from 1.1 percent of high school staff to 6.0 percent, a steeper rise than the one from 0.3 percent to 1.1 percent between 1961 and 1971.) The heterogeneity became even greater when Rindge merged with High and Latin in 1978.

In the combined and more comprehensive school, recognition of diversity marked the way students got along with each other. The tradition of different groups controlling the various school entrances came to an end. Interracial dating aroused less ire than it had in the late 1960s. Student committees chose music to replace bells, and the recordings reflected musical preferences of both blacks and whites. The rise of girls' sports righted the previously lopsided distribution of athletic honors. (In other schools, seating for lunches and for assemblies became less sex-segregated, as did teachers' lounges.)

The school responded sympathetically to diversity in several ways. Administrators frequently adopted the style and substance of the Pilot and Cluster experiments. In particular, there was more concern for a caring school climate. The Fairness Committee welcomed complaints from both students and teachers, and the Youth Advocacy Program featured peer counseling on in-school as well as community problems. The Blue Room was a place where students could go when they felt the need to scream and shout and talk with a sympathetic adult. By 1980, there was variable credit for work in the guidance office under a counselor's supervision. The Teacher-Advisory Program offered two credits; students discussed personal and school issues with a teacher to develop "a sense of togetherness and community within the high school." Ten credits were available for a course named Life Styles, which had no prerequisites. Its aim was "to help you develop insight into your actions and feelings through the study of common life experiences." There were twenty credits for K-100, which the catalogue called "more than just a course; it is a community." Indeed, it was the old Cluster School, renamed and scaled down to forty-five students. Adolescent parents enjoyed their own program, with life skills, child development, and an exercise class with special breathing and stretching techniques. Although enrollments for these optional courses were small, their mere existence signaled an unprecedented concern for affective needs. No course catalogues from the 1940s or 1950s included anything comparable.

The therapeutic commitments also affected staffing. The guidance department mushroomed to twenty full-time and three part-time counselors; nine worked exclusively with alternative and special programs. A "teacher support team" of three faculty members and one psychiatrist, formed in 1977, met with teachers against whom complaints had been filed. New administrative councils frequently made use of quasi-psychological phrases to describe their work — action plan, support mechanisms, goal setting, expectation reinforcement. The security force grew apace, but often they identified with counselors more than with the police. In a decade of flat enrollments and tight budgets, the social services were an area of growth, not retrenchment.

Probably the greatest impact of Pilot and Cluster was the legitimation of other special programs. The number of different options in 1980 prompted one writer for the student newspaper to suggest that each diploma be from "Cambridge maybe Rindge maybe Latin probably kind of sort of in a way." In 1976, a conservative Independent school board member crusading for a "neo-traditional voluntary fundamental school" stated that "we are asking for an alternative we feel safe with," one that emphasized discipline and the basics. For the chronic failures in the elementary grades, there was the Achievement School, designed to mainstream them into the high school they would otherwise never enter. For those with academic and attendance problems, there was the Enterprise Co-op Program, with each day split between employment and courses. A work-study program for juniors and seniors also divided their schooldays, and a community-based learning program offered choices between local colleges, internships, and jobs. The early commitment to diversity within a group faded with the rise of programs targeted for specific populations. Even the Pilot School became a more homogeneous place over time, because the widespread interpretation of its early years as evidence of liberal values prompted many middle- and upper-class parents to send their children there. The central administration encouraged the growth of the special programs. One assistant superintendent publicly said that if enough people wanted it, he would design a curriculum for "running naked through the woods."

Not everyone on the staff welcomed the new initiatives. The curriculum changed more rapidly than the staff. Many tenured older faculty resented the innovations. Commenting on students, a senior

English teacher paraphrased St. Thomas Aquinas when he sniffed, "Heaven is no longer the same for all, but it must be equally pleasant." Another conservative complained with more bitterness:

> If I grab a kid in the hall, they'll send me to a shrink. Get a conference! Adjustment counselors! The counselors excuse everything instead of just saying, wise up, your old man is a bum. Smarten up, or you'll be one too. If a kid wants to run up that wall and across the ceiling, I have to let him. So I say, fire the guidance counselors. Fire the adjustment counselors. They tell me if a kid cuts my class every day, I'm not a good teacher. They think every moron in the country needs a high school diploma. The whole place is crazy. Cambridge hasn't hired a teacher in fifteen years; they're all weirdos.

In truth, Cambridge in those years hired many excellent teachers, including several with Harvard doctorates. Several Pilot and Cluster veterans became respected administrators, and their influence ensured a secure place for various reforms. Yet the new order continued to irk the old guard. They saw the empowerment of the formerly disenfranchised as a restriction of their own influence, but they voiced their anger at other adults. The classroom cease-fire caused sniping to break out elsewhere.

"They Have to Care"

Some teachers boast that East High School in Denver, Colorado, survived racial turmoil in the late 1960s because the school was already diverse. It is true that East's student population changed in the early 1960s. The completion of new high schools siphoned off many bright middle-class whites. Median test scores plunged between 1959 and 1962, leveled out briefly, then fell again in 1968, dropping in nine years from the eighty-first to the fifty-sixth percentile nationally. Once featured in the *Atlantic Monthly* as an outstanding school, East became academically average and largely black (36 percent compared with 10 percent systemwide), and its yearly pupil transience rate was three times that of the new high schools in Denver.

But the program of studies was not simultaneously transformed. In a school where 65 percent of the class of 1964 entered college, the annual dropout rate was a substantial 17 percent. Not much was done to hold the dropouts. The 1966 accreditation team considered the meager vocational offerings the worst part of the curriculum. In addition, the lower level social studies classes lacked special materials, and the remedial English class was a "bore." The students did not relish those courses. Taking the basic courses invited stigmatization, one English teacher recalled.

> The accelerated classes were always doing special things — you know, trips, parties, things like that — and I wanted those things for my students too. So I thought, we'll have a party on the last day of school. I told them, "We'll all go on the lawn today." Well, I think they wanted to but, my goodness, they didn't want to be seen together! I'll never forget that. It was a shock to me.

Like most city dwellers in the 1960s, Denverites feared desegregation. In 1964, 69 percent of the white parents favored neighborhood schools; only 26 percent preferred open enrollment. The social worker at East used to get calls from nervous parents anxious to know whether their children were dating blacks. In 1969, when blacks and Hispanics accounted for 39.6 percent and 6.6 percent, respectively, of the East population, the school board passed a controversial student reassignment plan. The impact on East would have been more, not fewer, whites, but the white residents near East were so incensed by the means — busing — that they were sharply divided. The 1969 school board election turned on the busing issue, and several candidates inflamed white fear by ranting against "forced mandatory crosstown busing on a massive scale." The controversies about busing (here and elsewhere) put many parents on edge, even if their own schools were not yet transformed. People were no longer sure that their previously tranquil school, populated by their neighbors' usually well-behaved children, would remain a safe citadel. What did sacrifice for a home in the Right Area mean if some liberal judge could let the hooligans into the middle-class sanctuaries or, worse yet, order their own children into enemy territory?

The new board rescinded the previous plans and introduced voluntary student transfers. That device was one of many that a district court in 1973 considered evidence of racism on the part of the Denver school board. The judges decried gerrymandered zones, mobile classrooms (in trailers) sent only to black schools, and color-conscious staffing of minority schools.

Early in 1969, before that decision, members of the Black Student Association at East petitioned for soul food in the cafeteria, demanded reinstatement of blacks suspended for an entire year, and protested alleged racism among the faculty. The 1968–1969 school year featured Panthers with bullhorns, a walk-out, friendly meetings with black professional football players, and, toward the end, the appearance of soul food in the cafeteria. Initial agreements included a semester of black history, and later ones called for weekend retreats to the mountain cabin of the principal, who impressed some staff as too lenient. One teacher complained, "Many of us wanted more order and more discipline. Kids were running through the halls, and he never let us know that bothered him. At least he should have told us that he was trying to control things."

Concessions to black protesters were only the first steps in moving the curriculum in the direction of relevance and choice. By the mid 1970s, East offered an array of innovative programs: executive internships, career education, housing rehabilitation projects, eco-seminar (in the mountains), Senior Seminar (nature plus interpersonal skills), Hold Youth (dropout prevention), and the Mutual Agreement Program (for truants). Within the traditional departments, especially English, minicourses and electives proliferated. Overall, the 160 courses offered in the mid 1950s doubled by the early 1970s. Students in need of special services also received closer attention. Jay Breen, East's social worker, recalled that "during orientation week my first year [1958], a counselor told me, 'Don't worry about me referring any cases to you because I don't believe in social workers.'" By the 1970s she had scores of referrals, many urgent. "I can have a plan drawn up for the day, and nine times out of ten I don't come anywhere near it. I have to drop what I'm doing and deal with emergencies." Her jurisdiction included the emotionally disturbed, learning disabled, teens in foster homes, the hard of hearing, the hospitalized, as well as students troubled by competitive anxieties, family stress, pregnancies, and other complications. "I've felt many times as if I worked in a mental hospital." She saw the kind of adolescents who twenty-five years earlier rarely graduated from, or even began, high school.

East's self-consciousness about diversification was expressed in, and legitimated by, psychological shorthand. Senior Seminar, for example, was modeled on Outward Bound, originally a program to toughen World War II sailors so that they could survive if they were capsized. "Now the technique is used to avert the loss of meaning in life rather than prevent wartime loss of life." That uncritical language was quite different from the stern ("needs to know limits") and solicitous ("tends to be oversensitive") description of "The High School Teenager" on page two of the 1955 student handbook at East. John Astuno, a former principal, estimated that 20 percent of the students had some form of learning difficulty. "Once, they'd flunk out or be thrown out, but now we try to keep them. So teachers have to be warm human beings; they have to care."

Caring was rarely defined, but in practice it meant openness about personal experiences. As an English teacher exclaimed, "There's nothing they won't write on a piece of paper! Why, I got one this morning, a poem on sex. I don't believe that anyone would have handed that in ten years ago." Not all the revelations were voluntary. During her intake examination of ninth-graders, the school nurse asked the freshmen whether they were sexually active.

The frankness of expression was defended as a beneficial dose of realism. Life out there is not much different from daily life in here; high school is not a place apart. As the former principal led a tour of the school, he walked by the cooking class. There was a bottle of wine in the display case. Astuno stopped, shrugged his shoulders, and said he had decided not to try to remove the bottle. "That's the real world." Likewise, it was acceptable for a girl in the 1981 yearbook to announce, in the caption to her picture as a Senior Top Ten, that she was going to attend Stanford University in order to "obtain a degree in radical organizations." That assertiveness was no more threatening than the candid appraisal of the principal in the 1976 yearbook.

Whatever their politics, students at East in the 1970s went to an orderly school. The sort of strife seen in the late 1960s, when

Black Panthers urged students to tear the building down, was gone. This was a safe environment, where students felt secure (although some neighbors apparently did not. In 1979, the local Sambo's restaurant barred East students during the breakfast hours). Not only was the school safe; the climate was relaxed. As one gym teacher said, "Teachers are closer to the youngsters now . . . The staff became a little freer with the kids." A math teacher agreed: "The atmosphere now is lighter, less grave, than it used to be."

Light enough so that students were not hassled about spotty attendance. Twenty years earlier, students who missed twenty days or more per year would have been expelled without hesitation. In contrast, the state law later implied that absences were not, by themselves, sufficient cause for failure. Some teachers disliked the mild attendance policy, but in the words of John Astuno, "If I tried to keep ninety-four or ninety-six percent, instead of eighty-eight percent, I'd lose too many kids." Reinstatement of the old regimentations would have alienated too many students. The attendance issue was a reminder that psychosociological sensitivity can foster a hands-off response to many problems. People can leave each other alone with consequences other than harmony and good cheer. Several teachers reported that frankness in the classroom was not the same as camaraderie. Students may have written and talked about their private lives, but that did not necessarily lead to intellectual give-and-take. One English teacher said, "There's so little real togetherness. There's a feeling that it is not *in* to be friends with the teacher. It's not *in* to recite in class. Your friends won't like you if you joke with the teacher. They're so passive."

Student passivity was not a priority issue, because in fact it promoted stability. School men at East and elsewhere vividly remembered the chaos and uproar of the late 1960s. Black demands and student protest had disrupted many previously tranquil schools. Most administrators tried hard to re-create order. The therapeutic innovations were intended to contribute to the restoration of efficient routines. In other words, the mellowing of the high schools, less a cause than an effect of the tumult of the late 1960s, became, in the 1970s, an important element in defusing the unrest that had spawned it.

But every now and again, the mellowing invited the disorder.

When the 1981 Spirit Week at Denver East featured a Sixties Day, with students headbanded and befeathered, disruption threatened the usual calm. In keeping with the theme of the day, a dozen students walked to the main office during the morning announcements to borrow the P.A. system so that they could announce a demonstration outside. As the group approached the office, the principal was crossing the hall. "Well, he totally blew his cool," one teacher exclaimed. To a girl wearing a button saying JOAN BAEZ, PRESIDENT, he barked, "Joan Baez, president of what? How dare you say president of the United States."

The last thing Astuno wanted was a return to the spirit of the 1960s, by either students or staff. When Astuno came to East in 1974, he was fully aware that the faculty was stubborn and independent. He immediately enforced some previously ignored rules. One math teacher recalled, "The first day I forgot to sign in, he came down and got me out of a sophomore orientation group, right in the middle of class, and told me to go to the office. I thought he was kidding! I slapped him on the arm and said, 'Oh sure, I'll do that by mid-morning.' He said, 'You will do that *now*.'" Astuno also disciplined students — no hats, no loud radios — but the faculty chafed at his style. Some staff had no reason to complain, but they did. The fiercest anti-Astuno staff member taught some evening classes in a lab building unconnected to the main structure. Frequently he read a newspaper during class as students worked on their own. He sometimes kept a desk drawer open during class so that he could read the textbook for a university course he was taking. Astuno knew of these derelictions, and one day he walked into the class, took the newspaper, and asked, "What's this? Your lesson plan?" A grievance charge followed. That teacher later drew up a "no confidence" resolution, and 70 percent of the faculty voted against Astuno. Twenty years earlier, the teacher would have been silenced by a transfer or pressured to quit, and open faculty protest would have been very unlikely.

The informality apparent in many classrooms and in the corridors was not as evident in the relationship between staff and administration. That unevenness was not just a function of personality. It may be that for some parts of a high school to become more flexible, other parts have to be rigid and controlled. As the superintendent

127

of the San Francisco schools said in 1972, "It takes more planning, more guidance, more watching to create good open educational and informal programs than it does to run a traditional program." The firmness of an Astuno, in other words, was not simply the administrative counterpart of the classroom martinet of the 1930s or 1940s.

"It Used to Be They'd Be Gone"

San Diego High alumni, when talking of their school, often juxtaposed its distinguished early history with tumultuous recent times. In honor of the school's centennial, in 1982, an article, "The Way We Were," featured vignettes of teachers and alumni from the 1930s and 1940s. At that time a student body of thirty-eight hundred middle-class teenagers, most of them white, compiled strong athletic, extracurricular, and academic records. Famous graduates included Art Linkletter, Gregory Peck, and Raquel Welch. In both numbers and quality, this was the flagship school of the city. The building was an imposing Victorian structure covered with ivy and surrounded by manicured lawns. The teachers were also well groomed (the men wore coats and ties), and they had strict disciplinary standards. For instance, an industrial arts teacher failed one student who, driving by school later, flipped him a middle finger. The teacher related the incident to the football coach, who was furious. Several days afterward, in the middle of a school assembly, the coach took the kid to the principal's office. He was suspended for five days.

The erection of new high schools in this rapidly growing city, coupled with an influx of Hispanics and blacks, changed the school population before the eruptions of the late 1960s. By 1968, San Diego High was half white, one-quarter black, and one-quarter Hispanic. Parental incomes ranged from very high to very low, and the average IQ score was a decidedly average 103. The school responded cautiously to these demographic changes and altered neither the curriculum nor the school philosophy. There was some tinkering — the appointment of one bilingual counselor, the use of team teaching and paperbacks in English, "zipper applications" in home economics — that paralleled the modest changes introduced during the same years at Denver East and the Cambridge high schools.

Protests flared in the 1968–1969 school year. Black students vilified S.D.H.S. as racist and demanded more black teachers, more black coaches, more counselors, black literature courses, black paraprofessionals, and a black student center. One black counselor printed protest literature on school stationery and encouraged demonstrations. At a pep rally with students from Lincoln High, which was 99 percent black, students chanted, "Kill the whites," ordered the teachers to leave, and spat on an American flag. In the cafeteria, black students occasionally dumped food on the floor. Although Chicano agitation was minimal, others felt free to act out. Dope was smoked on the front lawn by the hippies, and students practicing witchcraft brought black cats and put a hex on the school. The faculty became polarized; many felt the demands and the protests were outrageous. The principal, one year from retirement, was less adamant, and the only demand he flatly denied was the one for a black student center.

The protests ended as quickly as they began, but they left marks on the school. Some innovations — team teaching, modular scheduling, eighteen English electives in place of junior- and senior-year requirements, contract experimental math, independent study, and coed gym — were fashionable changes tried at schools unscathed by the late 1960s' protests. But other initiatives at S.D.H.S. addressed the special needs of minority students and chronic absentees who were not previously considered special. Bilingual classes were offered in business, math, science, and social studies. The Barrio Station provided tutors for habitual absentees. The school also introduced a no-credit grade for students who did passing work when at school, but attended so rarely that they were failing their courses. To avoid stigmatizing the students, the special education department was renamed the special learning department. Throughout the school, the practice of ability grouping was sharply reduced.

All of that was light years from the S.D.H.S. of 1940, when the principal wrote, in the school newspaper, that nothing in the curriculum took the place of hard work and innate talent. The key to success then was said to be effort and intelligence; by the early 1970s, with a diverse student body, the school accepted more of the responsibility for students' success (though 56 percent of the 1973 student body failed a proficiency test at the sixth-grade reading level).

No one was more affected by the expansion of the curriculum and the consideration of minority needs than the counseling department. In the 1960s, some of the guidance staff impugned the abilities of Hispanics. One counselor said to a science teacher, "I'm putting this Mexican kid in your class, but frankly, I've never seen one who's any good." Chicanos were rarely urged to meet college representatives; counselors steered them instead to junior colleges. When a Hispanic student, Hector Torres, formed an organization to arrange contacts between Hispanics and representatives of four-year colleges, an administrator twice threatened to transfer him to a night school for dropouts. The demonstrators of 1969 protested the placing of minority students into lower ability sections, but in the early 1970s an about-face irked some of the more conservative staff. Black counselors reportedly placed some minority students in courses supposedly above their ability and background, and, it was said, encouraged mediocre students to apply to college. The introduction of a motivational adviser, peer counseling, and Saturday morning counseling expanded the power of the department, and some teachers groused that the new initiatives were not sufficiently teacher-oriented.

The restoration of order accompanied the commitment to inclusiveness. The 1973 accreditation report said that 53 percent of the students noted that theft was a "serious problem"; by the end of the decade, the atmosphere was quiet enough to permit the school to reduce the security force by half. There were still occasional episodes of disruptiveness — radios and tape recorders on campus, students carrying chains, loiterers near the gym, typewriters missing from the business department, and racist graffiti. But minor disturbances were tolerable as long as they did not spark the sort of major confrontations witnessed in the late 1960s. Giving a teacher the finger after school had once been a serious violation of propriety. By the 1970s, individual improprieties were not the same as (and thus mattered less than) the taboo on institutional disorder. As one teacher harumphed, "Twenty years ago, smoking a cigarette was good for a three-day suspension. Now kids can have dope and all that will happen is a talk with the parents."

The maintenance of order in a diversified and caring environment was not universally appreciated. The 1973 evaluation revealed that many students were unaware of both traditional and innovative aspects of their school. Can students suggest new courses? Sixty-one percent did not know. Are drugs a problem here? Forty percent had no opinion. Can racial and ethnic problems be discussed with teachers and administrators? I don't know, answered 44 percent. Do you know how to join a club? No, replied 52 percent. Is there a districtwide student rights policy? Fifty-nine percent did not know. Those figures indicate a pervasive disengagement from high school. That was one form of relaxation many students chose and the school allowed. Nobody forced students to take advantage of the many available opportunities; it was up to them to make the move.

The persistence of poor attendance was the major symptom of the students' weak commitment to S.D.H.S. By 1975, approximately 33 percent were out of their assigned class (the ditching was period truancy rather than day cuts). A new school policy set an automatic F for fifteen or more unexcused cuts; attendance improved immediately. But several years later the state legislature said a school could not fail a student on the basis of poor attendance alone. One parent-lawyer, aware of the new law, threatened to sue the school when his daughter received a midterm progress report saying that "she deserves a B but I have to give her an F because of absences." The principal decided not to fight back. In line with its humane orientation, the school had not relied solely on a stern attendance policy. In September 1977, Program Change drew 120 students with poor attendance records. They had multicultural instruction, signed contract lesson plans, and received motivational counseling. Although Program Change was a generous alternative to either expulsion or failure ("It used to be they'd be gone and that was the end of it"), the issue of attendance nevertheless continued to provoke hostility — among the staff. In the opinion of many S.D.H.S. teachers, lax enforcement of attendance rules meant jelly-fish principals unable or unwilling to press students. But in the opinion of some administrators, attendance figures accurately gauged the teachers' ability to interest and motivate their class. Administrators and teachers wound up accusing each other more than the students and their parents.

Another problem was the failure of the achievements of the 1970s to dispel occasional bad publicity. The public's impression of S.D.H.S. remained negative. In the 1981–1982 Gallup Poll on education, 26 percent of the San Diego respondents — three points higher than the national average — said lack of discipline was their school's worst problem. The director of alumni affairs had to meet one fearful alumna at a downtown store and escort her to the campus, where she wanted another escort from the security force. Several faculty committees recommended more publicity for special programs; they knew that articles on beer drinking on the front lawn (written by a reporter who simply drove by the school) perpetuated the terrible and inaccurate image. So did the declaration by a judge that S.D.H.S. was unsafe; he based his assessment on "incident reports," the number of which measured enforcement zeal more than the true degree of school safety.

However, the restoration of quiet on campus did not mean that the adults sat in peace with each other. Inside S.D.H.S., some departments were isolated from others. The rapid turnover of principals and vice-principals created uncertainties about front office policy, and encouraged some staffers to believe they would outlast any administrator. The vocal and critical school board publicized conflicts that either had not existed or once were settled quietly. The court's role in desegregation irritated many residents, and the strength of teachers' unions also fueled conflict. Disorder had not been eliminated; it had been displaced. Students may not have knifed each other, but adults needled other adults. The student apathy evidenced by nonattendance contrasted with the bickering of the adults.

"They've Taken This Fear Out"

At first glance, the history of Cleveland Central Catholic High School seems tame. Student militants and black activists never threatened the school, which served a blue-collar Polish-American neighborhood in the city. The "serious" protest was a P.A. announcement by freshmen upset by the cancelation of their prom. One teacher sponsored an underground newspaper (*Fudge*) and urged everyone to attend an Earth Day rally. The administration co-opted both issues — by bragging about the paper, and by asking the science department to run an assembly on ecology. Nor was the C.C.C. faculty as aggressive as their counterparts in the Cleveland public schools. Few faculty joined the local union. Once when the union called a strike, almost no C.C.C. staff honored it. The union representative then was not close with his colleagues, which hurt the strike, but the union remained unappealing, even under different leadership. Still, this faculty had cause for complaint. During the slapdash scheduling of the 1970s, some teachers had three preparations when others carried five. Some teachers took their classes to Dairy Queen; others gave science lectures to over two hundred students. The different styles of five principals in thirteen years irritated many.

Though its faculty avoided strikes, C.C.C. did not escape the late 1960s and early 1970s unscarred. The merger of four small parish schools into the consolidated and comprehensive diocesan high school was so difficult that this comparatively quiet school saw itself as rudderless.

In fact and in spirit, the four high schools that merged in 1969 were not comprehensive. Each school was small; the enrollments ranged from 250 to 578. Three of the four original schools limited their guidance staff to one half-time position. Academic opportunities were also sparse. When the 1968 Ohio legislature raised the minimum number of courses that high schools had to offer, from forty-five to fifty-five, not one of the four schools satisfied the new standard. Indeed, only the two largest met the old requirement. To satisfy a provision of the 1968 law stipulating that individual differences of students should be addressed, St. Michael's provided only one class (in prealgebra), and St. John Cantius, likewise, had one course in basic math. Moreover, not everyone was welcome in the parochial high schools. In a 1964 study of adolescents with IQs below 90, a Sister reported that these students thought the teachers did not care about them, and they also felt snubbed by other students. Not everyone had to associate with everyone else. Asked whether "persons of one race or creed have the right to live in a neighborhood restricted to this race or creed," 39 percent of the religion teachers in the system in 1969 agreed.

The merger satisfied the stiffer 1968 state standards, but it did more than comply with the new ruling. The founders envisioned a four-campus comprehensive high school devoted to good personal relations, individualized instruction, and independent study. Those goals justified several unusual strategies: mandatory enrollment in group dynamics and art appreciation courses, grading based on innate ability as well as achievement, and flexible scheduling. The merger entailed renovations and additions costing $2.7 million; only some special programs roped in state funds, but the principal was close enough to the bishop to secure generous appropriations for this experiment. When classes began in the fall of 1969, students found 137 different courses, twice the total (sixty-nine) offered by the four parent schools. The 1970 yearbook reprinted a list of all the courses, which ranged from horticulture to fashion design to business law, real estate, speed reading, aeronautics, Polish, and court reporting. As Bill Kelley, a Spanish teacher, said, "Everyone felt he was teaching something special." What looked good for the students also felt good to the staff.

Along with the respect of diversity was concern for good human relations. In the words of one parent, "They've taken this fear out and replaced everything with love." Guidance services expanded, embracing prevocational as well as precollege planning. On the report cards, a grade for nonacademic behavior carried equal weight with the traditional mark.

In contrast with the 1970s, the psychological work of the 1950s and 1960s had been modest. In 1955, the superintendent of the Cleveland Catholic schools privately complained of the aggressive administrator of the Catholic Guidance Bureau, who criticized teachers and wanted social workers rather than regular teachers to run the reading clinic. In 1960, the Catholic Counseling Center, an outpatient service staffed by social workers, received 552 applications for counseling, but 162 applicants were never seen, because of the long delay in processing new cases. That center grew in the 1960s; its 1968 budget was ten times the 1956 appropriation. But the staff's philosophy was cautious. As one of the social workers said of his colleagues, "With adolescents they don't want to stir up additional conflicts. Treating reality problems, setting limits and controls, is a lot of their work."

Major changes deserved extensive discussion, and small planning groups of the C.C.C. faculty had months of meetings. The enthusiastic principal who coordinated the planning, Father Fiala, was so committed to comprehensiveness that he envisioned a Russian-language center for C.C.C. "It all sounded very exciting," recalled Pat Lange, a math teacher. But she also noted that "not one thing was said about management." What looked nice on paper got smudged by bus wheels because the logistics of offering courses at four sites confounded Father Fiala. The modular system, with long blocks of time for some courses and briefer daily sessions for others, complicated the scheduling. One year, the students did not receive their schedules until October, when the superintendent finally ordered the principal to tighten up the makeshift arrangements. That same fall, several classrooms under construction were unusable until December, which also hampered the scheduling. Teachers and students had to travel from campus to campus, often leaving class early or arriving late. Within the school, not everyone got along well. Many coaches resented the principal's selection of rivals as head coaches. Students accustomed to athletic rivalry let the competitiveness linger. What further fragmented this school were the differences among the powerful building administrators. Each campus reflected the idiosyncrasies of the person in charge. One place was notoriously strict; another was so loose that the principal had to order the yearbook pictures retaken because almost no one was wearing the school uniform.

Like Denver East, San Diego High, and Cambridge Latin, C.C.C. endured a period of disorder. In each school, the restoration of order became the first priority. At the first three schools, the disorder was an important cause of the more sympathetic response to diversity. What with Black Panthers jumping on teachers' desks and demonstrations on the front lawn, a school like East had to deal with disruption. At C.C.C., in contrast, the disorder was initially the effect of the voluntary move toward comprehensiveness, affective education, and student choice.

By the early 1980s, C.C.C. was much more efficient, thanks to a strong principal and his experienced assistants. But it was not as rigid as the Catholic high schools of twenty or thirty years earlier. The impression of looseness or rigidity depends on the point of contrast; the farther back one recollects, the less austere C.C.C.

seemed. Students in the 1980s were franker: "Many of them treat me like a peer," said one teacher. They talked about divorce and separation with more ease. A second teacher remarked, "I would never have thought of talking to the Sisters at my high school the way some of these kids talk to me." The distance between student and teacher was less than when nuns stood in the halls to be sure no one talked between classes. "They are less guarded and more honest now," reported another. Several teachers resented those familiarities, but most did not mind. Moreover, theology classes did not call for memorization and recitation of dogma. A theology teacher mentioned that more students were willing to ask "If there's a God, why is there so much suffering?" An assistant principal added, "There's more room for discussion now."

In some respects, C.C.C. resembled a high school from the distant past. Proud staff earned modest salaries, working-class parents sacrificed for their children's education, and attendance was a privilege rather than a right. Even the buildings were turn-of-the-century architecture. But C.C.C. was hardly immune to the changes in the wider world. The complications between administrators and the classroom relaxations found elsewhere also shaped the history of C.C.C. in the 1970s. It is true that the school staff stayed because they chose to, aware that they could have earned more in public schools. The disgruntled left. It is also true that student-teacher chumminess was tempered by mutual respect of a religious school atmosphere, which limited uninhibited self-expression. But even in this more traditional, more structured, more directive setting, there were parallels to the major shifts taking place in the public schools since the late 1960s.

Partial Transformations, Persistent Traditions

Different schools cannot share a precisely common past. Each institution has its own ethos, subject to change for many reasons. Comparable budgets, related courses, the same textbooks, and other similarities do not result in identical schools. Because of the substantial diversity among high schools, it is necessary to concentrate on major tendencies when summarizing and interpreting the recent history of secondary education.

One of these tendencies was the speed with which the changes took place. High schools of 1945 and 1965 were more alike than the schools of 1965 and 1975. The period of greatest change was short and stormy, although much of the basic structure of schooling was left untouched. The reorientation came about less through internal leadership than as a consequence of pressure from the wider world. Ferment in the society more than educational theorizing or pedagogical research accounted for upheaval in the high schools. Educators could not ignore the many issues that developed outside their corridors but affected their lives.

Dropping an American history textbook for an anthology of primary sources exemplifies the garden variety of change known to educators in the 1950s. Coping with growth was the foremost achievement of those years. The quantitative changes — new buildings, more teachers, bigger budgets — were more striking than any rethinking of fundamental principles. The high schools' ambience remained uneasy. The lives of the decision makers continued to be less regimented than those of the students and teachers, who were constrained by the middle-class rituals they observed every day.

Then quite suddenly this conservative institution took on much of the national liberal agenda. The vigorous pursuit of egalitarian reforms promised to clarify, expand, and protect the claims of the disadvantaged. Disparate groups — ethnic and racial minorities, the learning disabled, the poor, the physically and emotionally impaired, and teen-agers in need of social services — previously served in niggardly fashion now found a more comfortable place in secondary schools. Before, their place had been marginal; in the 1970s, their once tenuous hold on the schools' resources and respect grew firmer. As one political scientist put it, "Inclusion has to do with the reduction of asymmetries of power, influence, and authority." Policy makers treated youth as one of the disadvantaged groups, due to receive and to exercise, by virtue of earlier maturation, more privileges and rights.

In 1965, high school principals ranked "development of positive self-concept and good human relations" seventh of eight educational goals; by 1977, that same objective was second of ten. The new prominence of feelings and emotions went hand in hand with the heightened responsiveness to the rights of the disenfranchised. There was less regimentation and more choice, both academic and personal. Getting a hall pass became easier.

The modification of the old austerities was an important liberalization of schooling. The treating of kids more as adults — and the kids' acting less innocent — alarmed conservatives. Most school people praised the changes as sensitive and pragmatic accommodations to reality, but many outsiders perceived in them the collapse of authority, morals, and common sense. The direction of change was toward openness and informality, but they did not sweep the field. Frankness about sexuality evoked strong resistance in many towns. Irate residents of Muncie, Indiana, pressured national television to cut several minutes from "Middletown," a documentary series filmed in their city. The objectionable episode aired teenagers' discussions of sex. (Yet in the same town, there were seven porno stores, plus two stores selling *used* porno.) Moreover, the number of censorship cases rose in the 1970s. Some of the offensive books were well known; *Catcher in the Rye,* with its 222 *hell*s, twenty-seven *Chrissake*s, and seven *horny*s, had been a target for years. Less familiar were the books, written for young readers, that explicitly discussed drugs and sex. Less familiar were the controversial novels of Judy Blume that referred to menstruation and masturbation with an openness that sparked many protests against their purchase by school librarians.

In face of the challenges to conventional behavior, many nervous parents transferred their children to private schools in search of more adult oversight in an environment shielded against unsettling social change. After the late 1960s, the liberals felt more at home in public schools than did conservatives, and their educational philosophy displeased some conservatives.

The easing of the old controls was one of several issues in dispute between adults. On many questions there was more public conflict than before. In the same years that student-teacher relations softened, adults quarreled openly with each other. Matters previously evaded or settled by compromise behind closed doors began to cause visible confrontations. Teacher unions frequently pitted staff against administrators. Often outsiders were the antagonists, whether stingy taxpayers, well-educated parents, judges, media alarmists, or social scientists. The exchanges seemed especially shrill because the voices muffled in the 1940s and 1950s were now clearly heard. The calm of the past had been superficial and deceptive. The more recent cacophony was an honest representation of opinion.

Like the swing toward less stressful schooldays, the rise of the adversarial style was a partial transformation. Not everyone was swept up by contentiousness. A case in point was the popular exaggeration of the impact of unions. The media often pictured teachers and administrators at one another's throat. In contrast, the past was memorialized as peaceful and professional, with powerful principals presiding over harmonious and happy staffs. In truth, life without unions was far from perfect. In smaller districts, teachers needed the principal's support in times of unexpected intervention by either the superintendent or the school committee, yet that alliance was uncertain, because the principal was dependent on those superiors. In Houston in the early 1950s, conservative pressures terrified some teachers, but they could not share their anxieties with their principals for fear of reprisals.

Various constraints on the principal either predated teacher militance or had little to do with unions. Smaller districts meant closer supervision by the superintendent and more informal pressure from the community. Later, the early 1960s' curricular reforms gave rise to subject specialists for kindergarten through twelfth grade, and those coordinators were often less subservient than department heads. Moreover, high school principals could sidestep contract provisions, few of which were fully implemented in any school. On paper, firing a teacher required tremendous caution and calculation, but in practice informal pressures could neutralize the inept or ease them out. Union representatives squared off against the principal, but in daily life their relationship was often friendly. As Susan Johnson argued, many nonsalary provisions were "interpreted, bent, and informally renegotiated to fit the needs of the teachers, principals, and schools." This helps explain why, in a 1977 national survey of principals, union "specifications" were a serious or very serious problem to only 12.2 percent of the respondents, far behind paperwork (42.4 percent), student apathy (40.9 percent), and lack of parental involvement (40.4 percent).

The flexibility in union-administrator relations signaled the persistence of some of the traditional informalities. Just as the mellowing of student-teacher contact was partial, so too was the mellowing among decision makers. Not every aspect of administrative life was tightly constrained. Not every classroom was full of frankness and free of fear. Schools did not wholly abandon their past.

Still, administration became less tranquil as classroom climates softened. Student-staff relationships turned more agreeable, on the whole, in the same years that administrators and aggressive outsiders snarled at each other. Both developments entailed more openness than the circumspections of the past. People spoke about concerns previously not legitimate topics of public conversation.

The major changes of the last fifteen years promoted equity and equality for the disadvantaged. Student rights, teacher unions, a comprehensive curriculum, compensatory and remedial programs, and other initiatives empowered different groups unaccustomed to full participation in the schools. Instead of foisting middle-class white Protestant values on a captive audience, high schools began to respect pluralism more than ever before. In the 1940s, there was much earnest rhetoric about the school as a democracy, but little actual respect for cultural diversity. By the 1970s the commitments to equality were taken more seriously.

Equality did not escape the competing claims of other interests. Throughout the 1970s, school people sought to restore orderly efficiency while they enfranchised the dispossessed. That was a hard assignment, because the uproar of the late 1960s had been fueled, in large part, by the protests from the disadvantaged. Stability returned, but there were no resurrections of the strict unilateral peace treaties of the past. The new covenants featured a broader curriculum, less stereotyping, and more freedom. Episodes of school violence distorted the general satisfaction with the new arrangements.

But the ingenious truce extended few incentives for academic intensity. Relaxation and engagement were not necessarily synonymous. If they were, student passivity and lack of interest would not have been ranked by teachers as their worst problems. Nor would achievement scores in social studies have slipped during a decade when school people worked hard to promote tolerance, celebrate pluralism, and encourage diversity. The daily lessons of peaceful coexistence in heterogeneous schools did not translate to better civics scores. In 1976, 47 percent of the seniors did not know the number of senators per state. In 1979, almost 10 percent of the seniors could not find the United States on a world map. Often the lighter school atmosphere was misused as an excuse for lazy classrooms, where neither teachers nor students pushed each other very far. Too easily ignored was the fact that first-rate schoolwork had to involve struggle and tension. In spurning regimentation, many schools also rejected the process of evaluation bound up with schooling that was focused on academic achievement. "To see some as better was perceived as denying that the failures were victims," said one critic. The heightened sensitivity to rights and feelings fostered considerable sympathy for those previously victimized by educational inequities. There was much generosity in the grade inflation of the 1970s, but for some, learning how to profit and grow from failure might have been a better lesson than receiving an unearned passing mark.

Easygoing attitudes could encourage agreements to make life cozy for all. Being comfortable could mean that an analysis of Act III in *Macbeth* might slide into chitchat on television murder scenes. As one housemaster said, "We don't grab them and say, 'Hey, this just isn't enough.' We don't grab them — but at least they no longer try to grab us."

Epilogue

IN THE EARLY 1970s, several panels of distinguished people issued reports on the condition and prospects of American high schools. Each study applauded educators' recent commitments to more responsive, flexible, and unprejudiced schools. The alienation of many students from one aspect or another of schooling worried the groups. Each report explicitly repudiated James Conant's faith that larger high schools were better high schools. Impersonality was seen as a result of growth. Schools would be friendlier places, it was thought, if they shrank.

In line with these views, the reports also advocated strongly a dispersal of some of the school programs to other institutions. Partnerships with the workplace were preferable to elaborate in-school vocational programs, the argument went. Out-of-school education might make in-school education more attractive. The lines between school and society should be less sharp. Not only should the citadels be less crowded; they should occupy less space in a student's day. Variety and choice would let students find their way to profitable off-campus experiences.

Those proposals put the seal of approval on high schools' efforts to move away from the rigidities of the past. Whether a particular school reduced its size or featured on-site learning, all high schools at least knew that national spokesmen approved of the overall purpose of local activity. A school could become less regimented without elaborate workplace electives. High school could be made less authoritarian by a variety of means, and the opinions of the national panels were in agreement with the local initiatives.

The reports sidestepped the matter of adversarial relations among adults. The observers avoided the political contexts of secondary education, a curious omission in light of the attention paid to connections between schooling and the wider world. Even the estimated cost of the proposals was not provided.

Neither the commission reports nor the developments described in the preceding chapter satisfied the American public that all was well with their high schools. Instead of congratulating one another on the charitable inclusiveness of an institution designed originally for a small fraction of adolescents, an institution known in the nineteenth century as the "capstone" of the educational pyramid, Americans felt sure that high schools were deteriorating. Private school enrollments rose, fewer citizens voted *yes* in school finance referenda, and fewer bright undergraduates intended to become teachers. Year after year, the Gallup Polls reported lower approval of the public schools, and the dissatisfied rebuked the high schools more than the elementary schools or colleges.

The codeword for the widespread nervousness was "lack of discipline," which Gallup respondents throughout the 1970s and 1980s ranked as the worst problem of public education. The fears expressed a concern that the shifting configurations of authority in and around high schools actually marked the collapse of adult authority. The changes were not, in fact, that dramatic, but the public was uneasy with the emergence of a less directive secondary education. Instead of relaxed classrooms, many saw alarming lapses of self-control. The 1984 movie *Teachers* played to popular stereotypes of rowdiness, particularly in the scene where a student bit his teacher. The same film also caricatured faculty members prone to quarrel with one another. Hedonistic revelries or snarling nastiness seemed to many the inevitable, lamentable results of the disappearance of the old proprieties expected of both teachers and students. Not everyone welcomed the greening of the high school, and the skeptics called the renegotiations of nonaggression pacts "lack of discipline."

The SAT slump was seen as one of the deplorable results of

the breakdown of self-restraint. Articles about functionally illiterate graduates startled newspaper readers, as did a few well-publicized lawsuits by illiterate graduates charging their schools with malpractice. Like the perception of disorder, the anxiety about test scores was a superficial reading of the true state of affairs. Because so many factors affected the scores, it was unfair to scan the SAT results as if they were a thermometer, indicating sickness or recovery. Assessments more thorough (but less publicized) than the SATs revealed that in the early 1970s the largest decline in student achievement was in civics, but the loudest public lamentations bewailed mathematical, scientific, and reading deficiencies — notwithstanding the rise of the College Board Advanced Placement scores in both science and math between 1969 and 1979.

Few of the 1980s' state and national reports on education spoke directly to those concerns. There was a get-tough tone, but in respect to academics. Longer schooldays, longer school years, more homework, fewer electives, stiffer graduation requirements, and higher college entrance standards led the lists of reforms proposed by individual critics, blue-ribbon panels, and government commissions. Nervous comparisons with diligent Japanese students dramatized the dangers of softness: the lazy would get left behind in the race for technological superiority. America's survival would be at risk unless state legislatures turned serious and insisted on quantifiable standards and demonstrable competencies, a national commission warned. The rhetoric was more sophisticated than the minimum-competency testing movement of the mid 1970s, when minimums had a way of becoming ceilings rather than floors. But the underlying sentiment was similar — no more nonsense — as was the implication that standards and standardization were one and the same.

Promises to honor the commitments to equality forged in the 1960s and 1970s accompanied the crusade for high quality. A College Board booklet captured the twin objectives with its clever title, *Project EQuality,* pledging excellence and equality in full measure for all. Mortimer Adler's defense of the Socratic dialogue as a method of teaching vowed to avoid "abominable discrimination." No one suggested that higher hurdles might slow rather than speed the disadvantaged. Almost no one discussed the fate of students unable to meet harder graduation requirements, or considered how funding the new priorities would affect the expensive social services already established by many schools. Unions and bilingual education were so controversial that most commissions took no position on those volatile issues. The silence reflected a general lack of attention to the political and social constraints on education. (To be sure, several reports deplored de facto tracking, which closed college doors to students without giving the young people enough skills to secure good jobs. Good reasoning skills were expected of all; as the College Board said, "We will all be well served if educational excellence can be made possible, not just for the few, but for all students." Equality was often defined in terms of exposure to and participation in high-quality academics.)

Meritocratic attitudes also marked the proposals for different career ladders for teachers. Instead of salaries pegged to seniority and number of graduate course credits, the idea of master teachers and merit pay received unprecedented attention. The low test scores of prospective teachers underlined the need to reverse the social demotion of teaching as a career. The campaign for excellence would be doomed if the new recruits were not academically talented, but smart students knew the condition of teacher compensation and recoiled from a lifetime of modest earnings, uncertain job security, and dwindling prestige. In Indiana, for example, the average 1982–1983 entry salary was $12,048; a family of three earning $14,360 qualified for low-priced school lunches. In Indianapolis, the 1982 starting teacher salary was $3604 less than the pay of a novice painter in the schools. Many reports linked merit pay and higher starting salaries with tougher teacher education in order to upgrade the quality of new staff — but only a few educators chose to question state certification laws that precluded the recruitment of the smart uncredentialed candidates, who were wooed by some private schools. The process of "headhunting" — luring the best teachers from other schools with promises of high salaries — was considered unacceptable by most personnel directors. Even state and federal administrators supportive of free market competition hesitated to roll back the barriers against people like retired executives, unemployed Ph.D.s, or the bright undergraduate idealists once drawn to the Peace Corps (where on-site teacher training was extensive). Furthermore, the salary issue overshadowed the related matter of firing the incompetent, which nearly everyone in the field considered extremely difficult. Transfers were much easier to secure than dismissals. Staffing, as one administrator said, is "like playing Old Maid; you know, you pass off all your bad cards." Her principal agreed, and asked, "Can you think of running General Motors or Ford or Sears this way?"

In the past, the problem of teacher supply was periodically finessed by economics (during the Depression, teaching was relatively secure because of large enrollments), or by sexism (schools hired single women, underpaid to overemphasize virtue and propriety), or by war (male teachers got draft exemptions in the 1960s). Above all, steadily rising enrollments promised job security, which strongly appealed to many lower-middle-class candidates whose parents had worked erratically during the Depression. In the 1970s, declining birth rates and wholesale layoffs transformed teaching from a stable to a precarious career. Moreover, the swift expansion of colleges in the 1950s and 1960s increased the number of adults with degrees; the college graduate of 1970 had the same social status as the high school graduate of 1940. That meant that high school staff were not particularly special by virtue of their B.A. or M.A. The achievement of college graduation, fostered by near universal high school attendance, diminished rather than enhanced the prestige of those teachers who processed adolescents on the educational conveyor belt. The social demotion of teachers was modestly analogous to the eclipse of first-class rail travel by the airlines. As late as the 1930s, one Seaboard train had a swimming pool, and the Union Pacific dining car served fresh antelope steak. Those attractions faded as affluent vacationers and businessmen came to prefer the greater speed and comfort and lower cost of a fast plane flight. High school teaching never matched the prestige of a luxury train, but, like the railroad, its social position was relative, not absolute.

At one time, the emotional life of a teacher was suspect, not her intellectual attainments. By the 1980s, the public wondered about her head more than her heart. It is unlikely that better pay will restore teachers to the status they had in the early twentieth century, when some were addressed as "Professor" (a title that persisted into the 1950s for administrators). Whatever their economic fate, the old educational differentials they once enjoyed were gone, a reminder that changes affecting teachers were inextricably related to transformations in the wider world over which school people had little if any control.

Encouraging merit in the front office was another common reform theme. The literature on effective schools stressed what practitioners knew all along: good principals were crucial. Administrators in the building got a better shake than downtown central office personnel, who were criticized for distracting site people with too many regulations and superfluous paperwork. The exemplary principal was to be an instructional leader, a headmaster, not a harried bureaucrat. The reports occasionally suggested more staff participation in decision making, but the old hierarchical organizational models remained. Everyone solemnly agreed that change was impossible without teacher involvement, yet the major decisions continued to be made in the front office. The power wielded by college faculties was never granted high school teachers, despite reformers' pleas for more collegiality and interdepartmental contact.

The schools the principals ran were to be leaner places, according to many reports. *High School* and *A Place Called School,* written independently, both titled their chapters on school purpose "We Want It All," and argued that we should not. The high school, wrote the authors, should stop trying to be all things to everyone. Unprofitably burdened with too many tasks, high schools were to set priorities and focus energy and attention on academics. There was much denigration of the "smorgasbord" curriculum, unflatteringly compared with a sit-down dinner with little if any choice of menu. In particular, vocational education was not to be an entrée.

A retreat from comprehensiveness would have fostered smaller schools. In 1959, Conant fixed four hundred students as the minimum for a decent four-year school; in 1983, John Goodlad took the same figure as optimal. What was rarely discussed was whether small-school intimacies would loosen or tighten the demands of a more academic curriculum.

If the recommendations proved successful, they would have brought about a major change. In 1977, almost no principals reported decreases in the preceding five years in either required or elective courses. Throughout the 1970s, declining enrollments and budget cuts forced some systems to retrench, but few did so cheerfully or creatively. A broad curriculum served many institutional (if not intellectual) needs: it accommodated student diversity, gave teachers some variety of assignment, helped public relations, brought in outside funds and private grants, and justified administrators. In light of that heritage, at least some high schools could insist that old and new priorities were perfectly compatible. Would it not have been possible to justify social services on the same basis as this vision of a basic curriculum for all students,

> a study of those consequential ideas, experiences, and traditions common to all of us by virtue of our membership in the human family at a particular moment in history? These shared experiences include our use of symbols, our sense of history, our membership in groups and institutions, our relationship to nature, our need for well-being, and our growing dependence on technology.

That definition would have precluded the more inane state requirements, such as teaching the value of dairy products and kindness to domestic pets, but still left the door open for a range of courses and programs.

Uninspired instruction was an important concern of several critics keen on changing teaching methods. Reliance on lectures, worksheets, questioning for monosyllabic factual answers, and friendly nonacademic chatter often left no time for analysis and discussion, according to several studies. "Most teachers simply do not know how to teach for higher levels of thinking," John Goodlad grimly concluded. Even if they had the wit, many teachers lacked the will to go beyond the minimum. Teacher-dominated work main-tained order (and saved energy) at the expense of lively (and exhausting) intellectual dialogue.

To improve matters, Mortimer Adler urged a new school schedule flexible enough for small sections devoted to personalized coaching, Socratic-style seminars, and large group meetings for lectures. The books by Goodlad, Ernest Boyer, and Theodore Sizer also spoke to the importance of more versatile pedagogy, not an easy thing to achieve, given the need to retrain an aging teaching force. Their work highlighted life inside classrooms. They cogently challenged the premise of panels like the National Commission for Excellence that quantitative change, such as another year of mathematics, would necessarily produce qualitative changes. (As one principal quipped, "The drive for more requirements of the same subjects resembled an old cereal advertisement that pledged, If you don't like our product, return it and we'll send you two free boxes.")

Historical Parallels

Even though there were points of disagreement, the 1980s' reassessments have some similarities to the criticism of previous periods. Bursts of report writing usually follow periods of relative quiet; the pace of publication has not been constant since 1940. There were peaks, in terms of volume and influence, in the mid 1940s (*Education for ALL American Youth, General Education in a Free Society*), from 1953 to 1959 (from Arthur Bestor to James Conant), the late 1960s and early 1970s (beginning with individual exposés, ending with several panel reports), and the early 1980s. There was never silence in the intervals, but most of the activity then was in-house tinkering and fine-tuning: life adjustment projects in the late 1940s, curricular experiments in the early 1960s, and various optional programs in the mid 1970s. The earlier reports catalyzed much of that work, but the major reports did not, by themselves, initiate the major changes. (Progressive experiments began well before 1944; science, math, and foreign language enrollments began to rise before Sputnik; flexible scheduling predated the endorsements of alternative programs.)

A second parallel was in the tone of the reports. *A Nation at Risk* sounded the alarm by invoking a formulaic rhetoric of crisis, with sentences like "If an unfriendly power had attempted to impose on America the mediocre educational performance that exists today, we might well have viewed it as an act of war." It is noteworthy that the working title was *Education and the 21st Century,* which lacked the immediacy that would capture public attention and convey the urgency of the writers' message. A more dramatic title would provide "originality," the staff felt.

The final title did indeed help draw attention, but it was hardly original. Previous writers had also shouted warnings from the watchtower. Book titles like *Our Children Are Cheated, Quackery in the Public Schools, Death at an Early Age, Crisis in the Classroom,* and *The Literacy Hoax* are a sample of the cries of emergency. The exact definition of the crisis varied from author to author. The antiprogressives singled out the pernicious theories of education school professors, whereas Charles Silberman pinpointed the stupefying mindlessness of classroom instruction. Some observers deplored the process; others faulted the results. Some related international security to education; others claimed domestic strength was imperiled. Whatever their differences, most writers depicted a decline from a better past. Their history memorialized supportive parents, stricter discipline, rigorous standards, and better-educated graduates.

Furthermore, the language of crisis was a political strategy, most frequently used by nonscholars eager to bring about change. The books by journalists, university presidents, school board members, and ex-teachers were not relatively dispassionate descriptions based on systematic research. Often they were partisan interpretations, and in the twentieth century crisis rhetoric has been a staple of political language. As Garry Wills wrote of President Kennedy, "Since the charismatic leader's special powers grow from special dangers, the two feed on each other. For some crises to be overcome, they must first be created." In education, the crisis rhetoric tried to jar the complacency of people unconnected with schools, who cared little about Socratic seminars and resisted higher taxes for raising teachers' salaries. (Indeed, for many of the 1980s' reforms, there was no clearly identifiable, let alone mobilized, constituency.) During the stormiest years of school desegregation, for example, the percentage of people aware of the racial composition of the nearest high school fell. The crisis rhetoric sought to rouse the sluggish — but rarely let on, as Conant told President Eisenhower in 1959, that apathy itself is a form of crisis. That might have insulted the very audience being wooed.

One group the reports rarely tried to court were the students. Usually benevolent adults assumed that students would embrace interesting new programs, whether core courses, advanced physics, work-study, or other novelties. It is striking that so few reformers tried to probe the habits and allegiances that could subvert well-intentioned change. Most students cared primarily about friendships, sports, sex, television, and music. When asked by Goodlad's staff in 1977 what they liked best about high school, students chose "nothing" ahead of either "teachers" or "classes I'm taking." Within the curriculum, they enjoyed art, gym, and vocational classes more than the academic courses. That situation was not new. In the late 1950s, another period of adult crusading for academic rigor, the favorite career fantasies of students had little to do with the life of the mind. The girls preferred modeling, and many boys wanted to be famous athletes. At any time, those who evolved strategies to encourage academic excellence seemed to ignore student preferences instead of directly considering whether to accept, challenge, or evade them. The state legislature could mandate eight years of math and science, but if P.A. announcements continued to interrupt classes to promote the afternoon pep rally, then more emotional investment in calculus or chemistry was unlikely. The rock star Frank Zappa once said that high school is a state of mind. In teen-age minds, what mattered was not the tough curriculum proposed by the reports. Being with one's friends was as critical as anything to students. There is evidence that friendship groups in the 1970s became somewhat more numerous (and less antagonistic) than the former tendency toward an in-out dichotomy, but that was the sort of change the commissions did not ponder. It was not clear why another required course would increase student investment in their course work, decrease their fascination with the curriculum of television, with its overstimulation and passivity, or rival the attractions of long hours spent at afterschool jobs.

Historical Changes

If there are some similarities between past and present periods of high school reform, there are also several major differences. The authors of the literature of reform in the last twenty years had more contact with high schools than their predecessors. In the mid 1940s, the commissions that drafted *Education for ALL American Youth* and *General Education in a Free Society* were elite groups whose teaching experiences were mostly in universities. Only a minority of the Educational Policies Commission were practitioners, and the deliberations in *General Education* were devoted more to abstract discussions than to testimony from school people. In fact, at one meeting Professor Howard Mumford Jones urged his colleagues to spend more time inside high schools, but his advice was not heeded. In the 1950s, professors like Arthur Bestor and Jacques Barzun wrote about schools, but so did indignant school board members, Admiral Hyman Rickover, Conant, and others. Some of the writings relied on experience, but school visits like Conant's were the exception, not the rule. Ridiculing an article from an education journal was more common than observing a classroom.

In the 1960s, voices from the inside reached an attentive audience. On the one hand, journalists like Fred Hechinger, Martin Mayer, Charles Silberman, and Peter Schrag described flesh-and-blood teachers. Their books were full of well-chosen vignettes, deft etchings of many schools rather than portraits of a few, and their reportage offered a range of useful insights rather than sharply focused interpretations. On the other hand, teachers also spoke, often bitterly, of their frustrations and disappointments. Autobiographical accounts by John Holt, George Dennison, James Herndon, Jonathan Kozol, and others described stultifying urban bureaucracies but also lauded the idealistic staff brave enough to battle conservative administrators, to create places of learning and joy in otherwise bleak institutions (often elementary and junior high schools, which was where many Great Society reformers thought change had to begin).

The major statements written recently drew more extensively on, and contributed to, scholarly research. In the early 1970s, several panels of experts issued reports that tapped historical, economic, and sociological data. At the same time, government funding to evaluate federally sponsored programs increased the scope of the literature. Field work, in particular, became more acceptable and widespread. Instead of tabulating questionnaires or spending a day or two at each of many schools, educators began to spend weeks and months in a few schools in the belief that complex organizations are as hard to understand as the distant tribes studied by anthropologists. The new literature came to command more scholarly respect than reportage. The Boyer, Goodlad, and Sizer studies relied on observations and interviews rather than one-shot testimony from outside consultants. Even Mortimer Adler's panel followed its manifesto with practical work in several school districts; forty years ago, its first book would have concluded rather than begun the project. These large-scale investigations marked more than a redirection of educational research; they also signaled a belief that prominent insiders could be trustworthy critics. It is hard to imagine an education school dean like John Goodlad in charge of empirical research in the 1950s designed to lead to consequential reform. The "educationists" refused to do quantitative studies that might challenge cherished progressive assumptions about good schools.

Alongside those shifts in research design and personnel (but only partially explained by them) was the rethinking of education as a form of social engineering. In the past, the lines between education and social theory were often indistinct. James Conant linked high school reform to larger issues, such as fostering social mobility for the brightest and simultaneously promoting mutual respect between students headed for different futures. In the 1960s, open school advocates wrote eloquently of the risk of alienation among people growing up in a world dominated by heartless bureaucracies. To a man like the poet and social critic Paul Goodman, pedagogical change should have gone hand in hand with a transformation of the entire culture. In the same period, liberal politicians like Lyndon Johnson promoted education as the most powerful weapon in the fight against poverty. Commentators of the 1980s made smaller claims for the social impact of educational reform. Achievement promised a competitive edge against rivals, but no one touted stiff graduation requirements as the solution to problems like racism. Whatever enchantment existed was a "romance with utilitarianism," as the head of the Council for Basic Education, A. Graham Down, has said.

Whether or not educational reform connects with grand visions of social change, any major redirection of secondary education will be hard to achieve. Many people are perfectly pleased with the smorgasbord curriculum; the 1983 Gallup Poll reported that driver education and computer training drew equal support as required classes. Change will occur very tentatively, as it has in the past, when the idea of less directive and less austere schooling took years to affect teacher-student relations — and even so, the shifts were incomplete and controversial. There are bound to be howls of protest from all the factions slighted by the 1980s' emphasis on academic excellence. In some Midwestern states, girls' full-court basketball has had a more powerful constituency than the proponents of Socratic dialogue. What the other kind of cheerleaders face is the task of mobilizing public support for changes whose payoff is not as immediate, as visible, or as much fun as the big games on Friday night and Saturday afternoon. Orderly schools with tight discipline matter more to many people than orderly thinking, and therefore change, which is usually neither tidy nor orderly, will probably continue to be slow and uneven.

Acknowledgments
Sources
Notes
Index

Acknowledgments

A FACT about American education too rarely acknowledged is the generosity of the teachers and administrators in the high schools. I am particularly grateful to William Mangan, Edward Sarason, and Diane Tabor (Cambridge Rindge and Latin); the Reverend Neil O'Connor (Cleveland Central Catholic) and Sister Rosemary Hocevar (Diocese of Cleveland); John Astuno (East High School) and LaRue Belcher (Denver Public Schools); and Robert Amparán and Johanna Plaehn (San Diego High School) for scheduling my visits and retrieving school documents for me to read. Shorter trips to Buckingham, Browne and Nichols, Greater Lawrence Regional Vocational-Technical High School, Hinsdale Township High School Central, Newton North High School, Watertown High School, and the Phillips Academy at Andover were also informative.

Many people assisted with archival research. Mrs. Grace Conant granted me access to the James B. Conant Papers (Harvard University Archives) related to his studies of American education. Gary Saretzky alerted me to other Conant letters in the Henry Chauncey Papers at the Educational Testing Service Archives. Worth David, Dean of Undergraduate Admissions at Yale, let me read the correspondence of his predecessors. The former vice-chairman of Scholastic, Inc., Jack Lippert, guided me through corporate records. The National Education Association Archives, previously run by Alice

Acknowledgments

Morton, hold the transcripts of the Educational Policies Commission meetings. Ralph West provided accreditation reports written for the New England Association of Colleges and Secondary Schools. Patricia Albjerg Graham, Dean of the Harvard Graduate School of Education, gave permission to read the Francis Spaulding Papers (Harvard University Archives). Harvard University granted me restricted access to the papers of the Committee on the Objectives of General Education in a Free Society, which Helen Kessler previewed for me. Thomas Geary at Coronet Films in Chicago shared several dozen movies with me.

I am indebted to William Carr, Alden Dunham, John Finley, John Gardner, Harold Howe II, Francis Keppel, Nathaniel Ober, and Betty Weatherby for answering questions about James Conant. Letters from Merle Borrowman, R. Freeman Butts, John B. Carroll, and David Riesman supplied additional information.

I spoke on behalf of A Study of High Schools before many different groups, and their reactions to my arguments refined and modified many of my ideas. Veteran administrators related experiences I would never have found in libraries. I thank the men and women I met at the Berkshire County (Massachusetts) Association of Superintendents of Schools, the Commission on Educational Issues, the Connecticut State Department of Education, the Connecticut Association of Curriculum Development, Glen Urquhart School, Cornell University's Rural School Program, Dwight Englewood School, Emmanuel College (Boston), the Farmington (Connecticut) Public Schools, the Grant Wood Area Educational Agency (Cedar Rapids, Iowa), Harvard University, the Independent Schools Associations of the Southwest and the Central States, Loyola University (Chicago), the Macomb (Michigan) Association of Secondary School Principals, the Massachusetts Teachers Association, Michigan State, the Midwest Modern Language Association, the Minnesota Council of Foundations, Northern Illinois University, the Pennsylvania Educational Research Association, Suffolk County (New York) School Board Institute, United States Department of Education, University of Chicago, Vanderbilt Advanced Study Program, Wellesley College, and the York Township (Illinois) Public Schools.

Parts of the manuscript were presented to the American Historical

Association (1982), the History of Education Society (1982), the Council for Basic Education (1983), and the National Association of Independent Schools (1984). A different version of chapter 3 was published as "The American High School Today: James Bryant Conant's Reservations and Reconsiderations," in *Phi Delta Kappan,* May 1983. "The Less Things Change" (*Independent School,* May 1984) and "America's Golden Age of Education" (N.A.S.S.P. *Bulletin,* September 1984) drew from various chapters.

I owe large debts to the readers of earlier drafts of this book. Marvin Lazerson (University of British Columbia) and David Tyack (Stanford University) wrote painstaking critiques on short notice. Barbara Brenzel (Wellesley), James Crouse (University of Delaware), Patricia Albjerg Graham (Harvard University), Gerald Grant (Syracuse University), Robin Lester (Trinity School, New York), and Joel Perlmann (Harvard University) evaluated individual chapters, as did my colleagues David Cohen, Eleanor Farrar, Diane Franklin, Cal Kolbe, Blair McElroy, and Barbara Neufeld. Seven good friends — Robert Danly, Bruce Fenner, Jonathan Harr, Charles Ormsby, Louis Picarello, Steven Rodermel, and David Winn — sent their shrewd advice. Especially helpful was the editorial advice from Houghton Mifflin, generously supplied by Austin Olney, Richard Todd, and Frances Apt. From first outline to final draft, Arthur Powell and Theodore Sizer improved every page they read.

The expertise as well as the friendship of everyone associated with A Study of High Schools eased the burden of research and writing. Grants from the Charles E. Culpeper Foundation, the Carnegie Corporation of New York, the Commonwealth Fund, the Esther A. and Joseph Klingenstein Fund, the Gates Foundation, and the Edward John Noble Foundation supported the work. Research assistants Joan Cawood, George Lowry, Mike Lyden, Betsy Parsons, and Bill Ubines deserve my thanks, as do our indispensable administrative assistants, Pat West-Barker and Cal Kolbe, and fellow researchers Richard Horn and Martha Landesberg. I learned much from the detailed field notes of Richard Berger, Ruben Carriedo, Helen Featherstone, Diane Franklin, Ellen Glanz, Peter Holland, Barbara Neufeld, Patricia Wertheimer, Lauren Young, and Mary Jane Yurchak. Eleanor Farrar and David Cohen chaired the debriefing sessions after each round of field work; their comments and questions raised issues that otherwise I might have missed.

The encouragement and advice of the project's directors, Arthur Powell and Theodore Sizer, are appreciated more than I can ever tell them. The fact that such men care so deeply about American education is in itself good reason for optimism about the high schools' future.

Sources

THE FOURTEEN-HUNDRED-ODD field notes dictated by the staff of A Study of High Schools shaped my understanding of secondary education in the early 1980s. Reading the notes on classroom observations as well as interviews with students, parents, teachers, and administrators reminded me how research "from the bottom up" can uncover otherwise inaccessible material. Consequently I chose for historical study four of the fifteen high schools visited by my colleagues.

My research in those schools combined oral history with analysis of published and unpublished sources. At each high school I requested an hour with teachers and administrators who had been there for at least fifteen years. Those taped interviews yielded fifty-two field notes. I also asked for post–1940 copies of accreditation reports (including the self-studies that preceded the outsiders' visits), files of the student newspaper, and back issues of the yearbook. In professional libraries (Denver and San Diego), central administrative files (Cambridge), and archives of a diocese (Cleveland), I found much additional material — committee reports, correspondence, memoranda, curricular guides for teachers, newspaper clippings, and photographs.

Just as intriguing as local sources were the archives of different institutions that support, and are supported by, high schools. I examined the records of a college admissions office (Yale College), commercial publishers (Scholastic, Inc., and the American Book Company), and an audiovisual company (Coronet). For professional associations, I read files at the National Education Association and the New England Association of Colleges and Secondary Schools. Outsider reports on the condition of education have become an institution of sorts; my case study of one report relied on the James B. Conant Papers (Harvard University), the Henry Chauncey Papers (Educational Testing Service), and interviews.

For the reader interested in learning more about American high schools, the

Sources

following published sources cover a range of topics. These books and articles tend to describe what happened inside schools rather than observers' opinions on what should take place. Often educational writing, particularly before the 1960s, bore little resemblance to day-to-day life.

For the years between 1880 and 1940, the standard work is Edward A. Krug's thorough two-volume *The Shaping of the American High School* (Madison, Wisconsin, 1964, 1972). Krug's study is full of useful information, but he rarely linked high schools to changes in the society and offered too little analysis of his material. A more vivid description of changes between 1890 and 1925 is the classic case study by Robert S. and Helen M. Lynd, *Middletown* (New York, 1925), chapters 13 to 15. A broader look at turn-of-the-century developments is in chapters 6 to 10 of David Nasaw's *Schooled to Order* (New York, 1979).

For the 1930s, the twenty-eight-volume National Study of Education (Washington, D.C., 1932–1933) is helpful, as are the detailed National Education Association *Research Bulletins*. The United States Office of Education published many valuable studies, especially the biennial surveys. Francis Spaulding, *High School and Life* (New York, 1938), summarized the massive Regents' study of education in New York State. The ambitious Eight-Year Study (1932–1940), a curricular reform sponsored by the Progressive Education Association, is described in *Thirty Schools Tell Their Story* (New York, 1943). For a lucid comparison of the 1930s and 1980s, see David Tyack, Robert Lowe, and Elisabeth Hansot, *Public Schools in Hard Times* (Cambridge, Massachusetts, 1984).

For an overview of elementary- and secondary-school and university education since World War II, Diane Ravitch's *The Troubled Crusade* (New York, 1983) is the place to begin. Shorter interpretations are Joseph Adelson, "What Happened to the Schools?" (*Commentary*, March 1981), Tommy Tomlinson, "The Troubled Years" (*Phi Delta Kappan*, January 1981), and Theodore R. Sizer, *Places of Learning, Places of Joy* (Cambridge, Massachusetts, 1973), chapter 1.

In light of the high schools' swift growth, it is useful to read Daniel Boorstin's remarks on "our continuously energetic effort to give everybody everything" (*Democracy and Its Discontents,* New York, 1974) and the subsequent loss of poignancy (*The Americans: The Democratic Experience,* New York, 1973). Martin Trow's "The Second Transformation of American Secondary Education" (*International Journal of Comparative Sociology,* September 1961) examines the important transition from a "mass terminal" to "mass preparatory" institutional mission. Inclusiveness spawned new problems, according to David K. Cohen and Barbara Neufeld, "The Failure of High Schools and the Progress of Education" (*Daedalus,* Summer 1981), and solved some old ones (Henry Steele Commager, "A Historian Looks at the American High School," *The School Review,* Spring 1958). Astute comments by foreigners on American inclusiveness are in John N. Wales, *Schools of Democracy* (East Lansing, 1962) and J. E. Strachan, *New Zealand Observer* (New York, 1940).

For understanding the managers of growth, knowledge of the partial eclipse of nineteenth-century pietistic zeal by twentieth-century administrative science is essential. Here the basic books are David Tyack's *The One Best System* (Cambridge,

Massachusetts, 1974) and David Tyack and Elisabeth Hansot, *Managers of Virtue* (New York, 1982). A knowledge of progressive terminology makes it easier to understand most administrators. For the rhetoric, Lawrence A. Cremin, *The Transformation of the School* (New York, 1961) is still reliable; for the practices, Larry Cuban, *How Teachers Taught: Constancy and Change in American Classrooms* (New York, 1984) is persuasive.

For any period, autobiographies are scarce. The best of the lot is Leonard Covello's *The Heart Is the Teacher* (New York, 1958), a well-written reminiscence of studying, teaching, and administering in New York City high schools. Jesse Davis, *The Saga of a Schoolmaster* (Boston, 1956), and Finis Engelman, *The Pleasure Was Mine* (Danville, Illinois, 1971), evoke the early-twentieth-century faith in scientific efficiency. From principals, the best recollections are Frank P. Whitney, *School and I* (Yellow Springs, Ohio, 1957) and C. S. Keister, *The Principal of the Thing* (Philadelphia, 1970). From teachers: Joan Dunn, *Retreat from Learning* (New York, 1955), Dorothy R. Robinson, *The Bell Rings at Four* (Austin, 1978), and Charles G. Rousculp, *Chalk Dust on My Shoulders* (Columbus, Ohio, 1969). From school psychologists: the autobiographical series of articles in *Journal of School Psychology,* 1981–1983.

Good modern histories of individual high schools are hard to find, and the best ones examine private schools. For Deerfield and Choate, see John McPhee, *The Headmaster* (New York, 1966), and Peter Prescott, *A World of Our Own* (New York, 1980). Susan Lloyd, *A Singular School* (Hanover, New Hampshire, 1979), is a thorough study of Abbot Academy, eventually merged with Phillips Academy, the subject of Frederick Allis, *Youth From Every Quarter* (Hanover, 1979). *The Walled Garden* (Boston, 1982) is Charles Merrill's account of the Commonwealth School, which he founded in 1958. Histories of other renowned Eastern boarding schools vary in quality but they do abound. A model use of primary sources, from Illinois public schools, is "A History of Social Services Delivered to Youth, 1880–1977," by Michael W. Sedlak and Robert L. Church (Washington, D.C., N.I.E. Report, 1982). The alternative schools born in the late 1960s and early 1970s attracted much scholarly attention, especially in dissertations. The best published work is Ann Swidler's *Organization Without Authority* (Cambridge, Massachusetts, 1979), a case study of two California schools. For the ideology of "open education," see Neil Postman and Charles Weingartner, *Teaching As a Subversive Activity* (New York, 1969).

Case studies of small towns and suburbs are invaluable for an understanding of public high schools. James West [pseud.], *Plainville USA* (New York, 1945); Arthur J. Vidich and Joseph Bensman, *Small Town in Mass Society* (Princeton, 1958); Alan Peshkin, *Growing Up American* (Chicago, 1978); Peter Davis, *Hometown* (New York, 1982); and Theodore Coplow et al., *Middletown Families* (Minneapolis, 1982), capture the local orientation of village schooling. Herbert J. Gans, *The Levittowners* (New York, 1967), is a meticulous participant-observation of a lower-middle-class New Jersey suburb. The opposite coast is examined in Bennett Berger's *Working Class Suburb* (Berkeley, 1960); and for an upper-middle-class Canadian suburb, comparable to many American suburbs, see John R. Seeley,

Sources

R. Alexander Sim, and E. W. Loosley, *Crestwood Heights* (Toronto, 1956). There are remarkable anecdotes about urban schooling in Peter Schrag, *Village School Downtown* (Boston, 1967), and David Rogers, *110 Livingston Street* (New York, 1968). University professors often led outside evaluations of urban school systems, and the scores of published reports bulge with information (and opinions) from progressive-minded authors.

The tradition of journalists describing and assessing schools dates from the classic *The Public School System of the United States* (New York, 1893) by Joseph M. Rice. There are valuable vignettes in Benjamin Fine, *Our Children Are Cheated* (New York, 1947), Martin Mayer, *The Schools* (New York, 1961), Fred and Grace Hechinger, *Teen-Age Tyranny* (New York, 1963), Peter Schrag, *Voices from the Classroom* (Boston, 1965), Charles Silberman, *Crisis in the Classroom* (New York, 1970), and Gene Maeroff, *Don't Blame the Kids* (New York, 1982).

Sometimes schools are discussed in the literature on adolescent values and behavior. The standard history is Joseph Kett's admirable *Rites of Passage: Adolescence in America 1790 to the Present* (New York, 1977). For the late 1930s and early 1940s, Allison Davis and John Dollard, *Children of Bondage* (Washington, D.C., 1940), and August Hollingshead, *Elmtown's Youth* (New York, 1949), are basic, as are James Coleman, *The Adolescent Society* (New York, 1961), and Dwight Macdonald, "A Caste, A Culture, A Market," *The New Yorker,* November 22 and 29, 1958. (Coleman found less stratification on the lines of class than did Hollingshead; we need more studies of the intervening years to know how and why class became less important.) Shorter but more provocative school portraits are in Edgar Z. Friedenberg, *The Dignity of Youth and Other Atavisms* (Boston, 1965), and Jules Henry, *Culture Against Man* (New York, 1963). A wonderful reminiscence of adolescence in Iowa in the 1950s is Sue Allen Toth, *Blooming* (Boston, 1978). In his witty *Is There Life After High School?* (New York, 1976), Ralph Keyes stresses the intensity of the "innie" and "outie" peer stratifications in high school. That point is pictured, hilariously, in the 1974 *National Lampoon* parody of a 1964 high school yearbook. Recent descriptions of what it feels like to be a student suggest less intensity than Keyes found for the 1950s and 1960s: see Philip Cusick, *Inside High School* (New York, 1973), and Ellen Glanz, "What Are *You* Doing Here?" (Washington, D.C., 1979), both good on docility; Ralph Larkin's polemical *Suburban Youth in Cultural Crisis* (New York, 1979); and two lively books by young writers who "passed" as students — David Owen, *High School* (New York, 1981), and Cameron Crowe, *Fast Times at Ridgemont High* (New York, 1981). No one interested in youth culture should forget the history of popular music. Simon Firth, *Sound Effects* (New York, 1981), and Charlie Gillett, *The Sound of the City* (New York edition, 1983), are first rate.

For students' own accounts of high schools, there is little besides the spate of radical protest in the late 1960s: John Birmingham, ed., *Our Time Is Now* (New York, 1970), Diane Divoky, ed., *How Old Will You Be in 1984?* (New York, 1969), and Marc Libarle and Tom Seligson, eds., *High School Revolutionaries* (New York, 1970). There are no portents of revolution in the collection by David Mallery, *High School Students Speak Out* (New York, 1962).

Judicial rulings shed light on conflicts in scores of different schools. Readable technical articles include Richard L. Berkman, "Students in Court," *Harvard Educational Review* (November 1970), Stephen R. Goldstein, "The Scope and Sources of School Board Authority to Regulate Student Conduct and Status," *University of Pennsylvania Law Review* (January 1969), and Leon Letwin, "Regulation of Underground Newspapers on Public School Campuses in California," *UCLA Law Review* (October 1974). Crisp overviews are "Limited Monarch: The Rise and Fall of Student Rights," by Lawrence Friedman (Stanford, 1982), and Franklin Zimring's *The Changing Legal World of Adolescence* (New York, 1982). The judiciary also spurred desegregation, surveyed by J. Harvie Wilkinson III, *From Brown to Bakke* (New York, 1979), and Gary Orfield, *Must We Bus?* (Washington, D.C., 1978). There are admirable case studies in David Kirp, *Just Schools* (Berkeley, 1982). Even more technical than judicial decrees are the massive quantitative studies made possible by fast computers and powerful statistical methods.

The leading studies of achievement include books from Project Talent; James S. Coleman, *Equality of Educational Opportunity* (Washington, D.C., 1966); the National Assessment of Educational Progress (1969–   ); Christopher Jencks et al., *Inequality* (New York, 1972); James S. Coleman, Thomas Hoffer, and Sally Kilgore, *High School Achievement* (New York, 1982). Huge amounts of data were gathered by the National Longitudinal Study of the High School Class of 1972, High School and Beyond, and A Study of Schooling (analyzed in John I. Goodlad, *A Place Called School* (New York, 1983).

The periodic rediscovery of a crisis generated many books that tried to expose what really went on in schools. Although more reflective of the particular anxieties of outsiders than of daily life in classrooms, the reports of individuals and panels should not be ignored. In the mid 1940s, a Harvard committee wrote *General Education in a Free Society* (Cambridge, 1945), an unusually lucid statement of the unifying and differentiating tasks of secondary education. *Education for ALL American Youth* (Washington, D.C., 1944) made the same case but with less emphasis on academic rigor. In the 1950s, get-tough recommendations came from Mortimer Smith, *The Diminished Mind* (Chicago, 1954), Arthur Bestor, *Educational Wastelands* (Urbana, 1953), Albert Lynd, *Quackery in the Public Schools* (Boston, 1953), Jacques Barzun, *The House of Intellect* (New York, 1959), and Hyman Rickover, *Education and Freedom* (New York, 1959). The major report was James Conant's *The American High School Today* (New York, 1959). The next decade featured individual books about survival inside dreary urban schools, from teachers (John Holt, James Herndon, Jonathan Kozol), writers (Martin Mayer, Peter Schrag, Charles Silberman), and social critics (Paul Goodman, Edgar Z. Friedenberg). Although few of their writings claimed that the high school was an especially serious problem (often the 1960s' school improvement efforts focused either on early intervention, like Head Start, or on the expansion of college facilities), their antibureaucratic manifestoes became handbooks for many reformers.

Three blue ribbon panels, in the 1970s, endorsed various reforms designed to remove some walls between schools and society: James S. Coleman, ed., *Youth:*

Sources

Transition to Adulthood (Chicago, 1974) is more thorough and insightful than either John Henry Martin in *The Education of Adolescents* (Washington, D.C., 1976) or B. Frank Brown, *The Reform of Secondary Education* (New York, 1973). The evidence, analysis, and recommendations of the reports and the middle-class view of youth are questioned by Michael Timpane et al. in *Youth Policy in Transition* (Santa Monica, 1976). For thoughtful comments on previous cycles of criticism, see Michael Katz, *Class, Bureaucracy and the Schools* (New York, 1971), chapter 3, and his article, "Reflections on Metaphors of Educational Reform," in *Harvard Graduate School of Education Association Bulletin* (Fall 1980).

In addition to the major reports of the 1980s, discussed in the Epilogue, there are excellent portraits of various high schools in "The Arts and Humanities in America's Schools" (*Daedalus,* Fall 1983) and in Sara Laurence Lightfoot's *The Good High School* (New York, 1983). Philip Cusick, *The Egalitarian Ideal and the American High School* (New York, 1983), has keen insights on how good human relations rather than back-to-basics sustain orderly efficiency. In *Schooling in America* (New York, 1983) and the earlier *The Culture of the School and the Problem of Change* (New York, 1971), Seymour Sarason evoked the rituals and routines of schooling.

Notes

Interviews done as part of the field work of A Study of High Schools were coded by my colleagues in 1982 to ensure confidentiality. For convenience and consistency, I have adopted their codings, with the understanding that I would name the schools studied. Each high school granted me permission to do so. Field notes marked U are for East High School; Z is for San Diego High School; X, for Cleveland Central Catholic; Cambridge Rindge and Latin is R. I dictated the notes numbered in the 400s; other numbers indicate notes taken by my colleagues in A Study of High Schools. For more on the collection, transcription, and preservation of the notes, see *The Shopping Mall High School*, 325–332, 338.

1. Formalities

Page
iii The year 1940 in the subtitle could have been 1938 or 1942 or some other proximate year, because it falls roughly in the middle of a long period of institutional expansion, when high schools reaffirmed major commitments made earlier in the century. Although educators around 1940 busied themselves with little experiments, the to-ing and fro-ing was the bustle of redecoration rather than of rebuilding. In the classroom, the authority of the adults prevailed over the wishes of the students. In the front office, administration was less impartial than educators' rhetoric suggested. Those patterns were already in place in the years examined in the first two chapters. They present business-as-usual, not turning points or fresh starts.
1 "One teacher let me": Field Note U-009, A Study of High Schools.
1 "They're not afraid": Field Note U-407, A Study of High Schools.

Notes

2 1939 Pennsylvania case: *Horosko* v. *School District of Mt. Pleasant* 6A (2d) 866 (Pa. 1939), excerpted in *Court Decisions Under Teacher Tenure Laws 1932–1946* (Washington, D.C., 1947), 107–108.

2 "were circumscribed by taboos": August Hollingshead, *Elmtown's Youth* (New York, 1949), 130. Also Howard Beale, *Are American Teachers Free?* (New York, 1936); Florence Greenhoe, *Community Contacts and Participations of Teachers* (Washington, D.C., 1941); Edward A. Krug, *The Shaping of the American High School* (Madison, Wisconsin, 1972), 150–152.

2 the novel: Sophia Engstrand, *Miss Munday* (New York, 1940), 4, 115, 60, 205, 344; Frances P. Donovan, *The Schoolma'am* (New York, 1938); George Zellhofer, "The Image of the Public High School Teacher in the American Novel," unpublished dissertation, Loyola University, 1980.

3 "a class apart": Lois McFarland, "I'm Through with Teaching," *Saturday Evening Post,* November 9, 1946.

3 nervous and neurotic teachers: William H. Kilpatrick, ed., *The Teacher and Society* (New York, 1937), 87.

3 "dangerously unsuitable": Emil Altman, "Our Mentally Unbalanced Teachers," *American Mercury,* April 1941.

4 "A car is John," "We ain't prissy," and "If every teacher": Willard Waller, *The Sociology of Teaching* (New York, 1932), 409, 413, 455–456.

4 the Nazi wave: Benjamin M. Steigman, *Accent on Talent: New York's High School of Music and Art* (Detroit, 1964), 41.

5 Waller: *Sociology,* 383, 390.

5 Georgie Hinman: Frederick S. Allis, *Youth from Every Quarter* (Hanover, New Hampshire, 1979), 414–417.

5 W. H. Auden: Humphrey Carpenter, *W. H. Auden* (Boston, 1981), 265. Many of the students were as unusual as their instructors. Auden later told a friend, "Some of the boys are so rich that they have to be taken home by a master at the end of the term to prevent their being kidnapped." Other eccentric staff at St. Mark's are described by Edward T. Hall, *St. Mark's School* (Lunenberg, Massachusetts, 1967). For eccentrics in an elite public high school, see Philip Mason, *A Teacher Speaks* (New York, 1960), 57–61.

5 The 1934 survey: Frank W. Hart, *Teachers and Teaching* (New York, 1934).

6 Mrs. K.: Norman Podhoretz, *Making It* (New York, 1967), 8–11.

7 Covello: Leonard Covello, *The Heart Is the Teacher* (New York, 1958), 94. Covello never confused firmness and authoritarianism. He tried to dismiss a tenured teacher whom he considered "unsympathetic," "too prone to scold," "uncompromising," and "strictly formalistic." See Box 34, Folder 21, Leonard Covello Papers, Balch Institute, Philadelphia.

8 President Johnson: Robert A. Caro, *The Path to Power* (New York, 1983), 209.

8 Stenographic records: James Hoetker and William P. Ahlbrand, Jr., "The Persistence of the Recitation," *American Educational Research Journal,* March 1969.

8 St. Louis, 1939: George D. Strayer and N. L. Engelhardt, *A Report of a*

Survey of the Public Schools of St. Louis, Missouri (New York, 1939), 54. Also, Clyde M. Hill and S. M. Brownell, *Report of the Co-operative Study of the Lincoln Schools, 1945–1946* (Lincoln, Nebraska, 1947), 581–582.

9 "It's all up to you": *How Good Are Our Schools?* (1959), 28-minute black and white film, viewed at the National Education Association Archives.

9 Muzzey: David S. Muzzey, *History of the American People* (Boston, 1935), iii, 238. For a lively history of social studies textbooks, see Frances FitzGerald, *America Revised* (New York, 1980).

10 Book rentals: Paul W. Lange, *The Administration of Free Textbooks in City School Systems* (Chicago, 1940).

10 Tracking and grouping: In 1930, 49% of the high schools enrolled fewer than 200 students; too small to track, they required only some "constants." In larger schools, the typical pattern was choice between curricula, with every student regardless of track required to take an average of eight constants. That is, everyone would have American history, but usually with kids from the same track. Roughly 20% of all high schools required constants plus a major and a minor. (Those schools did not track.) Majors typically meant six semesters of course work; four courses constituted a minor. See A. K. Loomis, Edwin S. Lide, R. Lamar Johnson, *The Program of Studies,* National Survey Monograph no. 19 (Washington, D.C., 1933); Roy O. Billett, *Provisions for Individual Differences, Marking, and Promotion,* National Survey Monograph no. 13 (Washington, D.C., 1933). For comparable tracking practices in black and Catholic high schools, see Ambrose Caliver, *Vocational Education and Guidance of Negroes* (Washington, D.C., 1937), 24, and Brother William Mang, *The Curriculum of the Catholic High School for Boys* (South Bend, Indiana, 1941), 164.

10 Indiana girl: Hollingshead, *Elmtown,* 130.

10 The same snootiness: Ronald Corwin, *Militant Professionalism* (New York, 1970), 170; Hollingshead, *Elmtown,* 171.

11 classified students: Yes, but not totally, because the advanced sections often used the same books assigned to the average. Francis T. Spaulding, *High School and Life* (New York, 1938), 166; "High School Methods with Superior Students," N.E.A. *Research Bulletin,* September 1941.

11 Wives' IQ: Arthur G. Powell, *The Uncertain Profession* (Cambridge, Massachusetts, 1980), 210.

11 Tests in 1960: David Snedden, *American High Schools and Vocational Schools in 1960* (New York, 1931), 17.

11 Validity of tests: Stephen Jay Gould, *The Mismeasure of Man* (New York, 1981), chap. 6; Walt Haney, "Validity, Vaudeville, and Values," *American Psychologist,* October 1981; Tommy Tomlinson, "The Troubled Years: An Interpretive Analysis of Public Schooling Since 1950," *Phi Delta Kappan,* January 1981.

11 challenges to it were unacceptable: This is not to deny their occurrence. Smoking in lavatories, cutting study hall, and skipping gym class were the most frequent discipline problems faced by principals. Students' dutifulness was

rarely transferred to the substitute teacher, who received less respect than the custodians. See Carol J. Henning, "Discipline: Are Schools' Practices Changing?" *Clearinghouse,* January 1949; Nathan Goldman, *A Socio-Psychological Study of School Vandalism* (Washington, D.C., 1959), 83, 84.

11 "submission of the school" and "you teach me": Joan Dunn, *Retreat from Learning* (New York, 1955), 169, 161.

12 "There are parts": Charles Rousculp, *Chalk Dust on My Shoulder* (Columbus, Ohio, 1969), 163. For similar sentiments from college professors, see Joseph Epstein, ed., *Masters* (New York, 1981).

12 Lack of knowledge of American history: *New York Times,* June 21, 1942, and April 4, 1943.

12 National Teacher Examination: *The Training of Secondary School Teachers Especially with Reference to English* (Cambridge, Massachusetts, 1942), 13.

12 Education majors' scores: Dael Wolfe, *America's Resources of Specialized Talent* (New York, 1954).

12 The Quiz Kids: Ruth D. Feldman, *Whatever Happened to the Quiz Kids?* (Chicago, 1982), 359.

13 The evangelical legacy: David Tyack and Elisabeth Hansot, *Managers of Virtue* (New York, 1982).

13 Middletown's pep chapels: Robert S. Lynd and Helen Merrell Lynd, *Middletown in Transition* (New York, 1937), 292.

13 Previous generation's education and employment: Larry Cuban, *How Teachers Taught* (New York, 1984); Tamara K. Harevan and Randolph Langenbach, *Amoskeag* (New York, 1978); Edward A. Krug, *The Shaping of the American High School* (Madison, Wisconsin, 1964).

14 Films: It is hard to know how often teachers used films to replace rather than enhance the analysis of ideas. One clue is that in 1945–1946 nearly one third of all school films were viewed in an auditorium, a setting less conducive to serious discussion relating the movie to the course work. Silent films, a choice inviting if not requiring teacher engagement, were rented only one-fifth as often as films with sound. See "Audio-Visual Education in City-School Systems," N.E.A. *Research Bulletin,* December 1946.

14 "better off at work": "What People Think About Youth and Education," N.E.A. *Research Bulletin,* November 1940.

14 students' favorite part: J. Lloyd Trump, *High School Extracurriculum Activities* (Chicago, 1944), 92; *Evaluation of Secondary Schools — General Report* (Washington, D.C., 1939), 145.

14 For a lovely reminiscence of afterschool informalities, see John Updike, "A Soft Spring Night in Shillington," *The New Yorker,* December 24, 1984.

14 remove the coach: Trump, *Activities,* 108.

14 Enrollment figures: *Statistical Summary of Education 1939–40* (Washington, D.C., 1943), vol. 11, chap. 1.

15 French school enrollment in 1939: Paul Gagnon, "French Secondary Education," paper prepared for the College Board, November 1981. Great Britain: Harry Judge, *A Generation of Schooling* (New York, 1985).

15 Graduates aged twenty-five and above: *Historical Statistics of the United States, Colonial Times to 1970* (Washington, D.C., 1975), 380.

15 high school diploma in 1940: Richard P. Coleman and Lee Rainwater, *Social Standing in America* (New York, 1978), 75.

15 Some working-class parents: Joseph A. Kahl, "Educational and Occupational Aspirations of 'Common Man' Boys," *Harvard Educational Review,* Summer 1953; Talcott Parsons, "The School Class as a Social System," ibid., Fall 1959. The one-third figure is from *Training of Secondary School Teachers,* 7.

15 Teen-age employment: Paul Osterman, *Getting Started* (Cambridge, Massachusetts, 1980), 38, 51–74; David Tyack, Robert Lowe, and Elisabeth Hansot, *Public Schools in Hard Times* (Cambridge, Massachusetts, 1984), 116–132.

15 More students took the college-prep track: The disparity was particularly great in black high schools, where, in 1935–1936, 46.4% chose the academic course. See Caliver, *Guidance of Negroes,* 24.

16 Managerial positions: Randall Collins, *The Credential Society* (New York, 1979), 6.

16 just below economist: Robert W. Hodge et al., "Occupational Prestige in the United States, 1925–1963," *American Journal of Sociology,* November 1964.

16 *Partisan Review* editor: William Barrett, *The Truants* (New York, 1982), 215.

16 The percentage of male teachers: *National Survey of the Education of Teachers* (Washington, D.C., 1933), vol. 2, 24–25; "The Status of the Teaching Profession," N.E.A. *Research Bulletin,* March 1940.

16 Maryland adolescents: Howard M. Bell, *Youth Tell Their Story* (Washington, D.C., 1938), 134.

16 Teachers' background: W. Lloyd Warner, Robert J. Havighurst, and Martin B. Loeb, *Who Shall Be Educated?* (New York, 1944), 102.

16 a bit less happy: In an N.E.A. survey (Spring 1944), 7% of the women teachers and 11% of the men said they would "certainly" not become teachers if they were starting their careers; 12% of the women and 20% of the men "probably" would not choose teaching again. From "The Teacher Looks at Personnel Administration," N.E.A. *Research Bulletin,* December 1945.

16 junior college: Over half the staff there had some secondary school teaching experience, according to Leland L. Medsker, *The Junior College* (New York, 1960), chap. 7.

16 Salary differentials and educational achievements: "The Status of the Teaching Profession," N.E.A. *Research Bulletin,* March 1940; for teachers eager to retain the differentials, see Steigman, *Accent on Talent,* 59. The salary differentials had almost vanished by 1950, according to "Salaries and Salary Schedules of Urban School Employees, 1954–55," N.E.A. *Research Bulletin,* April 1955.

17 Progressive label: For distinctions between different kinds of progressives, see Lawrence A. Cremin, *The Transformation of the School* (New York, 1961), part 2; Cuban, *Teachers,* passim; Patricia Albjerg Graham, *From Arcady to Academe* (New York, 1967); Richard Hofstadter, *Anti-Intellectualism in*

Notes

American Life (New York, 1963), part 5; Diane Ravitch, *The Troubled Crusade* (New York, 1983), 43–80; David Tyack, *The One Best System* (Cambridge, Massachusetts, 1974), part IV.

17 litmus test: *Minnesota Teacher Attitude Inventory Manual* (New York, 1951).

17 "tense, pin-dropping atmosphere": Quoted in Robert H. Beck, *Beyond Pedagogy* (St. Paul, 1980), 178.

18 "need a glowing faith": *Handbook for the Application of Progressive Education Principles to Secondary Education* (Denver, 1936), 2.

18 Detroit: From Jeffrey Mirel's valuable "Politics and Public Education in the Great Depression: Detroit, 1929–1940," unpublished dissertation, University of Michigan, 1984, chap. 5.

18 Resistance to Progressivism: Cuban, *Teachers,* and Ravitch, *Crusade,* 43–80.

18 "a continuous attack": *Thirty Schools Tell Their Story* (New York, 1943), 172.

19 Are tempers hereditary?: *Manual for Teachers Working on Core Courses* (Denver, 1936), 42–45. The questions from junior high school students were the sort critics later pounced at as evidence of progressive foolishness: How can I learn dainty habits? How can I stop being so fussy about my food? How can I stop biting my lips?

19 Not easy to change: C. L. Cushman, "Conference Appraises Denver Secondary Program," in *Curriculum Journal,* November 1938; *Thirty Schools,* 163–212. For the modest impact of progressive experiments elsewhere, see Barry M. Franklin, "The Social Efficiency Movement Reconsidered: Curriculum Change in Minneapolis, 1917–1950," *Curriculum Inquiry,* 1982; Irving J. Hendrick, "California's Response to the 'New Education' in the 1930s," *California Historical Quarterly,* Spring 1974; Arthur Zilversnit, "The Failure of Progressive Education, 1920–1940," in Lawrence Stone, ed., *Schooling and Society* (Baltimore, 1976), 252–263. For one of the many surveys on the gap between theory and practice, see Albert I. Oliver, "Basic Goals for a Small High School: Theory and Practice," *School Review,* November 1950. From private testimony: One committee studying the teaching of English reported a "willingness of English teachers at least to listen to new ways of doing things" but found "slight use" of novel methods. See the December 6, 1939, minutes of the Committee on the Training of Secondary School Teachers in folder entitled Correspondence. Preparation of Teachers. 1940–1941. The committee's papers are in the Francis Spaulding Papers, Harvard University Archives.

19 The Columbia study: Paul R. Mort and Francis G. Cornell, *American Schools in Transition* (New York, 1941), 356.

19 "cling to stereotypes": Ibid., 288.

20 "Our point": *General Education in a Free Society* (Cambridge, Massachusetts, 1945), 170.

20 "We must go softly": Interview with John Finley, October 7, 1982; Committee of Detail, February 14–16, 1944, Exeter, in Records of the University Committee on the Objectives of General Education in a Free Society, Harvard University Archives.

21 Posture Week: H. H. Kohl, "A Successful Posture Week," *The High School Journal,* February 1940. Student council members elsewhere often played policeman. One survey found that three of every ten councilors also functioned as hall proctors. See *National Association of Secondary School Principals Bulletin,* March 1940.

21 TIME WILL PASS. WILL YOU?: Harold B. and Elsie J. Alberty, *Reorganizing the High School Curriculum* (New York, 1962), 213.

21 "The school must not be": Herbert G. Espy, *The Public Secondary School* (Boston, 1939), 433.

22 Elizabeth Taylor's books: Dick Moore, *Twinkle, Twinkle, Little Star (but don't have sex or take the car)* (New York, 1984), 136.

2. Informalities

Page

23 Metaphors of democracy: Patricia Albjerg Graham, *From Arcady to Academe* (New York, 1967), 81, 108.

24 indignant critics deplored: Diane Ravitch, *The Great School Wars* (New York, 1974), 107–158.

24 The credentialed professionals: David Tyack, *The One Best System* (Cambridge, Massachusetts, 1974), 78–216.

25 "We'd argue a point": Alan Peshkin, *The Imperfect Union* (Chicago, 1982), 47. For Peshkin's excellent case study of downstate Illinois localism, see *Growing Up American* (Chicago, 1978), especially 78–82.

25 Massachusetts boards: Neal Gross, *Who Runs Our Schools?* (New York, 1958), 15, 90.

26 "like most schools": "School Laws and Pressure Groups," in Gaffney Materials folder, Miracle Box 12, Conant Papers, Harvard University Archives.

26 short and positive reports: Interview with Ralph West, January 15, 1982; October 14, 1959, entry in "Minutes, Standing Committee of the Independent Secondary Schools of the New England Association of Colleges and Secondary Schools," Burlington, Massachusetts. The November 9, 1960, minutes noted that two Vermont schools had publicly announced that membership in the association was "purely social."

26 "bad setup": W. W. Livengood to F. H. Blake, March 2, 1940, Texas Adoptions folder, Box 213, American Book Company Papers, Syracuse University.

26 "those who liked our book": Henry Wilkinson Bragdon, "Dilemmas of a Textbook Writer," *Social Education,* March 1969.

27 Southern subterfuge: J. Harvie Wilkinson III, *From Brown to Bakke* (New York, 1979), 61–102.

27 transcripts: "Proceedings of the Twenty-fifth Meeting of the Educational Policies Commission, September 27–29, 1944, Skytop, Pennsylvania," 109–110, in the National Education Association Archives, Washington, D.C.

27 Aspiring administrators: Daniel E. Griffiths et al., "Teacher Mobility in New York City," *Educational Administration Quarterly,* Winter 1965.

27 Elmtown: August Hollingshead, *Elmtown's Youth* (New York, 1949), 183–184. Also, Howard S. Becker, "The Teacher in the Authority System," *Journal of Educational Sociology,* November 1953.

28 Superintendents: David Tyack, "Pilgrim's Progress: Toward a Social History of the School Superintendency, 1860–1960," *History of Education Quarterly,* Fall 1976.

28 Basketball and bonds: Reuben H. Gross, "Visit to High Schools in Macon County, Illinois," May 13, 1959, Illinois folder, Miracle Box 18, Conant Papers. Another of Conant's assistants, in a memo titled "Athletics," reported twirling scholarships at a major Ohio university. Curriculum-Athletics folder, Miracle Box 10.

28 old-timer in Hamilton, Ohio: Peter Davis, *Hometown* (New York, 1982), 51.

28 The minister's file: Hollingshead, *Elmtown,* 153.

28 cancel the dancing classes: Daisy L. Bishop (Principal, Broadway High School, Madison, Indiana), "The Question of the Church," in unmarked brown folder, Box 1, Papers for the Ambrose Caliver survey of Negro vocational guidance, National Archives. The pressures on Southern black principals are noted in Anne Moody's reminiscences, *Coming of Age in Mississippi* (New York, 1968), 165–166.

28 "I know evolution is correct": Peter Schrag, *Voices in the Classroom* (Boston, 1965), 42. For the persistence of laws against teaching evolution, see Dorothy Nelkin, *Science Textbook Controversies and the Politics of Equal Time* (Cambridge, Massachusetts, 1977).

28 Academic complacency: "Report of the Southern Illinois Group," Illinois folder, Miracle Box 5, Conant Papers.

28 Plainville: James West [pseud.], *Plainville, U.S.A.* (New York, 1945), 81.

29 Women might vote: Benjamin Fine, *Our Children Are Cheated* (New York, 1947), 29.

29 Onward and Walton: *Life,* October 16, 1950.

30 states' educational expenditures: David Tyack, Robert Lowe, and Elisabeth Hansot, *Public Schools in Hard Times* (Cambridge, Massachusetts, 1984), 81.

30 Ohio 1941: "Proceedings of the Educational Policies Commission, 9/14, 15/1941, Chicago," 340, National Education Association Archives.

30 Custodian's salary: Michael Usdan, "Report on Austin, Texas Visit of October 4, 1962," in Texas folder, Miracle Box 21, Conant Papers.

30 Illinois farmer: Springfield folder, Miracle Box 21, Conant Papers.

31 New York City cronyism: David Rogers, *110 Livingston Street* (New York, 1968); for similar portraits of Chicago, Washington, D.C., and San Francisco, see Larry Cuban, *Urban School Chiefs Under Fire* (Chicago, 1976).

31 Boston cronyism: Peter Schrag, *Village School Downtown* (Boston, 1967). For national-level offstage conflict resolution in this period, see Stephen K. Bailey, "Political Coalitions for Public Education," *Daedalus,* Summer 1981.

31 School politics: Robert Wood, *Suburbia* (Boston, 1958), 193.

31 New Trier: *Life,* October 16, 1950.

32 Frank Boyden: John McPhee, *The Headmaster* (New York, 1966), 79.

32 stop stammering: Clayton P. Alderfer and L. Dave Brown, *Learning from Changing* (Beverly Hills, 1975), 58.

32 High Mowing: "Visit to High Mowing School, Wilton, New Hampshire, October 28, 1966," in "Records, Committee of the Independent Schools," Burlington, Massachusetts. The accreditors were both amazed and amused by Mrs. Emmet, but in their report they noted that the history class they observed was surprisingly teacher-dominated for a supposedly progressive school. Even there it was hard to break from traditional instructional methods.

34 "He looks not at all Semitic": Charles M. Rice to E. S. Noyes, May 7, 1945, Folder 9, Box 41, Yale Admissions Office Records, Yale University Archives.

34 SATs: Claude Fuess, *The College Board* (New York, 1950). Students began to receive their scores directly from ETS in 1959, according to Frank H. Bowles, *Admission to College* (Princeton, New Jersey, 1960), 58.

34 night letter: E. S. Noyes to N. H. Batchelder, April 5, 1946, Folder 29, Box 43, Yale University Archives. Noyes also sent congratulatory notes to headmasters and principals whenever their graduates won academic or athletic prizes at Yale. See George W. Pierson, *Yale* (New Haven, 1955), 488.

34 Keeping posted: Dexter K. Strong to E. S. Noyes, March 1, 1946, Folder 36, Box 44, Yale University Archives; William Saltonstall to Edward Noyes, December 4, 1946, Folder 15, Box 42, ibid.

34 Weak candidates discouraged: The Reverend Norman B. Nash to E. S. Noyes, January 7, 1947, Folder 46, Box 45, ibid.

34 "G.G.B.'s MUSTS": G. Granville Benedict to E. S. Noyes, May 4, 1947, Folder 6, Box 41, ibid.

35 Abolition of Exeter's grades: Robert R. Ramsey, Jr., to Herrick M. Macomber, January 3, 1962, Folder 39, Box 49, ibid.

35 Background of the Educational Policies Commission: William Carr, *The Continuing Education of William Carr* (Washington, D.C., 1978), 54–73.

37 "man's age-old struggle": *Education for ALL American Youth* (Washington, D.C., 1944). The same moral seriousness was in most high school textbooks, according to Frances FitzGerald, *America Revised* (New York, 1980), 55–56.

37 Several historians: Lawrence A. Cremin, *The Transformation of the School* (New York, 1961), 328–332; Diane Ravitch, *The Troubled Crusade* (New York, 1983), 62.

37 Stoddard and Rankin: "Proceedings of the Educational Policies Commission, March 11–13, Chicago, Illinois," 261–262, National Education Association Archives.

38 extending elementary school practices: Whether the growth of six-year high schools extended elementary curricula upward or pushed secondary practices down is not known, but it is clear that junior-senior "combined" schools (grades 7 to 12) held a larger percentage of students in those grades, rising from 18.8% in 1930, to 24.4% in 1938, to 26.1% in 1946, to 35.1% in 1952. Most of the combined schools were rural. By 1952, three of every four were in towns under 2500, whereas progressive initiatives were most

evident in cities. Whether this combination weakened the higher grades, toughened the lower ones, or did neither, it created a blurring between upper elementary and lower secondary that was not comparable to the overlap between upper secondary and lower college in the 1930s and 1940s, years before the boom in junior college enrollments and before the surge of Advanced Placement courses. Figures are from Walter H. Gaumnitz and J. Dan Hull, "Junior High Schools versus the Traditional (8–4) High School Organization," *National Association of Secondary School Principals Bulletin,* March 1954.

39 "I am trying": "Proceedings of the Educational Policies Commission," 269–270.

39 "This whole issue": Ibid., 274. Bacon introduced many curricular reforms at Evanston High, not all of which required teachers with doctorates. In 1929, for instance, the school added courses in carpentry, drafting, driver education, problems of democracy, and problems of everyday living. See Marie C. Davis, *History of Evanston Township High School 1883–1958* (Evanston, Illinois, 1963).

40 "You give the indirection": "Proceedings of the Educational Policies Commission," 276, 275.

40 "I don't think it is practical": Ibid., 290.

41 George D. Strayer: Ibid., 301.

41 The voting: Ibid., 308–309.

42 theater of virtue: For a different comparison of education and theater, see David Cohen and Bella Rosenberg, "Functions and Fantasies: Understanding Schools in Capitalist America," *History of Education Quarterly,* 1977.

3. The Persistence of the Old Order

Page

44 "Business arithmetic is superior": Charles A. Prosser, *Secondary Education and Life* (Cambridge, Massachusetts, 1939), 15–16.

44 "lessons in preventive and therapeutic mental health": A. S. Clayton, "Mental and Social Adjustments of the Young," in Harl R. Douglass, ed., *Education for Life Adjustment* (New York, 1950), 75, 76.

44 "must learn to control": Ibid., 75.

44 Postsecondary enrollments: *Historical Statistics of the United States: Colonial Times to 1957* (Washington, D.C., 1960).

45 Rising aspirations: Martin Trow, "The Democratization of Higher Education in America," *European Journal of Sociology,* 1962.

45 "A boy who does not have": Earl McGrath, *Education* (Birmingham, 1951), 66.

46 "To try to adjust": Jacques Barzun, *The House of Intellect* (New York, 1959), 104.

46 Enrollment and graduation rates: *Historical Statistics,* 368–369, 379; *Biennial Survey of Education in the United States, 1950–52* (Washington, D.C., 1955), chap. 1.

47 strategic value of ambiguity: For a case study of the complexities of using junior colleges to ease students off the educational conveyor belt, see Burton Clark, *The Open Door College* (New York, 1960). It was unacceptable for the two-year colleges to proclaim openly one major responsibility: removing from higher education those who should not be there. Reducing college entrance rates for the marginal candidates appealed more to Life Adjusters than to students and their parents.

47 Eisenhower: "Proceedings, Thirty-fifth Meeting, Educational Policies Commission," 406, National Education Association Archives.

47 social skills: H. H. Remmers and D. H. Radler, *The American Teenager* (Indianapolis, 1957), 140.

47 Course enrollments: "Offerings and Registrations in High School Subjects, 1933–34," Office of Education *Bulletin,* no. 6, 1938; "Offerings and Enrollments in High-School Subjects," chap. 5, *Biennial Survey, 1948–50* (Washington, D.C., 1951); Grace S. Wright, "Core Curriculum in Public High Schools," Office of Education *Bulletin,* no. 5, 1950. The periodic national surveys of course enrollments are not reliable enough for truly rigorous comparisons. None of the returns was verified by outsiders. The 1948–49 survey used a 50% sample of the small high schools (under 500 students) instead of querying all of them; the sampling had not been done in 1933–34. Even after follow-up mailings, approximately 20% of the high schools never returned questionnaires. The 1933–34 report stated how many schools offered a particular course; the 1948–49 document omitted that useful information. Also troublesome is the 1948–49 survey's use of separate categories distinguishing four-year high schools from six-year high schools, thereby making it impossible to know how many 9th-to-12th-graders were in any given course. In addition, course titles changed over time. In 1933–34 vocational and nonvocational industrial arts were separate categories; they were combined in 1948–49. Public speaking became debate, radio, speech, and public speaking. There are problems other than comparability over time. Both surveys included half-year and full-year enrollments for each subject; but can we be sure some principals did not mistakenly include the former in the latter? If the figures were accurate, there is still no way to know what proportion of the enrollments reflect local and state requirements instead of student choice. And finally, because the data for each survey were drawn at just one point in time, it is impossible to know what percentage of the senior class, at one time or another during their high school days, took a particular course. We cannot assume that if, say, 22% took typing in one year, 88% of the seniors had taken it by graduation. Failures, dropouts, transfers, and other variables would affect the figures. In light of all those problems, the numbers from the national surveys should be used as an aerial snapshot rather than as a roadmap.

48 Psychology courses: T. L. Engle, "Objectives for and Subject Matter Stressed in High School Courses in Psychology," *American Psychologist,* February 1967; T. L. Engle and M. E. Bunch, "The Teaching of Psychology in High School," ibid., April 1956; Natalie Zunino, "The Teaching of Psychology in

American High Schools: What's Happening?" *Social Education,* March 1974.

48 "the study of me": Richard A. Kasschau and Michael Wertheimer, "Teaching Psychology in Secondary Schools" pamphlet, American Psychological Association, 1974; Margo Johnson, "The Teaching of Psychology in United States Secondary Schools" pamphlet, American Psychological Association, 1979.

48 the most popular textbook: T. L. Engle, *Psychology* (Yonkers, New York, 1950), 2nd edition.

49 "Poetry is offered": *The Training of Secondary School Teachers Especially with Reference to English* (Cambridge, Massachusetts, 1942), 103.

49 "regards an agreeable style": Ibid., 81.

49 Driver education: "The Status of Driver Education in Public High Schools, 1952–53," N.E.A. *Research Bulletin,* April 1954.

49 History teachers' use of audiovisuals: Richard E. Gross, "What's Wrong with American History?" *Social Education,* April 1952.

50 Popularity of nonacademic activities: After World War II, there was also an extraordinary expansion of school lunch programs. See Thelma G. Flanagan, "School Food Services," in Fuller and Pearson, eds., *Education in the States* (Washington, D.C., 1969).

50 Life Adjusters agitated noisily: Diane Ravitch, *The Troubled Crusade* (New York, 1983), 64–69.

50 "something like Progress in Democratic Smoke Abatement": Arthur E. Bestor, *Educational Wastelands* (Urbana, Illinois, 1953), 64.

50 Goslin's ouster: David Hulburd, *This Happened in Pasadena* (New York, 1951).

51 John Dewey, 1952: From the introduction to Elsa Clapp, *The Uses of Resources in Education* (New York, 1952).

51 Number of counselors: Arthur J. Jones and Leonard M. Miller, "The National Picture of Pupil Personnel and Guidance Services in 1953," *National Association of Secondary School Principals Bulletin,* February 1954; "Public School Programs and Practices," N.E.A. *Research Bulletin,* December 1967. National Defense Education Act funds for training counselors accounted for much of the increase. See Barbara B. Clowse, *Brainpower for the Cold War* (Westport, Connecticut, 1981), 155.

51 Number of school psychologists: James F. Magary and Merle L. Meachan, "The Growth of School Psychology in the Last Decade," *Journal of School Psychology,* January 1963.

51 Certification and training: Douglas T. Brown, "Issues in the Development of Professional School Psychology," Reynolds and Gutkin, eds., *The Handbook of School Psychology* (New York, 1982), 14–17.

52 Increase of full-time counselors: William C. Reavis, *Program of Guidance* National Survey Monograph no. 14 (Washington, D.C., 1933), 7–14; William H. Weigel, Jr., *Research in Secondary Schools* National Survey Monograph no. 15 (Washington, D.C., 1932), 27; also Rachel D. Cox, *Counselors and Their Work* (Philadelphia, 1945); Educational Research Service, "Research Units in Local School Systems," Circular no. 5, July 1965. For two weeks

of daily logs from a Cleveland principal in 1937, see Frank P. Whitney, *School and I* (Yellow Springs, Ohio, 1957), 118, 128.

52 Psychiatry before 1940: Richard Fox, *So Far Disordered in Mind* (Berkeley, 1982); Christopher Lasch, *Haven in a Heartless World* (New York, 1977), 12–23. For a review of the mental hygienists' emphasis on personality development as *the* purpose of education, see Sol Cohen, "The School and Personality Development: Intellectual History," in John H. Best, ed., *Historical Inquiry in Education* (Washington, D.C., 1983), 109–137. The idea of a therapeutic model of schooling was being followed by 1940, but by slighting daily practice, Cohen gives little sense of how the grand visions affected everyday experience in the 1920s and 1930s, when hygienists made their views known.

52 Postwar psychiatry: Robert Castel, Françoise Castel, and Anne Lovell, trans. by Arthur Goldhammer, *The Psychiatric Society* (New York, 1982), 59–61.

52 Malaise as well as pathology: Janet Malcolm, *Psychoanalysis: The Impossible Profession* (New York, 1981), 41, 102, 120; Lawrence Frank, *Society as the Patient* (New Brunswick, New Jersey, 1948). For more critical assessments, see Robert N. Bellah et al., *Habits of the Heart* (Berkeley, 1985), chaps. 3–5; Lasch, *Haven,* 96–98; and Philip Rieff, *The Triumph of the Therapeutic* (New Haven, 1966), 8–25. For critical assessments of Lasch and Rieff, see Peter Clecak, *America's Quest for the Ideal Self* (New York, 1983), 230–270.

52 Ministers' soothing sermons: Donald Meyer, *The Positive Thinkers* (New York, 1965).

52 General Motors' psychologists; personality tests: Douglas T. Miller and Marion Novak, *The Fifties* (Garden City, New York, 1977), 129, 141.

52 Novels, television shows, and movies: Mark Shechner, "Jewish Writers," in Daniel Hoffman, ed., *Harvard Guide to Contemporary American Fiction* (Cambridge, 1979), 202; Leo Braudy, *The World in a Frame* (New York, 1974), 64; Robert Sklar, *Movie-Made America* (New York, 1976), 255.

53 Early-twentieth-century guidance: For the recollections of a pioneer of vocational guidance, see Jesse Buttrick Davis, *The Saga of a Schoolmaster* (Boston, 1956), 176–207.

53 By the time of Sputnik: Aaron V. Cicourel and John I. Kitsuse, *The Educational Decision-Makers* (New York, 1963).

53 Students' choice for help: John C. Flanagan et al., *The American High School Student* (Pittsburgh, 1964), K-9; Claude W. Grant, "The Counselor's Role," *Personnel and Guidance Journal,* October 1954.

53 Psychologists' role in high school: See the valuable autobiographies by Francis A. Muller, "School Psychology in the USA: Reminiscences of its Origins," and Jack I. Bardon, "Personalized Account of the Development and Status of School Psychology," both in *Journal of School Psychology,* 1981. Also, John B. Carroll, "Educational Psychology and Educational Research," unpublished manuscript, copy courtesy of Prof. Carroll.

53 emotionally disturbed and socially maladjusted: *Statistics of Special Education for Exceptional Children and Youth, 1957–58* (Washington, D.C., 1961), 7;

Romaine Mackie, *Special Education in the United States* (New York, 1969), 43.

54 Lawrenceville School, 1947: Allen V. Heely, *Why the Private School?* (New York, 1951), 175, 177.

54 Arthur Clarke and Johnny Barto: Edgar Z. Friedenberg, *Coming of Age in America* (Boston, 1965), 74–92.

55 The amount of school construction: *Planning America's School Buildings* (Washington, D.C., 1960); David Tyack, Robert Lowe, and Elisabeth Hansot, *Public Schools in Hard Times* (Cambridge, Massachusetts, 1984), 105. For a parallel "crisis of supply," see Paul Starr, *The Social Transformation of American Medicine* (New York, 1982), 355–378.

56 Changing architectural styles: *American School Buildings* (Washington, D.C., 1949); Educational Facilities Laboratories, *High Schools 1962* (New York, 1962); *Seminars for the Study of Secondary Schools and the Community* (Cambridge, Massachusetts, 1956); Office of Education, *The Secondary School Plant* (Washington, D.C., 1956); the 1940–70 issues of *Architectural Record* (especially the September 1953 and October 1955 issues); and the files of the *American School Board Journal*.

57 points for toilet facilities: George D. Strayer, *The Report of a Survey of the Public Schools of the District of Columbia* (Washington, D.C., 1949), 316–317.

57 doubled as a gristmill: Dorothy R. Robinson, *The Bell Rings at Four* (Austin, Texas, 1978), 51; "Rural Teachers in 1951–52," N.E.A. *Research Bulletin,* February 1953.

57 Busing: The number of students bused doubled in the 1930s, rose 70% in the 1940s, and increased by a third in the 1950s; see Gary Orfield, *Must We Bus?* (Washington, D.C., 1978), 130.

57 Anonymity in larger schools: R. G. Barker and P. V. Gump, *Big School, Small School* (Palo Alto, 1964).

57 Stephen and Alexis: *Life,* March 24, 1958.

58 During the years of his Harvard presidency: James Bryant Conant, *Education in a Divided World* (Cambridge, Massachusetts, 1948), and *Education and Liberty* (Cambridge, 1953). Conant's "equality of status" slogan, from an interview with Alden Dunham, October 15, 1982, New York City.

60 "significant interaction": That phrase was not clearly defined in *The American High School Today* (New York, 1959); its absence or presence was extrapolated from student and staff comments made during short group meetings with Conant.

60 state of affairs elsewhere: State Department of Education, "What the Top Fifteen Percent Studied," January 1960, in Florida folder, Miracle Box 5, Conant Papers; *A Second Look at the Program of Education for the Gifted,* March 1959, in Illinois folder, Miracle Box 5, Conant Papers. In response to a Conant letter asking for examples of academically challenging programs in schools where less than 50% of the seniors went to college, the incredulous Idaho state department responded, "Where would you find such a school in

the United States?" From an untitled memo in Idaho folder, Miracle Box 5, Conant Papers.

60 "Most of the schools": James B. Conant, *American High School,* 40.

61 "the main Conant case": John Hollister, Memorandum for the File, November 26, 1957, Folder 25, Box 1, Conant Papers.

61 "First Thoughts" memo: "J. B. Conant's First Thoughts on Criteria for a Satisfactory Public High School," November 1957, Folder 25, Box 1, Conant Papers.

61 "social studies": "Trip Report, Lincoln High School, Manitowac, Wisconsin, November 4, 1957," Wisconsin folder, Miracle Box 21, Conant Papers.

62 bright but lazy: James Bryant Conant to Henry Chauncey, November 11, 1957, Tests and Testing folder, Miracle Box 15, Conant Papers.

62 Chauncey's associates: Henry S. Dyer, Memorandum for Mr. Chauncey, November 15, 1957; Robert L. Ebel, Memorandum for Mr. Chauncey, November 15, 1957; James E. Dobbin, Memorandum for Mr. Chauncey, November 18, 1957; Martin Katz, Memorandum to Anna Dragositz, November 22, 1957, all in Chauncey Papers, Educational Testing Service Archives, Princeton, New Jersey.

62 "I've got to be surer": James Bryant Conant to Henry Chauncey, April 1, 1958, Chauncey Papers, Educational Testing Service Archives.

62 discriminate between achievement and aptitude: James Bryant Conant to Henry Chauncey, July 25, 1958, in Folder 30, Box 1, Conant Papers. Conant also complained that test scores revealed nothing about mastery of a field: "Is there no way of expressing the results of an achievement test in terms of an 'absolute standard?' In the days of long ago, if one received an 'A' on a College Board examination in trigonometry, it was assumed that the student 'knew' trigonometry. If he received an 'E,' he certainly did not. What is one to say about the present scale of scoring?" Several years later, he raised the same issue. The clarity of the pass-fail achievement exams had some appeal for Conant. He wanted to see "you know it or you don't know it" tests in foreign language, math, and science, by which a 65 or 80 or 95 was not a position relative to other scores but indicated how much material the student knew. Conant felt there was a discernible "corpus of knowledge" that justified absolute standards of mastery and competence. James B. Conant to John B. Hollister, December 14, 1960, Hollister Papers, Educational Testing Service Archives.

63 yield per acre: Robert L. Ebel, Memorandum for Mr. Chauncey, August 4, 1958, Chauncey Papers.

63 "Some influential nontesting person": John E. Dobbin, Memorandum for Mr. Chauncey, October 6, 1958, Chauncey Papers.

63 Conant's commitment to grouping: His opinions changed a bit after he wrote *American High School.* In February 1959 he praised grouping on the basis of reading ability, and by July 1960 he expressed his reservations more bluntly: "Frankly, I am becoming more and more skeptical about the validity of an individual I.Q., although statistically I think the subject is sound. I think

that in my future writings I am going to make much less use of I.Q. than I did even in my First Report and confine myself more to levels of achievement in separate skills." But in 1959, after a year's study of high schools, Conant still yearned for aptitude tests as pure as possible, stripped of the contributions from family, neighborhood, teachers, and textbooks. See James B. Conant to William Gruhn, July 8, 1960, Folder 41, Box 3, Conant Papers.

63 Average-ability students: James B. Conant to F. T. Tyler, March 31, 1959, Academically Talented folder, Miracle Box 10, Conant Papers.

63 "for my money": "Trip Report — Ann Arbor High School, Ann Arbor, Michigan, November 14, 1957," Michigan folder, Miracle Box 21, Conant Papers.

63 Physics enrollments: "Trip Report — A. C. David High School, Yakima, Washington, March 3, 1958," Miracle Box 12, Conant Papers.

63 A first degree: James B. Conant to Frank S. Freeman, October 28, 1960, Folder G, Box 7, Correspondence 1957–64, Conant Papers.

64 IQ below 90: "Report of a Visit to York Community High School, Elmhurst, Illinois, September 1957," Miracle Box 18, Conant Papers.

64 a slow learner: James B. Conant to F. G. Lankford, Jr., March 2, 1959, Virginia folder, Miracle Box 6, Conant Papers. Also Arthur Gates to James Conant, June 11, 1962, in Folder G, Box 7, Correspondence 1957–64, Conant Papers.

64 scratched out "garages": "First Thoughts," 15.

64 trial balloons: "An Academic High School Within a Comprehensive High School," June 17, 1958, Folder 26, Box 1, Conant Papers. Two months earlier, Conant said a visit to Minnesota made him "flirt with the Rickover hypothesis of having Federal schools on a regional basis." Conant thought the baleful influence of progressive theorists at the University of Minnesota undermined the chances for special attention for the talented. He added, "I can imagine all the problems and howls if anybody really took Rickover's suggestion seriously." See "Trip Report — Austin High School, Austin, Minnesota, April 10, 1958," in Miracle Box 18, Conant Papers.

64 "proper labeling": "First Thoughts," 7, and "Trip Report — Washington Park High School and William Horlick Trade School, Racine, Wisconsin, November 6, 1957," Miracle Box 17, Conant Papers. The president of Columbia University's Teachers College warned Conant that the recommended program for the talented would become an academic track. See Hollis Caswell to James Conant, March 17, 1959, Folder C-E, Box 6, Correspondence 1957–64, Conant Papers.

65 "gives losers": A line in John Gardner, "Equality and Excellence," draft copy (with words of praise in the margins) in Folder F, Box 7, Correspondence 1957–64, Conant Papers.

65 "if everything": William Fels to James Conant, February 5, 1959, Folder F, Box 7, Correspondence 1957–64, Conant Papers.

65 "the heart and emotions": From "Annual Report, Clayton High School," in Missouri folder, Miracle Box 18, Conant Papers.

65 "As we advocate": Paul B. Diederich, "The Conant Report," in Tests and Testing folder, Miracle Box 15, Conant Papers.

66 "Altogether too many of us": Bernard S. Miller to James B. Conant, June 23, 1960, Folder 41, Box 3, Conant Papers.

67 Vocational education in Chicago: "Lessons from the Visit to Chicago," Chicago folder, Miracle Box 5, Conant Papers. The report for that November 1959 trip anticipated much of *Slums and Suburbs,* especially the tone of shock at the extent and complexity of urban problems. Conant later praised Dunbar High School there, in a letter to Lawrence Cremin, as evidence that a good vocational program "has to be seen to be believed." See Conant to Cremin, December 15, 1961, in Folder 45, Box 3, Conant Papers.

67 "largely social": "Some Reflections on the Place of Vocational Education in a Comprehensive High School Program," January 31, 1958, Folder 25, Box 1, Conant Papers.

67 student councils: "Trip Report — Ann Arbor High School," and "Trip Report, Lincoln High School," Wisconsin folder, Miracle Box 21, Conant Papers.

68 "For certain kinds of people": James Conant to William Cornog, February 26, 1959, Academically Talented folder, Miracle Box 10, Conant Papers.

68 Lunchroom anthropologist: Henry Chauncey hoped that Conant would hire a sociologist. "Notes on Conference with Ambassador Conant — New York City, December 20, 1956," Chauncey Papers, Educational Testing Service Archives.

68 "As I now review the situation": Revision of the Report, memo from Conant to Eugene Youngert, Bernard Miller, and Nathaniel Ober, November 4, 1958, Folder 27, Box 1, Conant Papers.

69 playing up the positive: "Confidential Supplement to J. B. Conant's *The American High School Today,*" January 12, 1959, Indiana folder, Miracle Box 5, Conant Papers.

69 "right kids?": marginal comment on Wilbur Young, "A Look at Mathematics and Science Education in Indiana Schools," Indiana folder, Miracle Box 5, Conant Papers.

69 "which doesn't seem to me": "Trip Report, Bloomington High School," October 16, 1957, Miracle Box 18, Conant Papers.

69 "professional people": James Conant to William Fels, February 21, 1959, Folder F, Box 7, Correspondence 1957–64, Conant Papers.

69 need for more professionals: James Conant to John Kenneth Galbraith, March 2, 1959, Folder G, Box 7, Correspondence 1957–64, Conant Papers.

69 "a life in New Rochelle": John Kenneth Galbraith to James Conant, January 2, 1959, ibid.; also, Galbraith, *A Life in Our Times* (New York, 1981), 91.

69 "I am frank to admit": Conant to Galbraith, March 2, 1959. Earlier Conant deliberations on women were similar. In discussing the 1950 Educational Policies Commission report on the gifted, he was unsure about how to revise a section that said it was impossible to know whether smart women made their greater contribution at home or at work. The commissioners voted to

delete the section, at which point Conant quipped, "Let's not take a chance and discuss it any further." Silence also marked Conant's position on admitting women to the Harvard Medical School in 1943. The faculty approved co-education by a 68–12 vote. In presenting the vote to the Harvard Corporation, Conant "explained that neither the Dean nor I was prepared to endorse the faculty vote, nor were we ready to oppose it." "Proceedings, Thirty-fifth Meeting," 379; James B. Conant, *My Several Lives* (New York, 1970), 381.

70 "not so sure about the girls": James Conant to Matthew Gaffney, November 4, 1958, Folder 27, Box 1, Conant Papers.

70 "If all the high schools": *American High School,* 40.

70 "the one most vigorously attacked": Conant memo to Frank Keppel et al., March 5, 1959; Conant, Memo to John Gardner, February 23, 1959, both in Folder 28, Box 1, Conant Papers.

70 Consolidation: John K. Cox, "School District Reorganization," December 1957; Donald G. Wallace to James Conant, December 19, 1961, Iowa folder, Miracle Box 5, Conant Papers.

71 "would have to fly our students": Tracy Brower to James Conant, February 19, 1959, School Size folder, Miracle Box 15, Conant Papers.

71 have students boarded: James Conant to Ralph G. Bohrson, December 17, 1958, Colorado folder, Miracle Box 5, Conant Papers.

71 improve small schools: James Conant to E. Foster Dowell, June 10, 1958, Oklahoma folder, Miracle Box 6, Conant Papers.

71 local pride: Matthew P. Gaffney to James Conant, October 9, 1958, Folder 27, Box 1, Conant Papers.

71 "the old one": James Conant to Merle Borrowman, July 24, 1964, Merle Borrowman folder, Miracle Box 16, Conant Papers.

71 "wrap the N.E.A. mantle": Bernard S. Miller to James Conant, October 12, 1958, Folder 27, Box 1, Conant Papers. William Carr, executive secretary of the N.E.A. from 1952 to 1968, tried unsuccessfully to persuade Conant to become deputy executive secretary. Interview with William Carr, December 29, 1983, Washington, D.C.

71 "the real work is done": John Hollister, Memo for the Files, June 6, 1958, Folder 43, Box 3, Conant Papers.

72 Publication of *Slums and Suburbs:* James Conant to Philip Hickey, March 22, 1961, Folder 43, Box 3, Conant Papers.

72 "problems raised by": Appendix F, Folder 26, Box 1, Conant Papers. *American High School* criticized formal tracking, but Conant soon came to appreciate its merits in large cities. When he visited St. Louis, where students were assigned to one of five tracks, he learned that too many mediocre black students tried to take foreign languages and mathematics. Administrators there preferred track placements rather than Conant's suggestion of "holding up standards and failing students," which they thought "unrealistic." Conant went away impressed: "On the basis of experience in St. Louis perhaps I should modify my statement about tracks as opposed to individualized programs when it comes to large cities." From "Trip Report, St. Louis, Missouri, December 13, 1959," Missouri folder, Miracle Box 21, Conant Papers.

72 "What we are trying to do": "Proceedings of the Special Meeting of the Educational Policies Commission, December 14–15, 1957," 41, National Educational Association Archives.

72 Conant's audience: Memo to John Gardner, Henry Toy, and Jack Hollister, September 16, 1958, Folder 27, Box 1, Conant Papers; also, James Conant to John Hollister, October 24, 1958, Folder 34, Box 2, Conant Papers.

73 Wider patterns of exercising power: For President Eisenhower's leadership style, see Fred I. Greenstein, *The Hidden-Hand Presidency* (New York, 1982).

73 presented the academic challenge: Roald F. Campbell and Robert A. Bunnell, eds., *Nationalizing Influences on Secondary Education* (Danville, Illinois, 1963); John A. Valentine, "The College Board and the Classroom," unpublished manuscript, chaps. 6–9.

73 1960–1961 enrollments: *Subject Offerings and Enrollments in Public Secondary Schools* (Washington, D.C., 1965); for the retarded, Mackie, *Special Education*, 43.

74 "The strategy was to find": Jerome Bruner, *In Search of Mind* (New York, 1983), 181.

74 Curricular revisions: Edward Fenton, lecture, Harvard University, March 17, 1983; William W. Goetz, "Curriculum-Making in a Suburban New Jersey High School from 1957 to 1972," unpublished dissertation, Columbia University Teachers College, 1982; Marvin Lazerson et al., *An Education of Value* (New York, 1985), chap. 2.

74 "This is an attempt": Martin Trow, in Melvin M. Tumin and Marvin Bressler, eds., "Quality and Equality in Education," bound mimeographed transcript of conference proceedings, 1966. For a case study of one school keen on audiovisuals to "rationalize the instruction," see David W. Beggs III, *Decatur-Lakeview High School* (Englewood Cliffs, New Jersey, 1964). The school seemed to assume that both students and teachers would founder, in the new "large group" lectures Decatur-Lakeview required, without the help of mechanical relief. "The color overlays were appealing to learners. The turning on and off of the machine was another call for mental attention." Earlier in the book the author claimed that a teaching machine "extends the teacher's skill as the X-ray machine broadens the physician's ability to perform his function." And "a description in words or print of an 'H' bomb explosion is a second-class experience for students compared to the actual viewing of the event on video tape." Abstract reasoning comes across, in Beggs's book, as impossible in large groups without gadgetry close at hand (see pp. 119, 96, 90).

75 The new social studies: Edward Fenton, lecture, Harvard, March 17, 1963.

75 even the brightest: *They Went to College Early* (New York, 1957), 73–76, 83.

75 The school culture: "To have a cheerleader nod to me was to have a good day; to have her stop to talk with me was to be destined for greatness." Bill Henderson, *His Son* (New York, 1982), 86. For the same priorities around 1970, see Joyce Maynard, *Looking Back* (New York, 1973).

75 Testing produced more losers than winners: Gerald Grant and David Riesman, *The Perpetual Dream* (Chicago, 1978), 197.

Notes

75 Competitiveness over college entrance: David Mallery, *High School Students Speak Out* (New York, 1962); Christopher Jencks and David Riesman, *The Academic Revolution* (New York, 1968), 109–110, 132, 164, 272–273.

76 "rights and authorities": "Teacher Opinion on Pupil Behavior, 1955–56," N.E.A. *Research Bulletin,* April 1956.

76 "Celery Stalks at Midnight": Evan Hunter, *The Blackboard Jungle* (New York, 1954), 169. For a study of teachers better able to establish control in the face of challenge, see Carl Werthman, "Delinquents in School: A Test for the Legitimacy of Authority," *Berkeley Journal of Sociology,* 1963.

76 "a withdrawal of energies": Tumin and Bressler, eds., "Quality and Equality," 5–19, 6–10; for junior high schools, see James Herndon, *The Way It Spozed To Be* (New York, 1968).

76 "we are allowing social dynamite": James B. Conant, *Slums and Suburbs* (New York, 1961), 2.

77 "talent presumably will realize itself": Tumin and Bressler, 2–17.

77 "The kid we used to call": Field Note U-400, A Study of High Schools.

4. No One Can Really Tell You What to Do

Page
80 Flora Rhind, "The Teacher and Zestful Living," *Harvard Educational Review,* October 1941.

80 Films about teachers: David M. Considine, *The Cinema of Adolescence* (Jefferson, North Carolina, 1985), chaps. 6–7; Molly Haskell, *From Reverence to Rape* (New York, 1974), 240–241, 250, 337–338.

80 N.E.A. survey: "The Status of the American Public School Teacher," N.E.A. *Research Bulletin,* Fall 1957.

80 Single teachers in one-teacher schools: "Rural Teachers in 1951–52," N.E.A. *Research Bulletin,* February 1953.

80 Gains by married women: For a good survey of women in the 1940s and 1950s, see Alice Kessler-Harris, *Out to Work* (New York, 1982), chaps. 10 and 11.

80 Extension of tenure: "Teacher Personnel Procedures, 1950–51," N.E.A. *Research Bulletin,* April 1952.

80 Hidden tape recorder: *Life,* April 26, 1963. For teachers' wariness of discussing evolution, see Dorothy Nelkin, *Science Textbook Controversies and the Politics of Equal Time* (Cambridge, Massachusetts, 1977).

81 No weekday movies, no sitting in laps: Lawrence M. Friedman, "Limited Monarchy: The Rise and Fall of Student Rights" (Institute for Research on Educational Finance and Governance, Stanford, 1982). Also, Stephen R. Goldstein, "The Scope and Sources of School Board Authority to Regulate Student Conduct and Status: A Nonconstitutional Analysis," *University of Pennsylvania Law Review,* January 1969.

81 Seniors' favorites: Cambridge High and Latin *Yearbook,* 1941.

81 "Well, I like stories": David Riesman, *Faces in the Crowd* (New Haven, 1952), 247. For evocative reminiscences of coming-of-age in the 1930s, see Russell Baker, *Growing Up* (New York, 1983).

81 Ricky Nelson: Scott Cohen, "Rick & Tracy Nelson," *Interview,* September 1984.

81 1950s' music: Simon Firth, *Sound Effects* (New York, 1981).

82 Record sales: Dwight Macdonald, "A Caste, A Culture, A Market," *New Yorker,* November 22, 1958.

82 Economic growth: Alan Blinder, "The Level and Distribution of Economic Well-Being," in Martin Feldstein, ed., *The American Economy in Transition* (Chicago, 1980), 415–479; Morris Janowitz, *The Last Half Century* (Chicago, 1978), 155; James Patterson, *America's Struggle Against Poverty, 1900–1980* (Cambridge, Massachusetts, 1981), 80.

82 Teen-agers' spending money: Macdonald, "Caste, Culture, Market."

82 Cars and telephones: *Historical Statistics of the United States: Colonial Times to 1970* (Washington, D.C., 1975), vol. 2, 716, 783.

82 Larger homes: Philip Longman, "Taking America to the Cleaners," *The Washington Monthly,* November 1982.

82 "They can do things": Robert J. Havighurst and Hilda Taba, *Adolescent Character and Personality* (New York, 1949), 38; for parallels in Southern black schools, see Allison Davis and John Dollard, *Children of Bondage* (Washington, D.C., 1940), 108; for Midwestern schools, see I. Keith Taylor, *High School Students Talk It Over* (Columbus, Ohio, 1937), 28.

82 Muncie's clothes: Robert S. and Helen Merrell Lynd, *Middletown in Transition* (New York, 1937), 445, 306.

82 By the 1950s: C. Wayne Gordon, *The Social System of the High School* (Glencoe, Illinois, 1957), 23; James S. Coleman, *The Adolescent Society* (New York, 1961), passim.

83 "Much is at stake": David Riesman, *The Lonely Crowd* (New Haven, 1950), 68. Jules Henry, *Culture Against Man* (New York, 1963) is good on the intersections of anxiety and pleasure resulting from status competition among teens. It is clear from his book that the fearfulness described in chap. 1 of this volume, especially the winning-and-losing judgmentalism of school, was not put in place only by adults, a point too often forgotten by some of the critics of the late 1960s. For another good description of rating and ranking, see Joyce Maynard, *Looking Back* (New York, 1973), 36–47.

83 Presley: Albert Goodman, *Elvis* (New York, 1981).

83 Greasers: Bill Henderson, *His Son* (New York, 1982), 86.

83 Natalie Wood's parents: Dick Moore, *Twinkle, Twinkle, Little Star (but don't have sex or take the car)* (New York, 1984), 246.

83 Juvenile delinquency and class: W. Norton Grubb and Marvin Lazerson, *Broken Promises* (New York, 1982), 159–160, 183.

83 Levittown's social life: Herbert Gans, *The Levittowners* (New York, 1967), 206–219.

84 "flaming youth": Joseph Kett, *Rites of Passage* (New York, 1977), 258. Ac-

cording to the former president of Scholastic, Inc., a mid-1930s' advertisement for Coca-Cola that featured an unchaperoned girl smoking a cigarette in a car stirred angry letters and cancelations. See "A Report on the 1975 Meeting of Scholastic's National Advisory Council," May 16, 1975, Scholastic Archives, New York City.

84 Child-rearing: the paragraph draws on Urie Bronfenbrenner, "The Changing American Child," in Eli Ginzberg, ed., *Values and Ideals of American Youth* (New York, 1961); Christopher Lasch, *Haven in a Heartless World* (New York, 1977), 109; Margaret Mead, "The Contemporary American Family As an Anthropologist Sees It," *American Journal of Sociology,* May 1948; Mary McCarthy, *Memoirs of a Catholic Girlhood* (New York, 1957); Robert R. Sears, Eleanor Maccoby, and Harry Levin, *Patterns of Child Rearing* (Evanston, 1957); Milton Senn, *Speaking Out for America's Children* (New Haven, 1977), 54; Celia B. Stendler, "Sixty Years of Child-Training Practices," *Journal of Pediatrics,* 1950; Elinor Waters and Vaughn J. Crandall, "Social Class and Observed Maternal Behavior from 1940 to 1960," *Child Development,* 1964; Martha Wolfenstein, "Fun Morality: An Analysis of Recent American Child-Training Literature," in Margaret Mead and Martha Wolfenstein, eds., *Childhood in Contemporary Cultures* (Chicago, 1955), 168–178; Viviana A. Zelizer, *Pricing the Priceless Child* (New York, 1985). I do not claim that the mellowing suddenly began in the 1940s; simply that a discernible trend was evident and getting stronger.

85 1950s' television: Leo Bogart, *The Age of Television* (New York, 1956), 69, 233, 241–252; Wilbur Schramm, Jack Lyle, Edwin B. Parker, *Television in the Lives of our Children* (Palo Alto, 1961); Joshua Meyrowitz, "The Adultlike Child and the Childlike Adult: Socialization in an Electronic Age," *Daedalus,* Summer 1984, for incisive thoughts on how TV "takes children beyond the informational limits once set by walls and parents." Both the Bogart and Schramm books suggest that television often brought about negotiations between children and parents to avoid quarrels over the time, programs, and amount of viewing. This bargaining diminished as children grew older. The negotiations had no counterpart during the school hours.

85 first-date kisses: Harold T. Christensen, "Dating Behavior As Evaluated by High-School Students," *American Journal of Sociology,* March 1952.

85 Adolescent conservatism: H. H. Remmers, ed., *Anti-Democratic Attitudes in American Schools* (Evanston, 1963); H. H. Remmers and D. H. Radler, *The American Teenager* (Indianapolis, 1957), 138, 183.

85 Priority of athletics: This is borne out by how school reimbursed for extra duties. More high schools (83%) paid coaches than compensated band and music directors (53%), dramatics coaches (36%), or newspaper sponsors (30%). See "Teacher Personnel Practices," N.E.A. *Research Bulletin,* April 1952.

85 Dick Clark's audience: Macdonald, "Caste, Culture, Market."

85 Boy Scouts: Kett, *Rite,* 266.

86 "There is little room": A. Harry Passow, *Toward Creating a Model Urban*

School System (New York, 1967), 316. Washington's superintendent was irritated that students "pay more attention to their friendship problems than to their studies" and he scorned "alley-type subjects" in the curriculum. See Carl F. Hansen, *The Four Track Curriculum in Today's High School* (Englewood Cliffs, New Jersey, 1964), 77, 109.

86 "All the English teachers": Michael Medved and David Wallechinsky, *What Really Happened to the Class of '65?* (London, 1978), 252; also David Mallery, *High School Students Speak Out* (New York, 1962), and Arno Bellack et al., *The Language of the Classroom* (New York, 1966).

86 conservative teachers: *What Teachers Think* (Washington, D.C., 1965), 38, 57.

86 Scholarly research: Charles Bidwell, "The School As a Formal Organization," in J. G. March, ed., *Handbook on Organizations* (Chicago, 1965); W. W. Charters, "The Social Background of Teaching," in N. L. Gage, ed., *Handbook of Research on Teaching* (Chicago, 1963), 804.

87 "Sweet Little Sixteen," by Chuck Berry. Copyright 1958, Arc Music Corp. Reprinted by permission; all rights reserved.

87 Janis Joplin's sex life: Myra Friedman, *Buried Alive* (New York, 1973), 22.

87 Petting: Ellen K. Rothman, *Hands and Hearts* (New York, 1984), 304.

87 *Up in Seth's Room:* Brett Harvey, "Boy Crazy," *Village Voice,* February 10–16, 1982.

88 Ames, Iowa: Sue Allen Toth, *Blooming* (Boston, 1978), 14, 116, 46, 42.

88 "gives signs of being excited": Arnold Gesell, Frances Ilg, and Louise Bates Ames, *Youth: The Years Ten to Sixteen* (New York, 1956), 268.

88 Premarital intercourse and teen-age pregnancies: Michael Rutter, *Changing Youth in a Changing Society* (Cambridge, Massachusetts, 1980).

89 threshold of maturity: Of course, pregnant girls before the 1970s relinquished their adolescence and were passed through to adulthood, whereas now the "mature" behavior does not automatically push the mother outside the protections afforded by continued schooling. For a lucid study of pregnant girls and schools, see Michael Sedlak, "Young Women and the City," *History of Education Quarterly,* Spring 1983.

89 Class differences: Wardell B. Pomeroy, *Dr. Kinsey and the Institute for Sex Research* (New Haven, 1982 edition), 469; Paul Robinson, *The Modernization of Sex* (New York, 1976), 94–95.

89 Abbot Academy: Susan Lloyd, *A Singular School* (Hanover, New Hampshire, 1979), 352, 366.

89 Drugs: "Drugs and American High School Students, 1975–1983" (National Institute on Drug Abuse, Washington, D.C., 1984).

90 Employment and homework: John C. Flanagan et al., *The American High School Student* (Pittsburgh, 1964), 5–8, 5–12; Noah Lewin-Epstein, *Youth Employment during High School* (Washington, D.C., 1981), tables 1.1, 3.6.

90 Homework time versus job time: One should not glorify study habits before the advent of TV, because a majority of students kept a radio on as they toiled. Schramm et al., *Television,* 72.

90 "gradually enlarged": Patricia M. Spacks, *The Adolescent Idea* (New York, 1981), 3; Kenneth Keniston, "Prologue: Youth As a Stage of Life," in Robert J. Havighurst and Philip H. Dreyer, eds., *Youth* (Chicago, 1975), 3–26. The historian Robert Wiebe defined the age-role changes as part of "the threat of unstructured relations between blacks and whites, youth and adults, citizens and officials, women and men. Rules of transaction were being violated and realms of privacy invaded." See *The Segmented Society* (New York, 1975), 170.

91 Fashion: Kennedy Fraser, *The Fashionable Mind* (New York, 1981), 246.

91 sixteen again: For thoughts on life as an endless mixer, see Sue Allen Toth, *Ivy Days* (Boston, 1984), 109–112.

91 *Personal Health for Girls:* Screened at Coronet Films, Chicago, Illinois, August 22, 1983. Coronet made and distributed a variety of audiovisual materials to elementary and secondary schools.

91 "to get their children": Marie Winn, *Children Without Childhood* (New York, 1983), 101; Daniel Yankelovich, *New Rules* (New York, 1981); Gerald Grant with John Briggs, "Today's Children Are Different," *Educational Leadership,* March 1983.

92 "a brutal machine": Charles A. Reich, *The Greening of America* (New York, 1970), 137.

92 Therapeutic techniques: Peter Clecak, *America's Quest for the Ideal Self* (New York, 1983), 145–155.

93 "The sheer revelation": Richard Sennett, *The Fall of Public Man* (New York, 1978), 269.

93 "What was for me": Thomas J. Cottle, "The Connections of Adolescence," in Jerome Kagan and Robert Coles, ed., *Twelve to Sixteen* (New York, 1971), 319.

93 less denial of personal problems: Joseph Veroff, Elizabeth Douvan, Richard Kulka, *The Inner American* (New York, 1981), 530–531.

94 "entitled to as much protection": Alan Levine, *The Rights of Students* (New York, 1973), 85.

94 "Strikes may be legal": James H. Tipton, *Community in Crisis* (New York, 1953), 84.

94 "The locker room": Lawrence Friedman, "Limited Monarchy," 12.

95 "humiliate and ridicule": Goldstein, "Scope and Sources of School Board Authority," 395. In Washington, D.C., a report on teen-age pregnancies recommended barring young mothers and fathers from junior high school graduations, and discouraged their re-enrollment. This proposal was written not by the head of a school department but by the chief of the Washington Disease Control Bureau. From *U.S. News and World Report,* December 12, 1958.

95 *Tinker* v. *Des Moines:* There were several major ambiguities in the Tinker decision. School men had the right to curb activities that would create "substantial interference with school work or discipline," but what did "substantial" mean? What of the girl in typing class with hair so long that her teacher could not tell if she surreptitiously peeked at the keyboard? Was it right to

use a double standard for school and society on the premise that antics harmless on the streets might be disruptive in school? Moreover, it was not clear whether the critical variable was student conduct or the reaction of others. What of the vocational students whose scraggly beards caused such a bad impression of the entire school that employers stayed away? Although courts usually condoned symbolic student gestures like long hair, armbands, and underground newspapers, judges were not so willing to let administrators broadcast their values. A principal who hung a Confederate flag in his office had to remove it, unlike the wide receiver from another school who wore a Confederate soldier's cap to a rally for the junior varsity team. See Ralph D. Stern, ed., *The School Principal and the Law* (Topeka, Kansas, 1978), 96–112; Friedman, "Limited Monarchy," 25; George Leonard, "Car Pool — A Story of Public Education in the Eighties," *Esquire,* May 1983.

95 "Is it not more vital": Richard L. Berkman, "Students in Court: Free Speech and the Functions of Schooling in America," *Harvard Educational Review,* November 1970.

95 fewer personal demands: The legal transformations were particularly jarring to parents of preteens. A case in point was the March 19, 1973, issue of *News Citizen,* a Scholastic publication for middle-schoolers. An article entitled "Have You Got Rights?" pictured students picketing and wearing buttons for free lunches and against wars, and ended with a quiz matching various student rights with five of the first ten amendments to the Constitution. The child would put the appropriate numeral next to "you need not salute the flag; your locker can be searched only for a good reason; you can print what you want in your newspaper; you can wear your hair however you wish and dress as you wish; you can wear any buttons, armbands or badges you choose." The magazine slipped by the usual rigorous editorial scrutiny, and its publication prompted hundreds of angry letters and phone calls, many canceling subscriptions. The publishers immediately reassured subscribers that the issue was a fluke, and they printed a follow-up piece on student responsibilities. A strenuous month of phone calls reduced the cancelations, which came mostly from Midwestern towns, but not before over 500 irate teachers and administrators had protested. As one woman said, "Parents are losing too! Only kids have rights!" Next to a paragraph on due process, she penciled, "Give them a bigger knife." Sources: May 21, 1973, Memorandum from Jack Lippert, Richard Robinson, and Sturgis Cary to All New York Staff Members; May 21, 1973, memo, Community or School Board Bans or Threatened Bans of Scholastic (both in Scholastic, Inc., Archives, New York City). See also Jack Lippert, *Scholastic: A Publishing Adventure* (New York, 1979), 387–392.

96 student satisfaction: John Birmingham, ed., *Our Time Is Now* (New York, 1970). Also Diane Divoky, ed., *How Old Will You Be in 1984?* (New York, 1969), and Kenneth Fish, *Conflict and Dissent in the High Schools* (New York, 1970).

96 Evaluations: "The Teacher Looks at Personnel Administration," N.E.A. *Research Bulletin,* December 1945.

Notes

97 knee socks: C. S. Keister, *The Principal of the Thing* (Philadelphia, 1970), 73.

97 N.E.A. and A.F.T. competition: Alan Rosenthal, *Pedagogues and Power* (Syracuse, 1969), 15–24, 69; Frederick M. Wirt and Michael W. Kirst, *Schools in Conflict* (Berkeley, 1982), 17. Outsiders as well as insiders organized. In New York City, board negotiations with the United Federation of Teachers bypassed the principals, who in turn formed their own associations. The specter of teachers and principals collecting dues spurred angry parents and citizens' committees to demand that they too be consulted about policy. As Albert Shanker paraphrased their argument, "First you meet with teachers, then you make a deal with them alone. The next year you bring the supervisors in; now you've got a conspiracy of both these sets of professionals, and the public is left out of it." In Melvin Urofsky, ed., *Why Teachers Strike* (New York, 1970), 187.

97 sink sponges: Susan M. Johnson, "Teachers Unions and the Schools," unpublished dissertation, Harvard University, 1982, 166.

97 No meeting without stated reason: Lorraine McDonnell and Anthony Pascal, *Organized Teachers in American Schools* (Santa Monica, 1978), 79.

98 chores remained: William J. Martin and Donald J. Willower, "The Managerial Behavior of High School Principals," *Educational Administration Quarterly,* Winter 1981; John Goodlad, *What Schools Are For* (Bloomington, Indiana, 1979), 95–104.

98 Informal interpretation: The indictments of poisonous relations sometimes willfully exaggerate the power of opponents, because that argument can excuse inactivity, as Seymour Sarason noted in his *The Culture of the School and the Problem of Change* (Boston, 1971), 126.

98 Privacy: McDonnell and Pascal, *Organized Teachers,* 44.

98 Southern resistance: J. Harvie Wilkinson III, *From Brown to Bakke* (New York, 1979); Gary Orfield, *Must We Bus?* (Washington, D.C., 1978); Robin M. Williams, Jr., and Margaret W. Ryan, *Schools in Transition* (Chapel Hill, 1954), 94, 145.

99 "I am finding": J. H. Fischer to James Conant, October 5, 1962, F folder, Box 7, Correspondence 1957–64, Conant Papers.

99 Impact of the 1964 Civil Rights Act: Gary Orfield, *The Reconstruction of Southern Education* (New York, 1969).

99 stiffer standards: David L. Kirp, *Just Schools* (Berkeley, 1982); Raymond Wolters, *The Burden of Brown* (Knoxville, 1984).

100 media coverage: In Ohio, "one woman called up on the radio and said that the teachers were swinging whips, screaming and yelling at the kids to keep them away. It turned out to be a kid in the yard playing in the vicinity of the teachers who had some kind of a toy airplane on the end of a string that you whirl around." See Robert G. Stabile, *Anatomy of Two Teacher Strikes* (Cleveland, 1974), 14.

101 Facilities as an index: Godfrey Hodgson, *America in Our Time* (New York, 1976), 464–465; Frederick Mosteller and Daniel P. Moynihan, eds., *On Equality of Educational Opportunity* (New York, 1972). Also Charles Lindblom

and David K. Cohen, *Usable Knowledge* (New Haven, 1979); Daniel Bell, *The Social Sciences since the Second World War* (New Brunswick, New Jersey, 1982).

102 "To claim to act": David Rothman, "The State As Parent," in Willard Gaylin et al., *Doing Good* (New York, 1978), 82.

5. We Don't Grab Them

Page

103 "It's the leg thing": *High School,* copy provided by Zipporah Films, Cambridge, Massachusetts.

104 Lack of contingency plans: Beatrice M. Gutridge, *High School Student Unrest* (Washington, D.C., 1969).

105 Student openness: One veteran New York City teacher caught the spirit of the reorientation: "Maybe kids 24 years ago didn't want to learn so much, either, but they pretended better. Today fewer kids pretend. When I was a new teacher, the older teachers were stiff. They were formal. On the whole, their lessons were rather boring. Today's people are much more comfortable with the kids." From the *New York Times,* June 15, 1983.

105 "What matters most": Lloyd W. Ashby and John A. Stoops, eds., *Student Activism in the Secondary Schools* (Danville, Illinois, 1970), 70. Also see Philip A. Cusick's fine *The Egalitarian Ideal and the American High School* (New York, 1983), a study of three Michigan high schools. "It was not rules, regulations, and policies that made these schools work; it was the myriad personal relations between staff and student [and] cordial relations rather than the ostensible subject matter could serve as the basis for order." See pp. 33 and 53.

105 values-clarification panel: Peter R. Greer, "Epilogue: A School Administrator's View," in Chester Finn, Jr., Diane Ravitch, and Robert T. Fancher, eds., *Against Mediocrity* (New York, 1984), 229.

106 Cambridge politics: Maureen A. Malin, "Educational Decision-Making in the City of Cambridge, 1960 to 1975: A Community Affair," unpublished dissertation, Harvard University, 1982, 47.

106 John Tobin: Ibid., 310, 315, 401; Field Note R-405, A Study of High Schools.

106 Local staff: Alfred Simpson, *Cambridge School Survey* (Cambridge, 1947), 327, 326, 356, 334.

106 The 1930s and 1950s: Field Note R-401; "Cambridge High and Latin School: Report of the Visiting Committee," April 6, 7, and 8, 1959, 11–13; "A Reply to the Recommendations Stated in the Report of the Visiting Committee," June 1959, 5–6.

107 Albania: Arthur M. Schlesinger, *In Retrospect* (New York, 1963), 81.

107 Advanced Placement: conversation with Henry Cotton, April 25, 1985.

107 Guidance, tracking, special education: Simpson, *Survey,* 143–147, 153–155; *Annual Report,* 1964; Edwin Powers and Helen Witmer, *An Experiment in*

the *Prevention of Delinquency* (New York, 1951) used Cambridge youngsters to document their association of truancy with delinquency.

107 Rindge's image: Field Note R-407, R-408.

108 Rindge graduates' choices: *Annual Report,* 1959.

108 Physics at both schools: *Annual Report,* 1963.

108 piecemeal change: *Annual Reports,* 1946–68.

108 But teachers still relied on recitation: "Visiting Committee, 1969," section D-7.

108 Free and alternative schools: Allen Graubard, *Free the Children* (New York, 1972); Neil Postman and Charles Weingartner, *Teaching As a Subversive Activity* (New York, 1969); Diane Ravitch, *The Troubled Crusade* (New York, 1983), 234–256.

109 Origins of the Pilot School: Elizabeth Binstock, "Innovation and Organizational Development Within a Bureaucracy: A Case Study of the Early Years of a Public Alternative High School," unpublished dissertation, Harvard University, 1976, 69–73, 82; Diane Tabor, "Background to the Great Debate," unpublished paper, 1972; Stephen Hamilton, "Staff Roles and the Development of an Alternative Public School," unpublished dissertation, Harvard University, 1976, 48.

110 Student-teacher closeness: Wendy L. Gollub and Fritz Mulhauser, *Cambridge Pilot School: First Year Report,* September 1970.

110 not one big happy family: Binstock, "Innovation and Organizational Development," 102; Judy Steinberg, "Two Papers on the Student Social Structure at the Pilot School," unpublished paper, 1971, 8, 25.

111 "faggot": The December 22, 1971, transcript is reprinted in the appendix to Robert C. Riordan's "Education Toward Shared Purpose: An Interpretive Case History of the Development of Goals and Practices in an Alternative Public High School," unpublished dissertation, Harvard University, 1977.

111 divisions among the staff: Tabor, "Debate," 7, 25.

111 "What can be done": Hamilton, "Staff Roles," 41–42.

111 Smoking by teachers: Tabor, "Debate," 10.

111 "the whole area": Binstock, "Innovation and Organizational Development," 123; "Cambridge Pilot School Program Self-Evaluation Report," May 21, 1971, 82–83, 87. In the summer planning sessions, anyone could call a "town meeting" if he or she secured a certain number of signatures — but it was never clear to whom the signatures should be presented! See Gollub and Mulhauser, *Report,* 29.

111 Suspension for vandalism: Binstock, "Innovation and Organizational Development," 120–121.

112 Theft of videotape equipment: Tabor, "Debate," 18; Riordan, "Education Toward Shared Purpose," 33.

112 Grading and attendance: Usually individual teachers were free to do as they pleased. In the words of one instructor, "Although this might have allowed for evolution of an effective procedure as different teachers tried out different methods, what happened was a reversion to the method least onerous to the teacher." In the third year, "least onerous" meant that daily cut slips

were sent to the parents, who could do as they saw fit. See Hamilton, "Roles," 60.

112 Good human relations: Gollub and Mulhauser, *Report,* 57, 94; Hamilton, "Roles," 67; Ray F. Shurtleff, "Administrative Problems? Cambridge Pilot School," *National Association of Secondary School Principals Bulletin,* September 1973.

113 "if you say yes or no": Binstock, "Innovation," 259. As Ann Swidler noted in her superb study of two California free schools, *Organization Without Authority* (Cambridge, Massachusetts, 1979), it was never clear who could make what demands of whom. Any form of decision making usually involved long and loud public discussion of private feelings. Students and staff prized participatory democracy, but they also wanted autonomy, self-direction, and uninhibited expressiveness. Similar themes of authority are discussed in Steve Bhaerman and Joel Denker, *No Particular Place to Go* (Carbondale, Illinois, 1972), and Gerald Grant, "The Teacher's Predicament," *Teacher's College Record,* Spring 1983.

113 "In the Pilot School": Arthur Lipkind, "An Ethical Perspective on the First Year of the Cluster School," unpublished paper, 1975.

113 full-time administrator: Binstock, "Innovation and Organizational Development," 188; Riordan, "Education Toward Shared Purpose," 50; Shurtleff, "Administrative Problems?" 76–82.

114 "See, there is no real American flag": David J. Swanger, "For Want of a Real Flag: The Public Hearing of the Cambridge Pilot School," *Harvard Graduate School of Education Bulletin,* 1971.

114 Staff-director tensions: Binstock, "Innovation," 309; Riordan, "Education Toward Shared Purpose," 127–166.

114 TV broadcast: Field Note R-403.

115 "that no one's feelings": Riordan, "Education Toward Shared Purpose," 100.

115 "I'd have to be": Ibid., 118.

116 "You get to say": F. Clarke Power, "The Moral Atmosphere of a Just Community High School: A Four-Year Longitudinal Study," unpublished dissertation, Harvard University, 1979, 207.

116 Tape recorder: Ibid., 71.

117 Respect but not friendship: Ibid., 257.

117 first weekly meeting: Elga R. Wasserman, "The Development of an Alternative High School based on Kohlberg's Just Community Approach to Education," unpublished dissertation, Boston University, 1977, 45.

117 "I like to cut": Power, "The Moral Atmosphere," 217–218, 232.

117 Drugs: Ibid., 229, 221, 277–285.

117 "If a disturbance": Rule 8–3 is also noteworthy: "The use of the word 'shut-up' tends to create unnecessary tensions in the meetings; therefore, it is recommended that it not be used in the Community Meeting." See Lipkind, "An Ethical Perspective," appendix 3.

118 "I have to judge your sincerity": Wasserman, "Development," 172.

118 "The slightest amount of caring": Ibid., 212. For more on how tolerance at Cluster discouraged indignation, see Christina Hoff Sommers, "Education

Without Virtue: Moral Education in America," *American Scholar,* Summer 1984, 381–389.

119 Spring 1970 protests: Field Note R-404. During demonstrations over the invasion of Cambodia, one coach told several of his team members to go outside and beat up the protesters. At Rindge, in contrast, students and staff stood at the windows and watched the High and Latin demonstrations. Observers credited the tranquillity to the presence of a large percentage of second- and third-generation Rindge graduates. Field Note R-112.

119 Principal brought suit: *Boston Herald American,* July 18, 1979.

119 1980 murder: *Boston Globe,* January 16, 1980.

119 Other forms of diversity: Field Notes R-108, R-112, R-124, R-102.

120 Unofficial recognition of diversity: Field Notes R-121, T-127.

120 Blue Room: Conversation with principal, June 6, 1984.

120 Course credits: From the 1981–82 course catalogue.

120 Guidance department: A major 1969 study of urban schools found "expand guidance services" first of all the curricular reforms with "potential for improving instruction." See table 6–7 in Robert J. Havighurst, Frank L. Smith, and David E. Wilder, *A Profile of the Large-City High School* (Washington, D.C., 1970).

121 "teacher support team": *Boston Globe,* August 12, 1979.

121 Psychological terminology: From the minutes of the academic cabinet and the headmaster's cabinet; also, School Committee Order CO-1542 and Field Note R-121.

121 Security force: Field Note R-121.

121 "Cambridge maybe Rindge maybe Latin": *Register-Forum,* February 28, 1978.

121 Pilot's homogeneity: Field Note R-408.

121 "running naked through the woods": *Boston Globe,* June 18, 1978. For a case study of the implementation of a similar strategy in California, see David Kirp, *Just Schools* (Berkeley, 1982), 173.

122 "Heaven is no longer the same": Field Note R-401.

122 "If I grab a kid": Field Note R-402.

122 Test scores: from Denver City School's Education Center. Conant's associate Eugene Youngert reported that East was "usually mentioned with respectfully bated breath" as an outstanding school. See "Trip Report — School Visits, Denver and Salt Lake City," Colorado folder, Miracle Box 18, Conant Papers.

122 an outstanding school: Wymond J. Ehrenbrook, "The Importance of the Individual," *Atlantic Monthly,* February 1965; "Re-evaluation Report of East High School," May 2–5, 1966, 4.

123 meager vocational offerings: "Re-evaluation," 29, 13, 31, 11.

123 "The accelerated classes": Field Note U-406.

123 Neighborhood enrollment preferred: *Report and Recommendations to the Board of Education School District Number One, Denver, Colorado* (Denver, 1964), table 16.

124 District court, 1973 decision: *Keyes* v. *School District No. 1.* The case is discussed in J. Harvie Wilkinson III, *From Brown to Bakke* (New York, 1979), 190–197.

124 1968–1969 black protest: For the opinions of a black student from East, see Paul Gayton's angry "Keep on Pushing," in Marc Libarle and Tom Seligson, eds., *High School Revolutionaries* (New York, 1970), 74–75.

124 "Many of us wanted more order": Field Note U-403.

124 innovative programs: East consistently publicized the alternatives devised to suit so many different groups. When observers failed to appreciate the responsiveness, the school was displeased. In the spring of 1978, CBS filmed life at East as part of a documentary, "Is Anyone out There Learning?" The student newspaper thought that CBS would concentrate on the school's special programs and not treat it as a typical school. *Spotlight,* September 28, 1978.

124 "during orientation week": Field Note U-402.

125 "Now the technique": "East High School Senior Seminar — 1973 Evaluation," 3.

125 Stern . . . and solicitous: *East High School Handbook for Parents and Pupils* (Denver, 1955), 2.

125 "Once, they'd flunk out": Field Note U-400.

125 "There's nothing they won't write": Field Note U-406.

125 Ninth-graders asked about their sexuality: Field Note U-309.

125 "That's the real world": Field Note U-400.

125 Yearbooks: *Angelus,* vols. 58, 63. By way of contrast, East and other student newspaper writers in the 1950s authored spoofing antifaculty pieces. One began, "The faculty of this high school have become too obnoxious and our school politicians increasingly corrupt." That sort of statement was not uncommon in the 1970s in straight editorials, but the article in question continued, "Have our teachers forgotten that their job is to amuse if not appease their pupils?" (*Spotlight,* March 20, 1952). Did the sharper definitions of student and teacher roles encourage that sort of writing? To quote Gerald Grant of Syracuse University, "We students could parody the uptight principal but we were careful when we did so because we knew he could throw us out." See "Today Children Are Different," *Educational Leadership,* March 1983. It is my impression that there was more satire, role reversal, and rituals with rearrangement of authority in the 1950s than the 1970s. Recently those inversions would have been too threatening. For pre-1970 annual variety shows featuring role reversals, see Marie C. Davis, *History of Evanston Township High School, 1883–1958* (Evanston, Illinois, 1963), 113; Benjamin M. Steigman, *Accent on Talent: New York's High School of Music and Art* (Detroit, 1964), 277; Anthony F. Visco, *Sixty Year History of Frankford High School, 1910–1970* (Philadelphia, 1973). For suggestive points on role reversals in Japanese high schools — which in many ways are as rigid as American schools of the 1940s, if not more so — see Thomas P. Rohlen, *Japan's High Schools* (Berkeley, 1983), 164. For parody in 1950s American popular music, see Albert Goodman, *Elvis* (New York, 1981), 118.

126 Sambo's: *Spotlight,* January 30, 1979.

126 "Teachers are closer to the youngsters": Field Note U-408.

126 "The atmosphere now is lighter": Field Note U-409.

Notes

126 "If I tried to keep": Field Note U-400.

126 "There's so little real togetherness": Field Note U-406. In a nationwide study of 1015 schools, James Coleman, Thomas Hoffer, and Sally Kilgore found that, although public schools more than parochial schools emphasize socioemotional matters, pupils rate "teacher interest" in students higher in the Catholic and other private schools than in public schools. See *High School Achievement* (New York, 1982), table 5.9.

127 Spirit Week, 1981: Field Note U-403.

127 "The first day": Ibid.

127 anti-Astuno staff member: Field Note U-409.

128 "It takes more planning": "National Advisory Council Meeting," May 12, 1972, Scholastic, Inc., Archives, New York City.

128 "The Way We Were": *San Diego* magazine, April 1982.

128 Flipping the finger: Field Note Z-405.

128 the average IQ: "San Diego City Schools Testing Services Department Report — District Testing Statistics, 1968"

128 Tinkering: "Visiting Committee Report . . . March 11, 12, 13, 1968"; "Evaluation — San Diego High School: A Report of Self-Appraisal, March 1968," 9. The school also practiced differential grading in English courses: the basic students had a C-minus ceiling, but accelerated sections usually received all A's and B's. See "Evaluation," 57.

129 1968–1969 protests: *Russ,* January 22, 1971; Field Notes Z-401, Z-405, Z-409, Z-410; for faculty polarization on the opposite coast, at the Bronx High School of Science, see Robert Rossner, *The Year Without an Autumn* (New York, 1969).

129 Curricular changes: *Russ,* December 4, 1970, May 23, 1973; "Report of the Visiting Committee, April 30 — May 2, 1973"; "Mid-Term Evaluation of San Diego High School, May 1978."

129 hard work and innate talent: *Russ,* March 29, 1940. That same year, the principal's handbook sanctioned support of Boy Scout troops. See *Handbook for Principals,* 24.

130 56 percent failed sixth-grade test: "Report of the Visiting Committee, 1973."

130 "I'm putting this Mexican kid": Field Note Z-402.

130 Hispanics and college: Field Note Z-409. For the "one less report card to make out" attitude toward dropouts, see Margaret Casey, "A Follow-Up Study of Selected Girl Drop-outs from the Senior High Schools of San Diego," unpublished M.A. thesis, San Diego State College, 1951.

130 Changes in counseling department: Field Note Z-401. But students remained lukewarm about the department, as indicated by answers on questionnaires filled out for the accreditors:

	1963	1968	1973
Excellent	28.0%	18.7%	17.4%
Good	37.0%	49.0%	28.2%
Fair	28.0%	23.0%	28.6%
Poor	7.0%	9.3%	25.8%

130 Order restored: "Instructional Council Minutes," April 21, October 20, 1980; "Faculty Advisory Committee Minutes," December 14, 1981, January 11, 1982.

130 "Twenty years ago": Field Note Z-268.

131 Disengagement and indifference: "Secondary Student Questionnaire — San Diego High School, 1973." On emotional disengagement a decade later, among Southern California youth, see Bret Ellis, *Less Than Zero* (New York, 1985).

131 Attendance policies: Field Notes Z-403, Z-402.

131 "It used to be they'd be gone": Field Note Z-268. For parallel shifts in the direction of less harshness in local law enforcement, see James McClure, *Cop World: Policing the Streets of San Diego* (New York, 1984).

132 Gallup Poll: "San Diego County Survey of Public Attitudes Toward the Public Schools, 1981–82," 4.

132 one fearful alumna: Field Note Z-401.

132 Bad publicity: "Instructional Council Minutes," November 19, 1979; "Faculty Advisory Committee Minutes," May 7, 1979.

132 Lack of protest: Field Note X-405.

133 The four schools before the merger: The Reverend Joseph E. Mach, "A Developmental History of Cleveland Central Catholic High School," August 1971.

133 not everyone was welcome: "Minutes of High School Supervisors' Meeting," December 21, 1964.

133 "persons of one race": "Religion Teachers Census-Attitudinal Survey," December 1968.

133 The merger: Mach, "A Developmental History," 37–54.

134 "Everyone felt": Field Note X-400.

134 "They've taken this fear out": "Report on Group Interview Sessions *Re* Catholic Education," January 1973.

134 School psychology, 1950s and 1960s: C. E. Elwell to Bishop Krol, October 12, 1955; "Adolescents and Their Problems, Their Wait for Service," May 21, 1960, entry in "Minutes, Cleveland Diocesan Guidance Council."

135 "It all sounded very exciting": Field Note X-404.

135 No schedules until October: Field Note X-408.

135 Coaches' rivalry: Field Note X-409.

135 Building administrators: Field Note X-411.

136 "Many of them": Field Note X-408.

136 "I would never have thought": Field Note X-410.

136 "They are less guarded": Field Note X-403.

136 "If there's a God": Field Note X-407.

137 "Inclusion has to do": Harry Eckstein, "Civic Inclusion and Its Discontents," *Daedalus,* Fall 1984, 127.

137 "development of positive self-concept": David R. Byrne, Susan A. Hines, Lloyd E. McCleary, *The Senior High Principalship* (Reston, Virginia, 1978), 45.

138 Sex in Muncie: Theodore Caplow et al., *Middletown Families* (Minneapolis, 1982), 162, 164.

Notes

138 Censorship: Joseph Nocera, "The Big Book-Banning Brawl," *The New Republic,* September 13, 1982.

138 Judy Blume: Brett Harvey, "Boy Crazy," *Village Voice,* February 10–16, 1982.

139 Uncertain alliance: James D. Laurits, "An Investigation by Observations and by Focused Interview of Teacher Attitudes Toward the Work Situation in a Large Public High School," unpublished dissertation, Harvard University, 1956, 41, 95.

139 Houston: "Unsolicited Letters *re* Bad Conditions in Houston," in Houston folder, Defense Activities file, National Education Association Archives, Washington, D.C.

139 Subject specialists: William W. Goetz, "Curriculum-Making in a Suburban New Jersey High School from 1957 to 1972," unpublished dissertation, Columbia University Teachers College, 1982.

139 "interpreted, bent, and informally renegotiated": Susan M. Johnson, "Teacher Unions and the Schools," unpublished dissertation, Harvard University, 1982, 241.

139 Unions as a problem: Susan Abramowitz and Ellen Tenenbaum, *High School '77* (Washington, D.C., 1978), 86.

140 Not every aspect . . . constrained: For a lawyer's analysis of why "proceduralism" is hardly the demise of authority, see Mark G. Yudow, "Implementing Due Process," *Wisconsin Law Review,* 1981, no. 5.

140 School violence: For a properly skeptical review of the literature, see Daniel L. Duke and Cheryl Perry, "What Happened to the High School Discipline Crisis?" *Urban Education,* July 1979.

140 Satisfaction: Even in the lower-track courses, students evaluated their schools as favorably as did students in the general and academic tracks. Their *self*-esteem, however, was lower than other students'. See Jeannie Oakes, *Keeping Track* (New Haven, 1985), 146.

140 Incentives for intensity: The problem was particularly acute in the average-ability sections. The "unspecial" are discussed in detail by Arthur G. Powell, Eleanor Farrar, and David K. Cohen in *The Shopping Mall High School* (Boston, 1985), chap. 4. Here, the comments will be from the point of view of a publishing company curious to find out why some English teachers canceled or let lapse their subscriptions to a magazine designed for average-ability students. In 1978, market researchers at Scholastic telephoned teachers throughout the country to learn why they dropped *Voice* magazine. Several teachers mentioned budget cuts. In tough times their schools were unwilling to buy "consumable" magazines, and they would not or could not ask students to pay for them. But why this particular way to economize? One factor was a modest migration of students to the ill-defined general track. As a teacher from Texas said, "We have to feed them smaller bites. There is a place for *Voice* when the class is near or on level, but there's little time for it when we have so much diversity." Rather than have slow readers struggle with *Voice,* some schools substituted less demanding Scholastic publications.

A second major influence was the rise of minimum competency tests in the 1970s. Schools were under pressure to bring a larger percentage of the weakest students up to specified achievement levels. From South Carolina: "We have the problem of exceptional demands upon us to meet certain fundamental objectives — fundamental literacy for all. We simply do not have the time to spend with a magazine that goes beyond the basics." According to a Missouri teacher, "We buy your magazines for those who are so far below grade that we salvage. Salvage, that is the name of the game." Other teachers of similar convictions suggested that Scholastic pitch its advertising to skills improvement: "Give us a safety belt in the way of demonstrable skills improvement. What we're up against is showing the establishment that supplementary materials are worthwhile . . . Your *Voice* is for the average student, and the vocal elements are not interested in him or her." Respondents did not criticize the magazine on grounds other than difficulty. Cancellations said more about local pressure than anything else. As the director of market research concluded, "The classroom teacher, confronted by mixed abilities, strange faces, and a mandate to perform, is understandably wary of a periodical which he or she assumes to be for the average student; there being no such animal facing her or him."

There was such an animal, but there was no strong spokesman for the average student. As one Scholastic vice-president said in 1980, "Schools can find money for the below-level reader, and even the gifted — but the average student must shift for himself or herself. Reminds me of federal taxation — the average wage-earner gets neither federal assistance nor tax loopholes." See "Voice" and "Market Research" files, Scholastic, Inc., Archives, New York City.

141 Civics scores: N.A.E.P., *Changes in Social Studies Performance, 1972–76* (Washington, D.C., 1978), 58, and Brian J. Larkin and Elizabeth A. Vander-Putten, *The Condition of Social Studies 1980* (Washington, D.C., 1980).

141 struggle and tension: Lyrically evoked in Richard Rodriguez, *Hunger of Memory* (Boston, 1981), chap. 2.

141 "To see some as better": Charles Murray, *Losing Ground* (New York, 1984), 184.

141 "We don't grab them": Field Note R-408.

Epilogue

Page

142 Several panels, early 1970s: B. Frank Brown, chair, *The Reform of Secondary Education* (New York, 1973); James S. Coleman, chair, *Youth: Transition to Adulthood* (Chicago, 1974); John Henry Martin, chair, *The Education of Adolescents* (Washington, D.C., 1974).

143 "capstone": Carl Kaestle, *Pillars of the Republic* (New York, 1983), 120.

Notes

143 "lack of discipline": Stanley M. Elam, ed., *A Decade of Gallup Polls of Attitudes Toward Education* (Bloomington, Indiana, 1978).

143 Test scores: Albert E. Beaton et al., *Changes in Verbal Abilities of High School Seniors, College Entrants, and SAT Candidates between 1960 and 1972* (Princeton, 1977); *On Further Examination: Report of the Advisory Panel on the Scholastic Aptitude Test Score Decline* (Princeton, 1976); Lawrence C. Stedman and Marshall S. Smith, "Recent Reform Proposals for American Education," *Contemporary Education Review,* Fall 1983.

144 get-tough tone: the major statement of this attitude was from the National Commission on Excellence in Education, *A Nation at Risk* (Washington, D.C., 1983). Many state commissions echoed the dire warnings.

144 "abominable discrimination": Mortimer J. Adler, *The Paideia Proposal* (New York, 1982), 15.

145 lack of attention to the political and social constraints: Stephen J. Graubard's cogent "Zeal, Cunning, Candor, and Persistence — To What Educational Ends?," *Daedalus,* Fall 1984; Paul E. Peterson, "Did the Education Commissions Say Anything?" *The Brookings Review,* Winter 1983.

145 "We will all be well served": *Academic Preparation for College* (New York, 1983), 2. The assumption that "the best education for the best is the best education for all" was challenged by several participants in a symposium on the Paideia Proposal; see *Harvard Educational Review,* November 1983.

145 Indiana salaries: H. Dean Evans, "We Must Begin Educational Reform 'Every Place At Once,' " *Phi Delta Kappan,* November 1983.

146 "like playing Old Maid": Field Notes Z-308, Z-317, A Study of High Schools.

146 Appeal of job security: Dan Lortie, *Schoolteacher* (Chicago, 1975), 36–37.

146 Trains in the 1930s: John R. Stilgoe, *Metropolitan Corridor* (New Haven, 1983), 54, 55. An analogy to trains also graced an essay by Edgar Z. Friedenberg, "Education," *American Quarterly,* Spring-Summer, 1983.

146 addressed as "Professor": Russell Baker, *Growing Up* (New York, 1983), 118; Jesse Davis, *The Saga of a Schoolmaster* (Boston, 1956), 303; B. F. Skinner, *Particulars of My Life* (New York, 1976), 144–147. Robin Lester, headmaster of the Trinity School in New York City, told me that people in rural Missouri in the late 1950s often called the superintendent "Professor." A principal in upstate New York had the same honor, according to Arthur J. Vidich and Joseph Bensman, *Small Town in Mass Society* (Princeton, 1958), 187.

147 "We Want It All": Ernest Boyer, *High School* (New York, 1983), chap. 3; John I. Goodlad, *A Place Called School* (New York, 1983), chap. 2. The same theme runs through Gene Maeroff's *Don't Blame the Kids* (New York, 1982).

148 A broad curriculum: We recall elective mania in the 1970s, but one national survey reported sizable increases in both required and elective courses between 1972 and 1977. See Susan Abramowitz and Ellen Tenenbaum, *High School '77* (Washington, D.C., 1978), 88.

148 basic curriculum: Boyer, *High School,* 95.

148 "Most teachers": Goodlad, *A Place Called School,* 237.

149 "The drive for more requirements": Personal comment, October 1983.

149 "If an unfriendly power": *A Nation at Risk,* 1.

149 working title: "Final Report Outline," October 26, 1982. Memo courtesy of a commission staff member.

150 History that memorializes: David K. Cohen, "Loss As a Theme in Social Policy," *Harvard Educational Review,* November 1976.

150 Crisis rhetoric: Garry Wills, *The Kennedy Imprisonment* (Boston, 1982), 171–172. For general discussions of crisis rhetoric, see Murray Edelman, *Political Language* (New York, 1977), Christopher Lasch, *The Minimal Self* (New York, 1984), and Dan Nimmo and James E. Combs, *Nightly Horrors* (Knoxville, Tennessee, 1985).

150 Apathy a form of crisis: James B. Conant to Dwight Eisenhower, January 23, 1959, Folder E, Box 7, Correspondence 1957–64, Conant Papers. A further complication is that crisis rhetoric and crisis situations can be used by schoolmen as part of the solution. This was true of the Cambridge public schools discussed in chap. 5. The 1980 murder was undeniably horrible, but the following fall there was room in the budget for a full-time "crisis counselor." In the Pilot School, crises usually increased student participation, made the school analyze its institutional identity, and forced clear-cut decision making. See *Cambridge Chronicle,* August 28, 1980; Robert C. Riordan, "Education Toward Shared Purpose," unpublished dissertation, Harvard University, 1977, 26; Elizabeth Binstock, "Innovation and Organizational Development Within a Bureaucracy," unpublished dissertation, Harvard University, 1976, 123–125.

151 what they liked best: Cameron Crowe, *Fast Times at Ridgemont High* (New York, 1981); Mihaly Csikzentmihalyi and Reed Larson, *Being Adolescent* (New York, 1984); Philip Cusick, *Inside High School* (New York, 1973); Ellen Glanz, "What Are *You* Doing Here? or Schooldays for the Teacher," Occasional Paper 26, Council for Basic Education, Washington, D.C., 1979.

151 Fantasies of late 1950s: James S. Coleman, *The Adolescent Society* (New York, 1961), 27–28.

151 Frank Zappa: Quoted in Ralph Keyes, *Is There Life After High School?* (Boston, 1976), 29.

151 friendship groups: Based on field notes from A Study of High Schools.

152 Professor Jones's advice: in Memorandum No. 97 to the Committee on the Objectives of General Education in a Free Society, March 16, 1944; Harvard University Archives.

152 Field work: For examples of its fruits, see Michael Huberman, "Recipes for Busy Kitchens," *Knowledge,* June 1982.

153 Paul Goodman: *Growing Up Absurd* (New York, 1960).

153 "romance with utilitarianism": A. Graham Down, "Inequality, Testing, Utilitarianism," *Education Week,* October 12, 1983.

153 Gallup Poll: *Phi Delta Kappan,* September 1983.

154 full-court basketball: For the political dimensions of Midwestern girls' sports, see Joseph A. Califano, *Governing America* (New York, 1981), 224.

Index

Abbot Academy, 89
Ability grouping, 10–11, 61–65, 105, 129. *See also* Tracking
Academically talented students, 12–13, 59, 60, 62, 73
Accreditation, 26, 33
Adler, Mortimer, 144, 148, 153
Adolescence: in the 1920s, 84; in the 1950s, 76, 79, 81–87, 125; perils of, 44, 134
Advanced Placement, 73, 107, 144
Alexander, Franz, 52
American Federation of Teachers, 97
Ames, Louise B., 88
Anti-intellectualism, 12–13, 28, 43, 47
Art, 69, 74
Astuno, John, 125–128
Auden, W. H., 5
Average ability students, 63, 200n

Bacon, Francis, 39
Barnette, 95
Barzun, Jacques, 46, 152
Beard, Charles, 35
Bell, Howard, 16
Benjamin Franklin High School, 7
Bennington College, 69

Berry, Chuck, 87
Bestor, Arthur, 50, 149
Bilingual education: in Cambridge, 119; in San Diego, 129; volatility of, 145
Blackboard Jungle, The, 76
Blacks, 28, 72, 110, 114, 119, 129. *See also* Desegregation
Borrowman, Merle, 71
Boston, 31
Boyden, Frank, 32
Boyer, Ernest, 148, 153
Boy Scouts, 85
Breen, Jay, 124
Brown v. Board of Education, 98
Bruner, Jerome, 74
Busing, 77, 123

California, 50, 80, 128
Cambridge (Mass.) High and Latin School: curriculum in 1950s, 107; racial conflict at, 119, 196n; staff in 1940s, 106
Cambridge (Mass.) Rindge and Latin School: celebration of diversity by, 120; electives in, 120; guidance department at, 120–121; senior faculty in, 121–122; special programs at, 121

Cambridge (Mass.) school board: members of, 106; and Pilot School, 113–114; and student protest, 119; and superintendent search of 1971, 114
Cardinal Principles of Secondary Education, 47
Carnegie, Dale, 49
Carnegie Corporation, 59
Catcher in the Rye, 138
Change, slow pace of: x, 21–22, 74–75, 104, 108, 123, 128, 137, 153–154
Chauncey, Henry, 76, 84
Chicago, 67, 72
Clark, Dick, 85
Class, social, 10, 15
Cleveland Central Catholic High School: counseling at, 134; curriculum of, 134; ideology of, 134; internal disputes at, 135; origins of, 133; scheduling for, 135; teacher unions at, 133
Cluster School (Cambridge, Mass.): attendance policy in, 117; discipline in, 117; divisions within, 116–117; expulsions from, 118; governance of, 116; ideology of, 116
College admissions: acceleration of, 75; from Eastern independent schools, 33–35; and financial aid, 16, 34, 75; and girls, 69; and minorities, 130; in the 1950s, 44–45, 75; transcripts for, 27
College Entrance Examination Board, x, 34
Columbia University, 19, 99
Committee of Ten, x
Comprehensive high school, retreat from: 142, 147
Conant, James B.: and ability grouping, 61–65; and *The American High School Today,* 59–73; and average ability students, 63; and college enrollments, 63; defense of comprehensive high school by, 59, 67–68; and girls' education, 69–70; national reputation of, 58; opposed to small schools, 70; pessimistic musings of, 68–69; and school politics, 71–73;

and selective high schools, 64; on urban education, 76–77; and vocational education, 67; writings on education by, 1933–1953, 58
Connelly, Edward, 108, 114
Consolidation, school, 29–30, 36, 57, 70–71, 80
Cook, Walter, 18
Core courses, 36–39, 41, 48
Cottle, Thomas, 93
Courses, enrollments in: from 1934 to 1949, 47–50, 177n; from 1949 to 1961, 73–74
Court cases, 2, 95, 119, 190n
Covello, Leonard, 7–8, 105, 168n
Crisis rhetoric, 149–150

Dennison, George, 152
Denver, 18. *See also* East High School
Desegregation: and black staff, 27; and Civil Rights Act of 1964, 99; in Denver, 123; in Northern schools, 100; and public awareness of, 150; in Southern schools, 98–99
Detroit, 18, 72, 100
Dewey, John, 51
Diederich, Paul, 65
Discipline, 54–55, 112, 116–118, 119, 128, 130, 132, 143
Down, A. Graham, 153
Driver education, 49, 74, 153
Dropouts, 15, 64, 75, 76, 121, 123, 124
Dunn, Joan, 11

East High School (Denver, Col.): changing student population, 122; desegregation at, 123; faculty-principal tension, 127; principal of, 125–128; racial conflict in, 124; special programs at, 124; truancy from, 126
Education for ALL American Youth, 35–43, 47, 109, 149, 151. *See also* Progressive education
Educational Policies Commission, 35, 47, 72, 73, 152, 183n
Educational Testing Service, 61–63, 65
Eisenhower, Dwight, 47, 150
Electives, 42, 49, 124, 147–148

Index

Elementary schools: architecture of, 56; curriculum of, 38
Eliot, Charles W., x
"Elmtown," 27
Emmet, Beulah, 32–33
Engle, T. L., 48
English, 44, 49, 58, 59, 60, 86, 107, 123, 124, 125
Engstrand, Sophia, 2
Enrollment in high schools: from 1900 to 1940, 14–15; from 1940 to 1950, 46
Equality of educational opportunities, as studied by social science, 100–101, 144–145
European schools, 15
Evangelical religion, 13
Extracurriculum, 14

Federal government: and curricular reform, 74; and Southern states, 99; and work programs, 15, 16
Fiala, Father, 135
Filmstrips, 14, 49, 91, 93, 170n
Fine, Benjamin, 29
Finley, John, 20
Foreign languages, 44, 45, 50, 59, 60, 63, 73, 74, 107
Fraser, Kennedy, 91
Fraternities, in high schools, 84, 94
Friedenberg, Edgar Z., 54–55
Friedman, Lawrence, 94
Frisoli, Frank, 114

Gaffney, Matthew, 25, 26
Galbraith, John Kenneth, 69
Gardner, John, 67, 70
General Education in a Free Society, 20, 149, 151
Gesell, Arnold, 88
Goodlad, John, 147, 148, 153
Goodman, Paul, 153
Goslin, Willard, 50
Goss v. Lopez, 96
Graduation, rate of, 14–15, 46
Guidance counselors: as administrators, 53; at Cambridge Rindge and Latin, 120–121; at San Diego High School, 130. *See also* Therapeutic mentality

Hansot, Elisabeth, 25
Harvard University, 11, 20, 58, 71, 106, 108
Hechinger, Fred, 152
Herndon, James, 152
High Mowing School, 32–33
High schools, in Japan, 144
Hinman, Georgie, 5
Hispanics, 128–130
Holt, John, 152
Home economics, 47, 128
Homework, 60, 90
Houston, 139
Hunter, Evan, 76

Ilg, Frances, 88
Illinois, 28, 30, 70, 71
Immigrants, 7, 46, 75
Independent schools: in the 1970s, 138; New England headmasters of, 32–35
Indiana, 10, 13, 29–30, 71, 82, 145
Intelligence testing, 11, 62–64, 181n
Iowa, 57, 70, 88

Johnson, Lyndon B., 8, 100, 105, 153
Johnson, Susan, 139
Jones, Howard Mumford, 152
Joplin, Janis, 87
Junior colleges, 16
Junior high schools, 40, 62, 74, 172n, 175n
Juvenile delinquency, 83

Keinon, Irwin, 1
Keister, C. R., 97
Kelley, Bill, 134
Kennedy, John F., 150
Kinsey, Alfred, 89
Kohlberg, Lawrence, 116
Kozol, Jonathan, 152

Lange, Pat, 135
Lawrenceville School, 54
Life Adjustment, 43–51, 53, 55, 58
"Leave It to Beaver," 84
Levittown (N.J.), 83–84

Linkletter, Art, 128
Local control, 28–32, 70–72. *See also*
  Consolidation, school
Loomis School, 34
Lynd, Albert, 50

McCarthy, Mary, 85
McGrath, Earl, 45
McGuire sisters, 85
Maddox, Lester, 100
Massachusetts, 25–26
Mathematics, 44, 50, 58, 59, 60, 63, 73,
  74, 133
Mayer, Martin, 152
Michigan, 63, 95
"Middletown," 13, 138
Miller, Bernard, 71
Minimum competency testing, 144,
  201n
Minnesota, 21, 50, 71
Mississippi, 82
Missouri, 65
Music, 69, 74
Muzzey, David S., 9

Nation at Risk, A, 149
National Defense Education Act, 73
National Education Association, 9, 32,
  35, 70, 71, 73, 75, 80, 86, 97
National Institute of Mental Health, 52
National Merit Scholarships, 32, 73, 75,
  97
National Science Foundation, 73
Nelson, Ricky, 81
New Hampshire, 32
New Trier High School, 25, 31, 32
New York City: high schools of, 6–7,
  11; Nazi teacher in, 4; school boards
  of, 3, 31
Nurses, school, 47

Off-campus curricula, 142
Ohio, 12, 28, 30, 133
Open education, 108–109

Parents, 14, 27, 45, 50, 82–85, 90, 91,
  94, 98, 100
Peale, Norman Vincent, 52

Peck, Gregory, 128
Pedagogy: as avoidance behavior, 45,
  46, 51, 76, 148; as drill and recitation,
  8–9, 13, 19, 43, 66, 107, 108; reform
  of, 19
Peer pressure, 21, 82–83, 120, 187n
Pennsylvania, 64, 110
Phillips Andover Academy, 34
Phillips Exeter Academy, 35, 107
Pilot School (Cambridge, Mass.): activities in, 110, 115; administration of,
  111–114; admission to, 109; attendance policy in, 112, 115; divisions
  within, 110–111; first graduation ceremony in, 115; grading policy in, 112,
  115; ideology of, 110, 113; increasing
  homogenization of, 121; origins of,
  108–109
"Plainville," 28
Podhoretz, Norman, 6–7
Powell, Jane, 21
Presley, Elvis, 81, 83
Principals, high school, 25, 27, 97–98,
  139, 147
Progressive education: and classroom
  climate, 17; conservatism of, 18, 35–
  36; criticism of, 20; impact of, 18, 51–
  57, 105, 175n; and independent
  schools, 32–33. *See also* Life Adjustment
Prosser, Charles, 43, 44, 48
Psychologists, school, 51–53
Psychology: as high school course, 48–
  49; influence of, 52
Puerto Rico, 82

"Quiz Kids" radio show, 12–13

Radcliffe College, 69
Rankin, Paul, 37–39, 41, 43, 47, 48
Relationships: austerity of, 1, 5–8, 36,
  53, 76, 86, 103, 133; warmth of, 14,
  68, 105, 109, 116, 125, 136, 143
Rickover, Admiral Hyman, 152
Riesman, David, 81, 83
Rindge Technical High School (Cambridge, Mass.): guidance in, 107; image as vocational school, 107–108;
  staff in 1940s, 106; tracking, 107

Index

Rivers, Mendel, 99
Role reversals, between students and teachers, 197n
Roosevelt, Franklin D., 55, 106
Rothman, David, 102
Rural schools, 28, 30. See also Consolidation, school

St. Louis, 8, 72
St. Mark's School, 5
San Diego High School: changing student population at, 128; local reputation of, 132; racial conflict in, 129; restoration of order at, 130; special programs at, 129; student apathy at, 131; truancy from, 131
Schlesinger, Arthur, Jr., 107
Schlesinger, Arthur, Sr., 20, 107
Scholastic Aptitude Test, 34, 59, 143–144
School administration before 1920, 24
School architecture, 21, 55–57
School boards, 24, 25, 26, 31, 72, 76
School climate, 75, 77, 86, 103, 115–116, 120, 126, 136
Schrag, Peter, 152
Science, 45, 50, 59, 63, 73, 74, 108
Self-control, 13, 16, 19, 42, 86
Silberman, Charles, 150, 152
Sizer, Theodore, ix–xii, 148, 153
Slick, Grace, 89
Social class: in the 1930s, 6–7, 16, 82–83; in the 1950s, 83, 84, 89; in the 1960s, 101
Social services, 120, 124–125, 148
Social studies, 59, 61, 123, 140–141
Special education, 119
Spock, Benjamin, 84
Sports: and girls, 120, 154; prestige of, 14, 28, 85, 174n
Sputnik, 53, 58, 68, 73
State governments, 30
Stoddard, Alexander, 40–41
Stoddard, George, ix, xii, 37–43, 48, 51
Strayer, George D., 41
Student-teacher relations. See Relationships

Students: employment of, 15, 121; knowledge of history, 12; protest by, 95–96; punishment of, 13; seating of, 13
Suburban schools, 31–32
Sullivan, Ed, 83
Superintendents, 25, 27, 30–31, 72

Taylor, Elizabeth, 21
Teachers: as advisers, 52; certification of, 145; conservatism of, 86; education of, 71; of English, 37–38; mental health of, 3–4, 80, 121, 146; mistrust of, 74; percentage male, 16; percentage married, 80; and reluctance to change, 19; salaries for, 16, 145; shortage of, 80; social status of, 16, 146; surveillance of, 2, 5, 79–80, 96–97; and tenure, 80, 145–146; testing of, 12, 17, 99; and unions, 133, 139
Teenagers: and alcohol, 92; and drugs, 88, 89–90, 92; jobs of, 90; legal rights of, 94–96, 191n; and sex, 84, 87–89, 92–94, 190n. See also Adolescence
Television, 85, 90, 150, 188n
Tennessee, 94, 98
Texas, 26, 30, 98
Textbooks: adoptions of, 10, 26; contents of, 9
Therapeutic mentality: of the 1940s, 39, 40, 44; of the 1950s, 48, 134; of the 1970s, 92, 118, 125, 137
Tinker v. Des Moines, 95, 190n
Tobin, John, 106, 108
Toronto, 110
Toth, Sue Allen, 88
Tracking, 10–11, 45, 105, 169n, 184n
Tyack, David, 25
Typing, 49, 58

Unions, 97–98, 133, 139, 145

Virginia, 98
Vocational education, 57, 60, 63, 64, 67–68, 147

Waller, Willard, 4, 5
Warner, Lloyd, 16
Washington, D.C., 86

Welch, Raquel, 128
Wills, Garry, 150
Wisconsin, 8
Wiseman, Frederic, 103
Wood, Natalie, 83

Yale University, admission to, 33–35
Youth culture: of the 1940s, 81; of the
1950s, 81–83, 85; of the 1970s, 151

Zappa, Frank, 151